Room At The Inn
South East England

Contents

ERE IS NOTHING WHICH
T BEEN CONTRIVED BY
BY WHICH SO MUCH HAPP
IS PRODUCED AS BY A G
TAVERN OR INN 17
SAMUEL JOH
1709–178

LOUIS JADOT

King George V

Inn Location Map

Welcome to...
Room At The Inn

The great capital city of London lies at the heart of the South East region, surrounded by beautiful and interesting counties to explore on that all-important weekend away from the hustle and bustle. Hampshire has the New Forest, Britain's best-loved woodland, and crystal-clear chalk streams; across the Solent lies the Isle of Wight, with its timeless, old-fashioned appeal. Sussex boasts the majestic South Downs and a variety of popular resorts, while in Kent lie the orchards of the Garden of England. Oxfordshire and Buckinghamshire have the beech-clad Chiltern Hills to discover. Dotted around this varied landscape you'll find delightful villages and some great country pubs and historic inns.

Not long ago the thought of staying overnight in one of these pubs or inns would conjure up images of cheaply furnished bedrooms, the smell of stale smoke, food and beer, and basic shared bathrooms at the end of dimly lit corridors. How things have changed over the last decade! Just flicking through this collection of stylish inns across the South East, it's clear to see that pubs are becoming our new breed of country hotels.

Many of the inns listed in these pages are owned by chef/patrons who have previously plied their trade in top restaurants, or there's a talented and ambitious chef at the stove. You'll find chalkboard or daily printed menus championing local, seasonal produce, be it fish and shellfish from day boats at Rye or Hastings and fresh crab landed at Selsey, traceable farm-reared meats like Kentish Limousin beef and South Downs lamb, locally shot game or organic vegetables from allotment holders in the same village. Even the time-honoured ploughman's lunch and cheeseboard selections offer exciting regional farmhouse cheeses like Oxford Blue and Golden Cross goats' cheese from Sussex. One or two inns have taken their commitment to support local producers a step further by opening small produce shops in adjoining buildings.

There have also been major improvements in the range and quality of both wine and beer. Gone are the days when there was only one red and one white wine by the glass and a basic list to choose from. Wines are now carefully selected to match the style of food being created in the kitchen. Chalked-up lists include wines from the many excellent small vineyards across the South, notably Nyetimber and Denbies Estates, offer decent tasting notes, classic vintages and often up to 20 wines by the glass. You'll also find scores of interesting and often outstanding hand-pumped ales from local independent micro-breweries, from tip-top Hopdaemon Incabus in Kent, to Triple FFF Moondance in Hampshire and Mighty Oak Maldon Gold brewed in Essex, and you must try the heady Organic Extra Dry Cider made at Sedlescombe Vineyard in Sussex.

So, having wined and dined well, just climb the stairs to sleep in a cosy and well-equipped bedroom. The furnishings, fabrics, cosseting extras and swish bathrooms once only found in posh hotels are now the norm in the classy inns within these pages. You'll find soothing heritage colours, plasma TV screens, digital radios, fresh coffee, home-made biscuits, goose down duvets and pillows and Egyptian cotton sheets on big beds, and spotless bathrooms kitted out with claw-foot baths, storm showers, fluffy bathrobes, under-floor heating and top toiletries. Bliss!

To add to your enjoyment of a weekend in the South East we've included details on places to visit, from National Trust properties and museums to glorious gardens and timeless villages. Ideas to keep active types amused range from balloon trips and where to play golf to information on local cycle rides and where you can hire a classic car for the day. Upmarket shops are not forgotten; we guide you to the best shopping towns, key antique shops, galleries and clothing boutiques and, perhaps, a local farm shop or deli for those all-important edible goodies and gifts to take home.

The final ingredient to a good weekend away is a country walk. So, having tucked into a hearty breakfast you can follow the suggested rural ramble. All of the mapped walks are between 3 and 8 miles long and within easy reach of the inn, some even pass the door. You'll find detailed directions, essential notes on the terrain, and the relevant Ordnance Survey map to take with you.

Walking in Safety

Each of the inns featured in this book has a specially selected walk that will guide visitors around a nearby place of interest. Before you embark on any of the walks, read the righthand panel giving at-a-glance practical information about the walk, including the distance, how much time to allow, terrain, nature of the paths, and where to park your car.

All of the walks are suitable for families, but less experienced family groups, especially those with younger children, should try the shorter walks. Route finding is usually straightforward, but the maps are for guidance only and we recommend that you always take the relevant Ordnance Survey map with you.

The Risks

Although each walk has been researched with a view to minimising any risks to walkers, it is also good common sense to follow these guidelines:

• Be particularly careful on cliff paths and in hilly terrain, where the consequences of slipping can often be very serious.

• Remember to check the tidal conditions before walking on the seashore.

• Some sections of the walk routes are by, or cross, busy roads. Take care here, and remember that traffic is a danger even on minor country lanes.

• Be careful around farmyard machinery and livestock.

• Be prepared for the consequences of changes in the weather, and check the forecast before you set out.

• Ensure everyone is properly equipped with suitable clothing and a good pair of boots or sturdy walking shoes. Take waterproof clothing with you and a torch if you are walking in the winter months.

• Remember that the weather can change quickly at any time of the year, and in moorland and heathland areas, mist and fog can make route-finding much harder. In summer, take account of the heat and sun by wearing a hat, sunscreen and carrying enough water.

• On walks away from centres of population you should carry a mobile phone, a whistle and, if possible, a survival bag. If you do have an accident requiring emergency services, make a note of your position as accurately as possible and dial 999.

• Many of the routes in this book are suitable for dogs, but observing your responsibility to other people is essential. Keep your dog on a lead and under control.

⇢	Walk Route	▢	Built-up Area
➊	Route Waypoint	▢	Woodland Area
– – –	Adjoining Path	👫	Toilet
☀	Viewpoint	P	Car Park
•	Place of Interest	⌂	Picnic Area
△	Steep Section		

The Seaview Hotel

Isle of Wight

Time at the Bar!
11am-11pm
Food: 12-2.30pm, 6.30-9.30pm

What's the Damage?
Main courses from £8.95

Bitter Experience:
Goddard's Special, Greene King Abbot

Sticky Fingers:
Children welcome; children's menu

Muddy Paws:
Dogs allowed in the bar

Zzzzz:
24 rooms, £120-£199

Anything Else?
Terrace, car park, apartments

The Inn

Just yards from the seafront, with its pebble beach and pretty assortment of sailing dinghies bobbing on the water, this handsome early Victorian hotel has a deck-like front terrace complete with flagpole and glorious Solent views. The nautical, shipboard theme continues in the bars – one wardroom-style, its walls crowded with photos of old ships, the other more rustic, with bare boards, dado pine panelling, a blazing log fire and all manner of maritime memorabilia festooning the walls. There are two restaurants to choose from – the cosy Front Restaurant that is traditional and quaint, and the Sunshine Restaurant and Regatta Room, a brasserie styled in nautical blue and white.

Top designers Keech and Green revamped existing bedrooms and designed seven new rooms in 2007, so expect rich fabrics, luxurious furnishings and a high level of comfort. Crisp white linen, slippers, bathrobes, intimate lighting, plasma screens and White Company toiletries are standard throughout, while new rooms have intimate, blue-lit bathtubs with flat-screen TVs shaped into the marble tiles at one end. For stunning sea views, book the Apartment Suite.

The Food

The seasonally inspired menus make good use of home-grown Island produce, featuring local asparagus, garlic, fish and seafood as well as home-grown herbs and venison from the hotel's own herd of deer reared at Carisbrooke. From the modern British restaurant menu, start with rabbit and duck terrine with poached fig salad, locally caught spider crab risotto with pink grapefruit, tarragon and parmesan crisp, or mussel and smoked salmon broth. For your main course, try line-caught sea bass with broad bean purée and herb oil, free-range duck breast with parsnip and vanilla purée and a prune and lime sauce, or, perhaps, the organic Island beef fillet.

In the bar or out on the pleasant terrace, quaff a pint of Island-brewed Goddard's Special and tuck into venison sausages, doorstep sandwiches or the famous and rather moreish hot crab ramekin. Leave room for a wicked dark chocolate tart served with warm chocolate soup and white chocolate ice cream, or a traditional favourite like sticky toffee pudding with butterscotch sauce and vanilla ice cream. Don't miss the excellent Sunday lunch in the restaurant.

What To Do

Shop

THE GARLIC FARM

If you are a devotee of this tasty wonder plant and intrigued by its ancient origins and wide range of culinary, health and mythical properties, then head here. Owner Colin Boswell has become certainly the UK's, if not Europe's, leading expert on garlic, and his passion and expertise have built a thriving food business offering the best range of garlic to eat, grow and learn about.

Newchurch, Isle of Wight PO36 0NR

01983 865378

www.thegarlicfarm.co.uk

ISLE OF WIGHT STUDIO GLASS

Situated along the beautiful St Lawrence Undercliff on the Island's south coast, this studio has been producing hand-blown glass to create decorative and functional vessels of all shapes and sizes since 1973. A highly imaginative and original approach is used in developing the glass to produce one-off designs, collections and commissions to order.

Old Park, St Lawrence,

Isle Of Wight PO38 1XR

01983 853526

www.isleofwightstudioglass.co.uk

OASIS INTERIOR LANDSCAPES

One of the most interesting shops on the Isle of Wight, bringing you a selection of Fairtrade goods – hand-made teak furniture, carvings, handicraft gifts and much more – imported directly from family enterprises in Bali and India.

Carpenters Road, Brading,

Isle of Wight PO36 0QA

01983 613760

www.oasis-iow.com

Visit

ISLE OF WIGHT OWL & FALCONRY CENTRE

Experience the thrill of falconry, one of the oldest sports in the world, in the grounds of historic Appuldurcombe House. At 650ft (200m) and with excellent sea breeze potential, the centre offers rising air currents that even the biggest of birds can appreciate. The centre also runs a number of courses for those keen to discover the thrill of falconry.

Appuldurcombe Farm, Wroxall,

Isle of Wight PO38 3EW

01983 852484

www.appuldurcombe.co.uk

MOTTISTONE MANOR GARDEN

This magical garden, planted to allow for climate change with colourful borders, shrub-filled banks and grassy terraces, is set in a sheltered valley with views to the sea and surrounds an Elizabethan manor house (tenanted). There are delightful walks on the downs over the adjoining Mottistone Estate.

Mottistone, Isle of Wight PO30 4EA

01983 741302

www.nationaltrust.org.uk

ROSEMARY VINEYARD

With 30 acres of vines, this is one of the largest British vineyards and makes the most of the Island's mild climate to produce a range of fine red and white wines, a sparkling wine, country wines such as elderflower, an award-winning elderberry liqueur, and juices made with 100% fruit.

Smallbrook Lane, Ryde,

Isle of Wight PO33 2UX

01983 811084

www.rosemaryvineyard.co.uk

Activity

HORSE RIDING

A professional and friendly yard that offers excellent escorted hacking in stunning countryside, as well as top-quality tuition with BHS-registered instructors. There's also a children's club.

Allendale Equestrian Centre

Newport Road, Godshill,

Isle of Wight PO38 3LY

01983 840258

PARAGLIDING

Learn from scratch or improve your paragliding skills in great surroundings with one of the longest-established paragliding schools in the country. Tandem flights, tow launch instruction and hill soaring, plus an interactive weight shift flight simulator, are on offer. Weekend or taster days are also available.

Butterfly Paragliding

The Terrace, Chale, Isle of Wight PO38 2HL

01983 731611

www.paraglide.uk.com

SEA ANGLING

Operated and owned by husband-and-wife team Chris and Priscilla Solomon, Cachalot Charters provides sea angling for experienced anglers, beginners, complete novices, school groups, clubs and individuals. The 34ft (10m) *Starfish* charter boat is fully equipped and inspected annually, providing all the necessary safety and comfort for passengers.

Cachalot Charters

Bembridge Harbour, Bembridge,

Isle of Wight

01983 874100 (booking kiosk)

01983 872185 (office)

www.cachalot-charters.co.uk

The Walk - Carisbrooke Castle, A Royal Prison

King Charles I was imprisoned in the castle until his trial and execution in London, 1648.

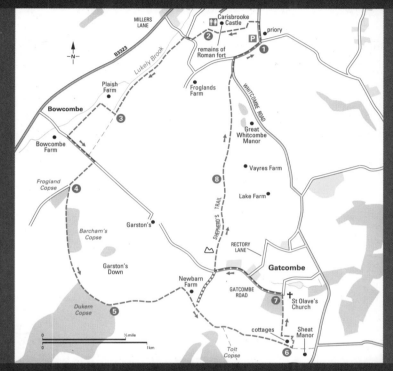

Walk Details

LENGTH: 6.5 miles (10.4km)

TIME: 2hrs 30min

ASCENT: 764ft (233m)

PATHS: Field and downland paths and tracks, some roads, 4 stiles

SUGGESTED MAP: aqua3 OS Outdoor Leisure 29 Isle of Wight

GRID REFERENCE: SZ 489876

PARKING: Car park close to Carisbrooke Priory

❶ From the car park (facing the Priory) turn left and walk along road. Take 1st lefthand footpath. Shortly veer left, ascending through trees. On reaching the castle, bear left; follow path alongside castle walls. Turn left towards car park; follow footpath ('Millers Lane').

❷ Turn right at road, pass Millers Lane; walk to stile and path on left ('Bowcombe'). Cross field to next stile; cross pastures, crossing several stiles. Level with Plaish Farm, reach stile and junction.

❸ Bear right; follow enclosed path, shortly bending left. At Bowcombe Farm, turn left. Follow signs ('Gatcombe'). Pass footpath on left; stay on track as it curves right, avoiding track ahead. Veer away from track at corner of Frogland Copse; follow field edge to the gate.

❹ Pass through trees to the gate; continue up the slope, skirting field boundary. Keep ahead in next field towards gate and bridleway sign. Walk along edge of Dukem Copse; look for turning on left to Gatcombe.

❺ Go through gate; along field edge. At path to Garston's, descend right; then left to gate. Follow bridleway for Gatcombe; turn right to Newbarn Farm. Bear right at entrance and, at lane, keep right along bridleway. At the edge of Tolt Copse ignore path right and bear left, soon to leave Shepherd's Trail, proceed along the bridleway towards Sheat Manor.

❻ Before the manor, at the junction of paths, turn left, following the path past cottages. Bear left and keep to the curving path as it ascends to woodland. Proceed through the wood and down to the lane by St Olave's Church.

❼ Turn left along Gatcombe Road, pass Rectory Lane, then turn right at the crossing of ways, rejoining Shepherd's Trail for Carisbrooke. Pass between properties and ascend through trees. Pass over the track; go through the gate; follow the path round lefthand field edge.

❽ Go through the gate; keep by the field edge. The path is later enclosed by fence and hedge to reach the sign ('Carisbrooke and Whitcombe Road'). Keep to the path and eventually reach the junction. Continue to reach the car park.

The Peat Spade Inn

Hampshire

The Essentials

Time at the Bar!
11am-11pm
Food: 12-2pm 7-9pm; Sun 12-4pm
(no food Sun evening)

What's the Damage?
Main courses from £10.50

Bitter Experience:
Ringwood Best,
Guest ales

Sticky Fingers:
Children welcome, smaller
portions available

Muddy Paws:
Dogs welcome

Zzzzz:
6 rooms, £110

Anything Else?
Terrace, garden, car park

The Peat Spade Inn, Village Street, Longstock, Stockbridge, Hampshire SO20 6DR

The Inn

Following months of searching for their perfect country inn, Andrew Clarke and Lucy Townsend snapped up the Peat Spade in summer 2005, quickly seeing the potential of the striking, red-brick and gabled Victorian pub. It overlooks a peaceful lane and idyllic thatched cottages in the Test Valley village of Longstock, only yards from the famous trout stream that attracts fishermen from all over the world. Here, they have created a classy country inn, one where you will find a relaxed atmosphere in the cosy fishing and shooting themed bar and dining room, a simple menu listing classic English food, and six sumptuous bedrooms. If you fancy fly-fishing, then Lucy can arrange a day with a ghillie on the Test, with a picnic hamper provided for lunch. The on-site fishing shop stocks all you'll need.

Book well ahead as the rooms have found favour with shooting parties and fishing folk, and you can see why – all have big beds with down pillows and duvets, deep easy chairs, flat-screen TV with DVD, wireless internet connection, and tiled bathrooms with glorious power showers and local Longbarn toiletries.

The Food

Naturally, given Andrew's background as head chef at Winchester's Hotel du Vin, good pub food is driving the business. As much local produce as possible is sourced, including free-range pork from Greenfields Farm near Andover and fruit and game from the Leckford Estate, while villagers bring in herbs, apples and vegetables from their allotments in return for a pint. The short simply described menu changes daily and lists some great pub classics.

Start with potted shrimps with toasted sour dough or game terrine with Cumberland sauce, then move on to braised faggots with green split-pea puree, rib-eye steak with chips and béarnaise sauce, Lancashire hotpot with pickled red cabbage, or halibut with Jerusalem artichokes and wild mushrooms. Finish with walnut and date pudding with caramel sauce, chocolate and cherry brownie with crème fraîche, or a plate of English cheeses served with quince paste. To drink, try a pint of Ringwood Fortyniner or one of eight wines by the glass from the carefully prepared list. Dine alfresco on the sheltered rear terrace on sunny summer days.

What To Do

Shop

DAIRY BARN FARM SHOP

Award-winning farm shop stocked with home-produced beef, lamb and pork from native British rare and minority breeds of livestock, home-made sausages (gluten free) and dry cured bacon, plus a full range of local produce including cheese, organic vegetables and bread, chutneys, jams and woollen goods.

North Houghton, Stockbridge, Hampshire SO20 6LF
01264 811405
www.dairybarn.co.uk

RIVER TEST SMOKERY

One of the best-known traditional trout smokeries in the country. Bring your catch here to be smoked or buy their cold-smoked trout and salmon, or smoked trout chowder.

Watch Estate, Coley Lane, Chilbolton, Hampshire SO20 6AZ
01264 860813
www.rivertest.net

WYKEHAM GALLERY

For paintings, watercolours and sculpture by contemporary artists, alongside pictures from 1880-1940 head for the Wykeham Gallery in Stockbridge, where the wide high street straddles the River Test and is lined with traditional tea rooms, picture and craft galleries. Here you'll also find Courcoux & Courcoux, one of Britain's leading provincial galleries for contemporary art. For unusual ideas for your home and garden go to Garden Inn, and for stylish crafts take a look in Broughton Crafts.

High Street, Stockbridge, Hampshire SO20 6HE
01264 810364
www.wykehamgallery.co.uk

Visit

HOUGHTON LODGE GARDENS

Twelve acres of tranquil gardens bordering the lovely River Test.

Houghton, Stockbridge, Hampshire SO20 6LQ
01264 810502
www.houghtonlodge.co.uk

MOTTISFONT ABBEY

Originally a 12th-century Augustinian priory, Mottisfont Abbey has a drawing room decorated by Rex Whistler and a walled garden with one of the finest collections of roses in the country. You can stroll through the elegant grounds beside a clear chalk stream, a tributary of the River Test.

Mottisfont Abbey, Mottisfont, Romsey, Hampshire SO51 0LP
01794 340757
www.nationaltrust.org.uk

WHITCHURCH SILK MILL

This lovely old mill in the country town of Whitchurch has been producing silk since 1830. The oldest working silk museum in the country, it operates on Victorian machinery. The shop stocks silk items and gifts.

28 Winchester Street, Whitchurch, Hampshire RG28 7AL
01256 892065
www.whitchurchsilkmill.org.uk

WINCHESTER

Join a tour and explore the city's historic streets on foot. From the cathedral, stroll through the close to the famous college, then through the watermeadows beside the River Itchen. Don't miss the Great Hall, home to the legendary Round Table.

Tourist Information 01962 840500
www.visitwinchester.co.uk

Activity

CYCLING

Pick up the packs of cycling routes available from local tourist information centres and explore the beautiful Test Valley on two wheels. Routes vary in length, terrain and difficulty so there is something for everyone. For an easy ride, cycle the old railway line from Stockbridge to Mottisfont.

www.hants.gov.uk/cycling

FISHING

Book yourself a day's fly-fishing tuition with a local ghillie on the River Test, Britain's finest trout stream. Lucy at the Peat Spade will arrange everything, right down to the picnic hamper for lunch.

RACING AT SALISBURY

One of the oldest courses in England, there's been horse racing at Salisbury since the 16th century – it's a very picturesque flat-racing course set in the Wiltshire downland, with a spectacular view of Salisbury Cathedral.

Netherhampton, Salisbury, Wiltshire SP2 8PN
01722 326461
www.salisburyracecourse.co.uk

The Walk - Murder in Harewood Forest

In search of Deadman's Plack, the spot where King Edgar murdered Athelwold.

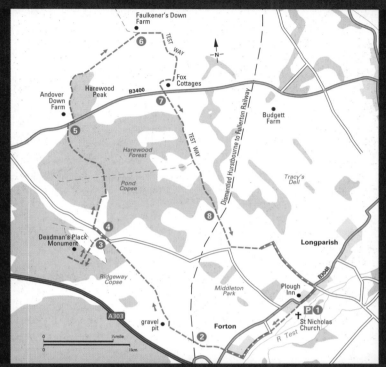

Walk Details

LENGTH: 7.5 miles (12.1km)

TIME: 3hrs 30min

ASCENT: 295ft (90m)

PATHS: Field, woodland paths and tracks, sections of Test Way

SUGGESTED MAP: aqua3 OS Explorer 144 Basingstoke, Alton & Whitchurch

GRID REFERENCE: SU 426439

PARKING: Car park at St Nicholas Church or by village hall

❶ Walk through the churchyard; exit via the gate; follow Test Way across water-meadow. Go through 2 gates. Turn left along the lane into Forton. Take sharp righthand bend by barn to T-junction. Pass through the gate opposite to the field path; bear right along the track.

❷ Cross the old railway; follow the track between fields. At the copse, leave track. Bear left with waymarker along field edge. Shortly, cross track to follow the path along lefthand edge of the field at base of shallow valley. At copse, keep left and continue to reach gate and lane.

❸ To see Deadman's Plack, turn left before gate. Follow the path uphill into woodland. Ignore 2 tracks on right. Take 3rd path. Where it forks, keep right; follow the path for 300yds (274m), take the path on the right leading to the monument.

❹ Retrace your steps back to lane. Turn left; after 50yds (46m), cross the stile in hedge on right; follow path between fields, by woodland. Bear left by birch trees to join main track through Harewood Forest. Keep ahead at crossing of paths by conifer tree. Eventually join the gravel drive leading to the B3400.

❺ Turn right then left up the drive to Andover Down Farm. Keep to the right of the farm and industrial site. Bear left at gates to the house; follow the track right. Head downhill towards Faulkner's Down Farm.

❻ At the farm, bear right along metalled drive, ('Test Way' – 'TW').

Proceed downhill. Turn right ('Private Road, No Thoroughfare') on to a track between fields. Go through gap in the hedge ('TW'). Follow lefthand field edge to stile near cottages. Bear left through the gate; follow the drive to the B3400.

❼ Cross the road and stile opposite. Follow the grassy track ('TW') beside arable land. Gently climb, then descend, to join a stony track. Shortly, bear left ('TW') along the narrow path to a metalled track.

❽ Turn left, cross the railway. Keep left at the fork on to a gravel track. Follow it left. Shortly reach a junction of tracks. Turn right ('TW') to reach Longparish. At village lane, turn right, passing the Plough Inn, back to the church or village hall.

The Wykeham Arms

Hampshire

The Inn

You'll find this fine 250-year-old brick building in the oldest part of the city, a stone's throw from Cathedral Close and the famous college. Oozing charm and always buzzing, the pub is patronised by an eclectic mix of drinkers and diners, from businessmen and barristers, clergy and college dons to tourists and well-heeled foodies. The rambling character bars and eating areas are furnished with old pine tables and old-fashioned school desks from Winchester College. They also boast four welcoming winter log fires, an impressive collection of hats, and fascinating pictures and military memorabilia adorning every available space.

Stylishly decorated and well equipped, bedrooms are split between the inn and St George, a 16th-century annexe across the narrow street. If you book a room above the bar, then choose Hamilton, with its rich fabrics and deep red walls lined with tasteful pictures, or Nelson for its grand four-poster bed. St George rooms are quieter and more contemporary – College Bakehouse Suite is decorated in cool blue, has an open fireplace, deep sofas and a big bed on the mezzanine.

The Food

Well-prepared modern pub food alongside more adventurous evening choices attracts food lovers from far and wide – evening booking is essential. Follow a city stroll or an amble through the water meadows with a satisfying lunch from the seasonally changing menu, perhaps smoked chicken salad, sea bass with rocket, parmesan and pesto dressing, cottage pie or a posh sandwich, say, roast beef with watercress and horseradish mayonnaise.

Cooking moves up a gear in the evenings, with the imaginative repertoire built around fresh ingredients. Begin with seafood bouillabaisse or spiced butternut and yellow pepper soup, and follow with baked cod wrapped in smoked bacon with a chive cream sauce, or rack of Hampshire lamb served with dauphinois potatoes and a redcurrant and mint jus. Finish with chocolate and cherry brownie with pistachio anglaise, or elderflower and white wine jelly with fresh fruit salad. Quaff tip-top ales from Fuller's or delve into the well-chosen list of wines, complete with personal and informative tasting notes; 20 are available by the glass.

The Essentials

Time at the Bar!
11am-11pm
Food: 12-2.30pm (1.45pm Sun),
6.30-8.45pm. No food Sun evening

What's the Damage?
Main courses from £6.50 (lunch), £12 (dinner), Sunday lunch £15.50 & £19.50

Bitter Experience:
Fuller's London Pride & Chiswick Bitter, Gales Butser & HSB

Sticky Fingers:
No children under 14

Muddy Paws:
Dogs welcome in bar & bedrooms

Zzzzz:
14 rooms, £105-£150; single £62-£115

Anything Else?
Garden, limited parking

What To Do

Shop

ALRESFORD
Stroll around the elegant little town of Alresford and you'll find art galleries, specialist food shops, antiques and interiors shops, as well as top-notch boutiques like Moda Rosa, for modern designer clothing, and Hêtre, for shoes from the world's leading designers.

Moda Rosa
35 West Street, Alresford,
Hampshire SO24 9AB
01962 733277

Hêtre
39 West Street, Alresford,
Hampshire SO24 9AB
01962 733312

CADOGAN & JAMES
Celebrity chef James Martin's delicatessen stocks a superb range of unusual cheeses, olive oils, freshly baked breads and speciality foods, and you can enjoy a cup of coffee at pavement tables. The stylish sister shop next door stocks quality country clothing and shoes, top designer names and cashmere.

31a The Square, Winchester,
Hampshire SO23 9EX
01962 877399

WINCHESTER FARMERS' MARKET
Stroll across the Cathedral Close on the second and last Sunday of the month and stock up on quality local goodies at the largest farmers' market in the country. Over 95 local producers showcase their goods – you can taste, try and buy everything from home-baked bread to fresh crabs from the coast and locally brewed ales.

Middle Book Street, Winchester, Hampshire
01420 588671
www.hampshirefarmersmarkets.co.uk

Visit

HINTON AMPNER
This elegant country house, set in superb countryside, is known for its fine gardens combining formality of design with informality of planting. Full of scent and colour, they offer walks with many unexpected vistas. The house contains outstanding furniture, paintings and objets d'art.

Bramdean, Alresford, Hampshire SO24 0LA
01962 771305
www.nationaltrust.org.uk

WINCHESTER CATHEDRAL
Awesome and full of interest, one of Europe's finest cathedrals, with the longest of all Gothic naves, this magnificent building dominates the city's compact and fascinating medieval centre. Treasures include many rare books, notably a wonderful 12th-century illuminated Bible, some spectacular architecture, and the tombs of Jane Austen, Izaak Walton and the early English kings. Don't miss evensong for an opportunity to hear the choir.

01962 857251 (Visitor's Centre)
www.winchester-cathedral.org.uk

WINCHESTER COLLEGE
Founded in 1382, Winchester College is believed to be the oldest continuously running school in the country. Join one of the guided tours that explore its medieval heart, including the Chamber Court, the 14th-century Gothic chapel, original scholars' dining room, and the 17th-century red-brick schoolroom, thought to have been designed by Sir Christopher Wren.

College Street, Winchester,
Hampshire SO23 9NA
01962 621209
www.winchestercollege.org

Activity

FISHING ON THE ITCHEN
Keen anglers wishing to cast a line for trout can buy half-day or day tickets at Avington Trout Fishery, one of the oldest stillwater trout fisheries in the country and renowned for its clear water stalking and big fish.

Avington Trout Fishery
Avington, Winchester, Hampshire SO21 1BZ
01962 779312
www.avingtontrout.com

TRAIN RIDE
Travel by steam or heritage diesel train through 10 miles (16km) of beautiful Hampshire countryside between Alresford and Alton on this preserved steam railway. All four stations are authentically 'dressed' in period style. There's a locomotive shed and picnic area at Ropley, and special events throughout the year.

Watercress Line
The Railway Station, Alresford,
Hampshire SO24 9JG
01962 733810
www.watercressline.co.uk

WINCHESTER WALKING TOUR
Pick up one of the leaflets at the Tourist Information Centre and take a self-guided walk around Winchester. Choose from the King Alfred City Tour, the Sunset Walk up St Giles' Hill for superb views over the city, and Keats' Walk, where you stroll through the Cathedral Close and water meadows to St Cross, which provided the inspiration for the poet's work.

Tourist Information Centre, Winchester Guildhall, High Street, Winchester, Hampshire SO23 9GH
01962 840500
www.visitwinchester.co.uk

The Walk - *Alfred's Ancient Capital*

Winchester's historic streets, Cathedral Close and the beautiful Itchen Valley.

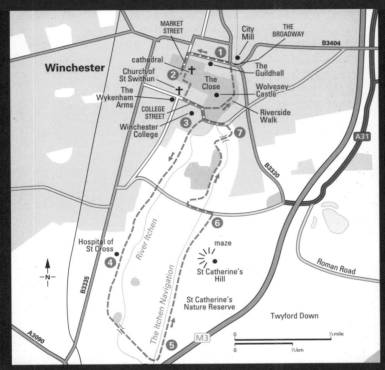

Walk Details

LENGTH: 3.5 miles (5.6km)

TIME: 1hr 30min

ASCENT: 499ft (152m)

PATHS: Established riverside paths through water-meadows, 3 stiles

SUGGESTED MAP: aqua3 OS Explorer 132 Winchester

GRID REFERENCE: SU 486294

PARKING: Pay-and-display car parks in city centre

❶ From King Alfred's statue on the Broadway, walk towards the city centre, passing the Guildhall (tourist information centre) on the left. Join the High Street, then in 100yds (91m), turn left along Market Street. Continue ahead into Cathedral Close to pass the cathedral main door.

❷ Turn left down the cloister, then turn right through the Close ('Wolvesey Castle'), to Cheyney Court and exit via Prior's Gate. Turn left though Kingsgate, with the tiny Church of St Swithun above, then bear left down College Street and shortly pass the entrance to Winchester College. Beyond the road barrier, bear right along College Walk then turn right at the end of the wall, along the track.

❸ Go left through the gate by the private entrance to the College. Follow the path beside the River Itchen for 0.5 mile (800m) to the gate and road. Cross over and follow the gravel path, alongside the tributary, to the gate and cross open meadow towards Hospital of St Cross.

❹ Keep left alongside the wall and through the avenue of trees to the stile. Proceed ahead along the gravel path to 2 further stiles and join the farm track leading to the road. Turn left and walk the length of the now gated road (traffic-free), crossing the River Itchen to reach the junction of paths by the M3.

❺ Turn left along the path. Pass the gate on the right (access to St Catherine's Hill). Keep left at the

fork and drop down to follow a narrow path by Itchen Navigation. Go through the car park to the road.

❻ Turn left across the bridge and take the footpath immediately right. Keep to the path beside the water, disregarding the path left (College nature reserve). Soon cross the bridge by the rowing sheds to join the metalled track.

❼ Turn left, then left again at the road. Follow the road left along College Walk then bear right at the end ('Riverside Walk'). Pass the Old Bishops Palace (Wolvesey Castle) and follow the metalled path beside the Itchen and up the steps to Bridge Street, opposite the City Mill (National Trust). Turn left and walk back to King Alfred's statue.

* Antony Gormley's *Sound II* sculpture, Winchester Cathedral, Hampshire

The Hawkley Inn

Hampshire

The Inn

Beware: approach the village of Hawkley from the west and you will experience tortuously steep and narrow lanes; instead head for Petersfield and follow signs off the B3006 north of the town to locate this friendly and unpretentious village local, tucked away well off the beaten track in unspoilt rolling countryside. First impressions are deceptive, for the simple and unassuming opened-up rustic front bar is not smart – but this is the charm of the place and the locals love it. You'll find big scrubbed pine tables topped with chunky candles, a 'listed' very worn carpet, the odd battered armchair, posters on nicotine-stained walls, and a mad moose head above the crackling log fire. Step into the rear dining room and you enter the 21st century, with its sandstone flagged floor and modern art on the walls.

Upstairs bedrooms are positively space age in comparison: sleigh or colonial four-poster beds have thick goose-down duvets and Italian Beltrami cotton sheets, there are plasma screens, free wi-fi/broadband access, and top-notch Hudson Reed-designed bathrooms. These classy rooms come as a big surprise and are hugely comfortable.

The Hawkley Inn, Pococks Lane, Hawkley, Liss, Hampshire GU33 6NE

The Essentials

Time at the Bar!
Food: 12-3pm, 5.30-11pm;
Sun 12-5pm, 7-10.30pm

What's the Damage?
Main courses from £7.50

Bitter Experience:
Ten changing guest ales

Sticky Fingers:
Children welcome in bar until 8pm

Muddy Paws:
Dogs welcome

Zzzzz:
5 rooms, £65-£120

Anything Else?
Terrace, garden, no car park

The Food

Chalkboards list the hearty range of traditional pub dishes. Everything is freshly prepared in the kitchen, from the filled rolls and generous ploughman's at lunchtime to the rustic evening meals that may take in the likes of curried parsnip soup, minted lamb casserole, spaghetti bolognese or pesto, cottage pie, grilled duck breast with green peppercorn sauce, or the delicious Sussex beef stew, served with spring greens, carrots and lashings of creamy mash.

Real ale aficionados regularly beat a path to the Hawkley Inn to sample the mind-boggling and ever-changing choice of ales (from local microbreweries) that flows through the 12 hand pumps on the bar. So, wash your casserole down with a pint of Goddards Special, or the full-bodied and malty Ballards Wassail, or perhaps a tankard of the dark, coffee-like Espresso from the Dark Star brewery in Sussex. Arrive on a Friday night and a local band may be playing, or a festival of local ale may be in full swing. In summer, sit and enjoy an alfresco pint at slate-topped tables on the front veranda or in the peaceful rear garden.

What To Do

Shop

BOSHAM WALK ART & CRAFT CENTRE

Overlooking Chichester Harbour, an Area of Outstanding Natural Beauty, Bosham is the perfect setting for this art and craft centre on the Sussex coast. Here you can wander around 20 shops and an art gallery to see where local artists and resident and visiting craftspeople make, display and sell their products. Or join one of the regular workshops for children and adults.

Bosham Lane, Bosham, Chichester, West Sussex PO18 8HX
01243 572475
www.bosham-walk.co.uk

NICHOLAS MOSSE & BURLEIGH POTTERIES

Nicholas Mosse and Burleigh Potteries use traditional hand skills so that each piece you buy is both beautiful and unique. Nicholas Mosse (based in southern Ireland) concentrates on hand crafting and decorating techniques developed in the 18th and 19th centuries, while Burleigh (from Stoke-on-Trent), is famous for blue-and-white earthenware. Situated next door to the ruins of Cowdray House.

River Ground Stables, Cowdray Park, Midhurst, West Sussex GU29 9AL
01730 810880
www.mosse-burleigh.co.uk

Visit

GILBERT WHITE'S HOUSE

Take a stroll round picturesque Selborne village and visit The Wakes Museum, much-loved home of 18th-century naturalist Gilbert White who, with his brother, cut the nearby Zigzag Path that climbs above the village. Opposite his house is the church, which has a window dedicated to him, depicting St Francis feeding the birds.

Selborne, Hampshire GU34 3JH
01420 511275
www.gilbertwhiteshouse.org.uk

HINTON AMPNER HOUSE & GARDENS

Garden lovers should make a trip to this elegant country house, best known for its masterpiece of 20th-century garden design. Manicured lawns and fine topiary combine formality of design with informality of planting, and the gardens are full of scent and colour. The house has an outstanding collection of furniture, paintings and *objets d'art*.

Alresford, Hampshire SO24 0LA
01962 771305
www.nationaltrust.org.uk

UPPARK

Imagine Uppark during the great days of the British Empire when Queen Victoria was on the throne and the mother of HG Wells was housekeeper here. Look out for a Grand Tour collection of paintings, furniture and ceramics in the elegant Georgian rooms. From its setting on the South Downs there are breathtaking views to the coast.

South Harting, Petersfield, West Sussex GU31 5QR
01730 825857
www.nationaltrust.org.uk

Activity

THE HANGERS WAY

This spectacular 21-mile (34-km) trail runs from Alton to the Queen Elizabeth Country Park south of Petersfield. Hardly a moment passes without a superb view. One of the route's highlights is Shoulder of Mutton Hill – the view from the top was described by the Edwardian poet Edward Thomas as 'sixty miles of South Downs at one glance'.

0800 028 0888
www.hants.gov.uk/longdistance/hangers-way.htm

JANE AUSTEN – THE EARLY YEARS GUIDED TOUR

Our most famous romantic novelist continues to enthral nearly 200 years after her death. As well as visiting her home at Chawton you can tour The Vyne near Basingstoke where she attended balls, visit Winchester Cathedral where she is buried or book a half-day tour illustrating her early life – she was born in the tiny Hampshire village of Steventon, near Basingstoke.

Hidden Britain Tours, 28 Chequers Road, Basingstoke, Hampshire RG21 7PU
01256 814222
www.hiddenbritaintours.co.uk

WATERCRESS LINE

Experience history in motion as you travel by steam or heritage diesel through 10 miles of glorious countryside between Alton and Alresford. Learn how to drive a steam train on a day's Footplate Experience Course, or join one of the regular real ale trains.

Mid Hants Railway, Alresford, Hampshire SO24 9JG
01962 733810
www.watercressline.co.uk

The Walk - Looking for Edward Thomas

Explore The Hangers - beech-clad hills and vales that inspired Hampshire's great poet.

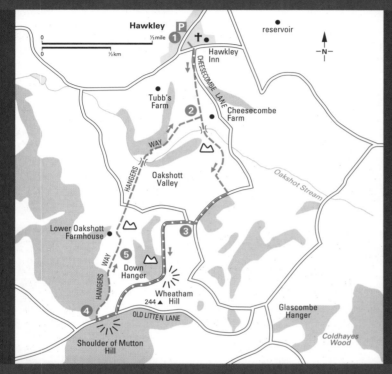

Walk Details

LENGTH: 3 miles (4.8km)

TIME: 2hrs

ASCENT: 682ft (208m)

PATHS: Field and woodland paths, rutted, wet and muddy tracks (in winter) and short stretches of road, 29 stiles

SUGGESTED MAP: aqua3 OS Explorer 133 Haslemere & Petersfield

GRID REFERENCE: SU 746291

PARKING: By village green and church in Hawkley

❶ With your back to Hawkley church, walk left beside the green to the road junction. With Hawkley Inn to your left, cross straight over and head down Cheesecombe Farm Lane ('Hangers Way'). Shortly, bear off right along the concrete path. Descend to the stile and keep straight on at the fork of paths, with Cheesecombe Farm on your left.

❷ Cross Oakshott Stream and keep left along the field edge beside woodland. Steeply ascend to the stile, keep right to a further stile, then turn left beside the fence and drop down to the track. Turn right, to reach the lane, then right again for 55yds (50m) to take the waymarked right of way beside Wheatham Hill House.

❸ Climb the long and steep chalky track up through Down Hanger (be warned, this track habitually gets very wet and muddy), with views unfolding east along the South Downs. At the top of Shoulder of Mutton Hill, turn right at the T-junction of tracks along Old Litten Lane. In 300yds (274m), take Hangers Way right over the stile. To look at the Edward Thomas memorial stone and appreciate the glorious South Downs views, continue along the track for 200yds (183m) and turn left with the waymarker. Pass beside the wooden barrier and then drop down to the clearing on Shoulder of Mutton Hill.

❹ On the return route, follow a short section of Hangers Way; this is a 21-mile (34km) long-distance trail that traverses the countryside of East Hampshire, from the Queen Elizabeth Country Park to Alton. Follow the Hangers Way trail as it descends through the edge of the beech woods and steeply down across lush meadowland, eventually joining the drive to Lower Oakshott Farmhouse and the road.

❺ Turn right, then go left over the stile and follow the clearly defined Hangers Way path through the Oakshott Valley, crossing stiles, plank bridges and some delightful meadows to reach the junction of paths before Cheesecombe Farm. Turn left to reach the stile and then retrace your steps back to Hawkley village green and your car.

The Crab at Chieveley

Berkshire

The Crab at Chieveley, Wantage Road, Chieveley, Newbury, Berkshire RG20 8UE

The Inn

The Crab is not actually in Chieveley but east of the village on the quiet B4494 Wantage Road. It's an enviable location, and views over the Berkshire Downs from the stylish terraces and beer garden make a favourable impression on visitors. Fish bar, restaurant, inn – all bases are covered – and the whole operation exudes an air of enthusiasm, thanks not least to the amiable and unpretentious David Barnard who hovers diligently and is thoroughly charming.

There's a strong Mediterranean feel to the pretty inner courtyard that leads to the bedrooms, which, in turn, plunder the world for decorative themes. From the jewel colours of the Raj-themed Indian Plantation to the fake fur of the Kenyan-themed Tree Tops, rooms are stylish and highly individual. Should your taste be more traditional, though, try Gleneagles, with its classic four-poster and tartan curtains. Contemporary bathrooms include five with a spa bath (the Moroccan-inspired La Mamounia has an eight-seat hot tub). Espresso machines and DVD players are standard issue, and many rooms have flat-screen TVs.

The Essentials

Time at the Bar!
12pm-12am
Food: 12-2.30pm, 6-9.30pm (7-9.30pm Fri & Sat)

What's the Damage?
Main courses from £12.50

Bitter Experience:
Fuller's London Pride, Timothy Taylor's Landlord,
West Berkshire Good Old Boy

Sticky Fingers:
Children welcome; smaller portions available

Muddy Paws:
Dogs welcome

Zzzzz:
14 rooms, £120-£200

Anything Else?
Terrace, garden, car park, conservatory

The Food

There are rug-strewn floorboards, large ornate mirrors and bright Mediterranean-inspired paintings on the walls, but it's the fishing nets, shells and fishing artefacts dangling from the ceiling that make it clear that seafood has long dominated proceedings here. And the kitchen certainly lives up to its promise, which is just as well: with nearly all seating given over to eating, the Crab is definitely more gastro than pub. An extensive list of hot and cold starters ranges from simple potted shrimps via giant Cornish king scallops with Thai butter to butter-poached lobster with mango and pak choi.

Main courses, meanwhile, might take in curried saffron bouillabaisse with tiger prawns, scallops and salmon, and Brixham sole goujons with Ratte potatoes and lemon salad. There's the odd nod to non-fish-eaters through organic rack of lamb or aged Angus beef fillet, and dessert options might run to passion fruit tart with frozen gin and tonic, or chocolate pavé with blood orange granita. Summer attractions include popular Sunday barbecues, and a crab and lobster festival held in July and August.

What To Do

Shop

HUNGERFORD

A busy, pretty market town with a number of eclectic shops. Benchmark Furniture (in nearby Kintbury) makes beautifully hand-crafted pieces for the home, while at Kitchenmonger you'll find all your cooking requirements. Hungerford Books is a delightful shop selling new and second-hand books, as well as gifts and cards.

Benchmark Furniture
Bath Road, Kintbury, Hungerford,
Berkshire RG17 9SA
01488 608020
www.benchmark-furniture.com

Hungerford Books
24 High Street, Hungerford,
Berkshire RG17 0NF
01488 683480
www.hungerfordbooks.co.uk

Kitchenmonger
8 High Street, Hungerford,
Berkshire RG17 0DN
01488 682158
www.kitchenmonger.co.uk

FARMERS' MARKET

Everything you buy at Newbury Farmers' Market is sold to you by those who produce it, all within a 30-mile (48-km) radius of Newbury. On the same day – first Sunday of the month – is an antique market at Kennet Shopping Centre in town.

Marketplace, Newbury, Berkshire

THE JELLY LEG'D CHICKEN

This light and airy gallery has quirky and innovative paintings, sculpture, jewellery and photography – much of it by local artists.

The Town Hall, Blagrave Street, Reading,
Berkshire RG1 1QH
0118 950 7926
www.jelly.org.uk

Visit

ASHDOWN HOUSE

This extraordinary 17th-century, Dutch-style house is famous for its association with the sister of Charles I, Elizabeth of Bohemia, who was nicknamed the 'Winter Queen'. The interior has impressive paintings of the period, and from the roof there are spectacular views over Ashdown Woods and the Berkshire Downs.

Lambourn, Newbury, Berkshire RG17 8RE
01793 762209
www.nationaltrust.org.uk

HIGHCLERE CASTLE

This is probably one of the finest Victorian buildings in the country, designed by Sir Charles Barry, who also designed the Houses of Parliament. Inside is an Egyptology exhibition relating to the fifth Earl of Carnarvon, who uncovered Tutankhamun's tomb. The castle dominates the grounds that were inspired by 'Capability' Brown. These have woodland and temple walks, and there's a fascinating Monk's Garden.

Highclere, Newbury, Berkshire RG20 9RN
01535 253210
www.highclerecastle.co.uk

SANDHAM MEMORIAL CHAPEL

This unique 1920s chapel contains Stanley Spencer's murals inspired by his experience of World War I – they took five years to complete and are possibly his best achievement. The surrounding orchard is carpeted with flowers, and there are views of Watership Down.

Harts Lane, Burghclere, Newbury
Berkshire RG20 9JT
01635 278394
www.nationaltrust.org.uk

Activity

BALLOONING

See the county from above. For a really special experience, charter your own champagne flight.

Floating Sensations
Upper Denford, Hungerford,
Berkshire RG18 9UD
01635 201007
www.floatingsensations.co.uk

GOLF

This beautiful 18-hole course takes in woodland and parkland, and is set against the backcloth of the Hampshire Downs. It runs from Greenham Common to Newbury Racecourse, and the vista from the 7th tee is breathtaking.

Newbury & Crookham Golf Club
Bury's Bank Road, Newbury,
Berkshire RG19 8BZ
01635 40035
www.newburygolf.co.uk

HORSE-DRAWN BARGE

What better way to discover the hidden charms of Berkshire than on a horse-drawn narrow boat on the Kennet and Avon Canal? Drift along at a relaxing pace through lovely countryside – and treat yourself to an on-board lunch.

Kennet Horse Boat Company
2 Rectory Cottage, Church Hill, Wickham,
Berkshire RG20 8HD
01488 658866
www.kennet-horse-boat.co.uk

HORSE RACING AT NEWBURY

Set in 360 acres of picturesque countryside, with a grandstand designed by Norman Foster.

Newbury Racecourse, Newbury,
Berkshire RG14 7NZ
01635 40015
www.newbury-racecourse.co.uk

The Walk - The Old Rectory at Farnborough

To the former home of a poet laureate, John Betjeman.

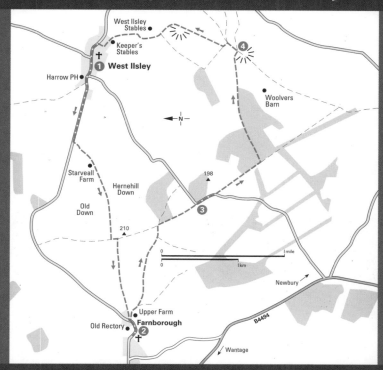

Walk Details

LENGTH: 7.5 miles (12.1km)

TIME: 3hrs

ASCENT: 150ft (46m)

PATHS: Bridleways, field paths, tracks and quiet lanes, no stiles

SUGGESTED MAP: aqua3 OS Explorer 170 Abingdon & Wantage

GRID REFERENCE: SU 471825

PARKING: Room to park in West Ilsley's main street

❶ Follow the road out of West Ilsley, heading west. Take the 1st bridleway on the left and make for the gate. Continue ahead with field boundary on right. Bear left at next junction, and then almost immediately right to follow the path across large field. Look for boundary corner ahead and keep ahead in next field, with fence on the right. Follow the path across the field to road by Upper Farm, veer left and walk along to Farnborough church and the Old Rectory.

❷ Walk along the road to the farm, rejoin track beside outbuildings and look for the waymark and galvanised gates after about 60yds (55m). The field footpath and 2 tracks can be seen here. Keep right, alongside the farm. Cut between the trees, bushes and margins of vegetation and cross the track further on. Continue ahead to a junction with byway and bridleway. Keep going through woodland, following Ilsley Downs Riding Route. Make for next junction, where you can see field beyond the trees, bear right and follow clear path through woods.

❸ Keep right at the road and when it bends right, keep ahead along the bridleway running across fields towards trees. At length, bridleway becomes byway. Keep ahead on reaching the bend and walk along to path on left. Take it into woodland and down slope. As you approach a gap in hedge, with field ahead, veer right to follow path running through trees. Eventually it climbs gently to a junction. Walk turns left, but it is worth stepping to right for several paces to admire timeless view of Woolvers Barn and Woolvers Down.

❹ Follow the byway, avoiding the public footpath on the right, and take the next bridleway on the left. Keep right at the next junction and cut through between the hedges. When the track bends left, there is a memorable view of West Ilsley sitting snug in its downland setting. Keep right at the next junction, following the track alongside West Ilsley Stables. Walk down to the path and turn left. As it bends right by the bridleway sign, go straight on by Keeper's Stables. Swing left as you reach the centre of West Ilsley and pass All Saints Church.

Carnarvon Arms

Berkshire

The Inn

Four months of careful refurbishment in 2005 saw the Carnarvon Arms, a rambling old coaching inn near the gates of Highclere Castle, reopen as a 'fine dining, traditional country inn' – one with a warm, contemporary and tasteful look. Today's incarnation has fresh, natural colours on the walls, bare boards and subtle lighting throughout; there are deep sofas in relaxing lounge areas, and a stylish, yet traditional feel to the extended bar. What's more, you'll find three real ales on tap, a raft of wines by the glass, and a bar menu listing traditional pub dishes.

The high-vaulted dining area is equally informal, sporting painted beams, rug-strewn boards, polished tables, an ornate fireplace, and Egyptian motifs inspired by Highclere Castle's Egyptian collection – brought back to the south of England from the Valley of the Kings by the fifth Earl of Carnarvon. Bedrooms are furnished and decorated with style and panache: all are comfortable and homely, featuring pale wood furnishings, plasma screens, internet access, and smart tiled bathrooms with top toiletries and power showers.

The Essentials

Time at the Bar!
11am-11pm
Food: 12-3pm, 6.30-9pm
(Fri-Sat 9.30pm), Sun 12-4pm,
6.30-8.30pm

What's the Damage?
Main courses from £7.95

Bitter Experience:
Greene King IPA,
Shepherd Neame Spitfire

Sticky Fingers:
Children welcome, children's menu

Muddy Paws:
No dogs

Zzzzz:
23 rooms, £79.95-£89.95

Anything Else?
Garden, car park

The Food

The fine dining side of the operation comes courtesy of executive chef Robert Clayton, whose skilled cooking, based on modern British cuisine, has seen him head up several Michelin-star kitchens, notably the Priory Hotel in Bath. Using local butcher meats, game from the Highclere Estate, fish from Brixham, and other ingredients from quality suppliers, Clayton's menus change with the seasons, although the odd dish changes on a whim to add interest.

The main menu is also available in the bar and you can order just a starter, perhaps scallops with asparagus and parmesan and balsamic dressing, or crispy braised duck leg with celeriac mash. Or go the whole hog and tuck into pan-fried turbot with confit fennel and red wine sauce, or shoulder of lamb with red wine sauce, followed by vanilla bean panna cotta with berry compote, or citrus bread and butter pudding. Conversely, if you fancy fish and chips or steak and ale pie in the dining room, then that's fine, too. The bar menu also offers sandwiches and classic pub dishes like home-made burger with red onion marmalade.

What To Do

Shop

ANTIQUES

Hungerford is the place to visit for antiques. The town has been well known for its antiques trade for many years, and today there are two sizeable centres, housing 80 individual dealers, several general antique shops and many specialists. All of the outlets are great hunting grounds for dealers, collectors and browsers of fine furniture, clocks, silverware, ceramics, pottery and a full range of decorative and utilitarian collectables.

Hungerford High Street, Berkshire
www.hungerford.co.uk

WEST BERKSHIRE BREWERY

The West Berkshire Brewery is a real rural success story. It was back in 1995 that local builder Dave Maggs and his wife Helen decided to start their own micro-brewery. It became so successful that they had to find larger premises in Yattendon. Today the brewery benefits from an extended brewhouse, new equipment and has a shop selling a good range of the company's excellent ales plus local ceramics and crafts.

Yattendon, Thatcham, Berkshire RG18 0UE
01635 202968
www.wbbrew.co.uk

Visit

HIGHCLERE CASTLE

Berkshire's largest house dates back to the first half of the 19th century and was designed for the third Earl of Carnarvon by Charles Barry, the architect of the Houses of Parliament. It was later home to the fifth Earl who opened Tutankhamun's tomb in 1922. The castle contains objects from other sites in Europe and is one of the county's major tourist attractions, and a popular wedding venue.

Highclere, Newbury, Berkshire RG20 9RN
01635 253210
www.highclerecastle.co.uk

SANDHAM MEMORIAL CHAPEL

This small red-brick chapel was built in the 1920s to house a series of fascinating but disturbing murals by the artist Stanley Spencer, inspired by his experiences in World War I. Influenced by Giotto's Arena Chapel in Padua, Spencer took five years to complete what is arguably his finest achievement. The chapel is in the care of the National Trust and it stands in a mature orchard enjoying beautiful views towards Watership Down.

Harts Lane, Burghclere, Newbury, Berkshire RG20 9JT
01635 278394
www.nationaltrust.org.uk

THE VYNE

It was in 1956 that the National Trust added this grand country house to their collection of historic treasures. Built by William Sandys, Henry VIII's Lord Chamberlain, between 1518 and 1527, The Vyne includes a Tudor chapel, a Palladian staircase and a variety of fine old panelling and furniture. There's also the chance to enjoy a woodland stroll in the grounds where you can discover the herbaceous borders, a wild garden and an example of one of the earliest summer houses.

Sherborne St John, Basingstoke, Hampshire RG24 9HL
01256 883858
www.nationaltrust.org.uk/thevyne

Activity

BALLOONING

What better way to see and appreciate the English countryside than from a hot-air balloon? One of the longest established hot-air balloon operators in the country, based near the M4, specialises in providing passengers with breathtaking views over rural Berkshire, Wiltshire and Oxfordshire. A variety of balloons take to the skies – from the smallest three-passenger size to the largest, which is capable of carrying 11 people.

01635 201007
www.floatingsensations.co.uk

FLY FISHING

Experience a day's fly fishing at one of the exclusive sites (Wherwell Priory or Mottisfont Abbey) along the beautiful River Test, one of England's finest chalk streams. Day rods can be booked on the river and private tuition for the day can be arranged on the Wallop Brook at Nether Wallop Mill.

Fishing Breaks, The Mill, Heathman Lane, Nether Wallop, Stockbridge, Hampshire SO20 8EW
01264 781988
www.fishingbreaks.co.uk

KENNET HORSE BOAT COMPANY

Enjoy the pace and tranquillity of a bygone era on this horse-drawn canal cruise along the Kennet and Avon canal to the west of the market town of Newbury. The boat journey offers some stunning scenery and an unmissable trip into the past as you discover the fascinating history of this restored waterway.

01488 658866
www.kennet-horse-boat.co.uk

The Walk - *High Above Highclere Castle*

A hilltop grave and a decorated chapel are just two of the features of this walk.

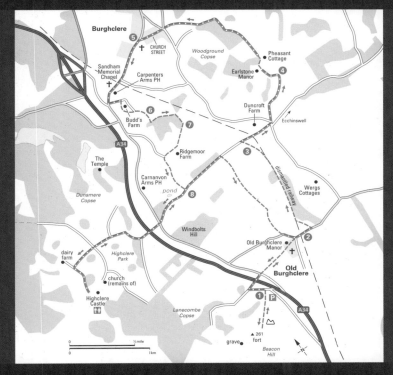

Walk Details

LENGTH: 6.5 miles (10.4km)

TIME: 3hrs

ASCENT: 767ft (234m)

PATHS: Tracks, field and woodland paths, some roads, 6 stiles

SUGGESTED MAP: aqua3 OS Explorers 144 Basingstoke, Alton & Whitchurch; 158 Newbury & Hungerford

GRID REFERENCE: SU 463575 (on Explorer 144)

PARKING: Beacon Hill car park off A34

INFORMATION: This walk is over the county border in Hampshire

1 Climb Beacon Hill at the start or finish. Leave the car park via the access road. Cross A34 bridge to T-junction. Take footpath opposite, downhill to gate. Walk along field edge to Old Burghclere. Pass beside church wall and Old Burghclere Manor to lane. Proceed ahead, cross railway bridge and take path left.

2 Keep to the lefthand field edge. Enter woodland. Shortly, bear left on to the track bed. Turn right. Follow the track to the bridge.

3 Bear left up the chalky path to the track. Turn right over the bridge. Descend to the lane, turn left then right, ('Ecchinswell'). In 50yds (46m), take the waymarked bridleway left. Keep to the path until the gravel drive. Turn left.

4 Follow the track to Earlstone Manor. Proceed through or close to woodland for 1 mile (1.6km) to road. Turn right, then left along Church Street in Burghclere, ('Sandham Memorial Chapel').

5 Turn left by the church; keep to the road, passing the Memorial Chapel and Carpenters Arms, before turning left along a metalled dead-end lane. Pass the cottage; take the footpath right between the gardens to stile. Skirt round Budd's Farm across 3 fields via 3 stiles; join the path through the trees to stile.

6 Turn right along the field edge, following it left in corner. Descend to fingerpost. Follow lefthand path into woodland. If the route is boggy, keep to the field edge, looking out for gap and path right into woodland. Cross to the stile keep ahead across field. Bear right through gap to field.

7 Ignore path to left. Continue, with woodland on right, to waymarker. Turn right towards Ridgemoor Farm. Pass pond to gate and track. Turn right, then where it bears right, go left on the sunken path to the track. To visit Highclere Castle, turn right to the road; cross the A34; enter parkland; follow drive to house. Retrace steps; keep ahead.

8 Turn left to the crossroads, then right. Head uphill; keeping to the undulating track for 0.5 mile (800m) to Old Burghclere. Turn left along the lane; then right along the drive to Old Burghclere Manor. Retrace your outward steps to the car park.

The New Inn

Berkshire

DESSERTS
Sticky Toffee Pudding £4.95
Vanilla Creme Brulee £4.75
Eton Mess £4.75
Dark Chocolate Torte £4.75
Selection of Ice Creams £4.25
Crumble £4.75
£5.95

The Essentials

Time at the Bar!
11am–11pm
Food: 12-2.30pm, 6.30-9.45pm
No food Sun evening

What's the Damage?
Main courses from £6.50

Bitter Experience:
Brakspear Bitter, Bee Sting

Sticky Fingers:
Children welcome; small portions
available

Muddy Paws:
Dogs welcome in the bar

Zzzzz:
6 rooms, £75-£110

Anything Else?
Patio, garden, car park

The Inn

The white-painted building with casement windows, peeping out from a steep-pitched tiled roof, is in a thoroughly rural location yet just 5 miles (8km) north of Reading. A beer garden and a perfect patio, shaded by a giant single parasol, make the most of the peaceful setting, while inside the decor is predominantly modern but still with all the trappings of an old English village pub – without the clutter. Expect lots of beams in the low-ceilinged bar, a large exposed brick fireplace, bare floorboards and cottage-style furniture. For many, this is the ideal retreat, combining good food with superb overnight accommodation.

Bedrooms and bathrooms have been given an ultra-modern lift with light wood floors, neutral shades of cream, brown and beige, crisp white linen, scatter cushions and throws on large, comfortable beds, as well as flat-screen TVs, DVD players and good lighting. All six rooms are named after grape varieties – Semillion, Shiraz, Merlot, for example – and vary in size. The best, Champagne, sports a state-of-the-art bathroom with a walk-in wet room and double sinks.

The Food

With a stylish, softly lit, beamed restaurant, where plain wood tables are simply laid and high-backed chairs are comfortable, this is obviously a pub where food takes centre stage. The menu is an ambitious collection of upmarket pub dishes with brasserie leanings: chicken liver parfait with spiced apple and brandy chutney, griddled black pudding with Dijon mustard sauce, fillet steak with creamy peppercorn sauce, cottage pie with cheddar and leek mash, and sea bass with sautéed leeks. The food is pitched exactly right for the surroundings, with the kitchen delivering fresh, honestly prepared dishes with bags of flavour.

Traditional roasts with all the trimmings keep Sunday lunch special, otherwise expect light bites, such as crayfish tail salad, deep-fried whitebait, ciabattas filled with smoked bacon and brie or smoked salmon and cream cheese, and more substantial plates of home-made lasagne, rib-eye steak burger served with smoked Applewood cheddar, caramelised onions and home-made chips, and Cumberland sausage and mash smothered in rich onion gravy.

What To Do

Shop

BOHUN GALLERY
Specialising in contemporary British fine art, this gallery exhibits paintings, sculpture, watercolours, drawings, original prints and ceramics. Artists represented range from the young and promising to recognised and respected figures. There is a lively and varied annual exhibition programme, plus a show of sculpture in the garden.

15 Reading Road, Henley on Thames, Oxfordshire RG9 1AB
01491 576228
www.bohungallery.co.uk

CHILTERN VALLEY WINERY & BREWERY
With vines first planted in 1982 on the slopes of the Chilterns, surrounded by beech woodland and overlooking the beautiful Hambleden Valley, Old Luxters is home to the Chiltern Valley Winery and Brewery, which produces fine wines and real ales.

Old Luxters Vineyard, Hambleden, Henley on Thames, Oxfordshire RG9 6JW
01491 638330
www.chilternvalley.co.uk

THE HERB FARM
A picturesque timber-framed local barn forms the centrepiece of this specialist herb nursery, where experienced staff grow a comprehensive range of herb plants to sell. There are also cottage garden plants and old-style roses, as well as herb-based products and hand-crafted items. The Saxon Maze adds extra interest.

Peppard Road, Sonning Common, Reading, Berkshire RG4 9NJ
0118 972 4220
www.herbfarm.co.uk

Visit

CLIVEDEN
Stroll through an impressive series of unique formal gardens in the footsteps of Anglo-American high society – Cliveden was once home to the Astors. An enchanting and unspoilt stretch of the Thames borders the garden and Italianate mansion, which is now a hotel. Rub shoulders, too, with a superb collection of sculpture and statues from the ancient and modern world.

Taplow, Maidenhead, Buckinghamshire SL6 0JA
01628 605069
www.nationaltrust.org.uk

MAPLEDURHAM HOUSE & WATERMILL
Depart from Caversham and arrive by boat at the historic home of the Blount family, a superb Elizabethan mansion set in a Thameside location in beautiful countryside. The watermill is the last remaining on the River Thames, and it still grinds flour for sale in the gift shop. Cream teas can be purchased in the Old Manor tea rooms.

Mapledurham Estate, Reading, Berkshire RG4 7TR
0118 972 3350
www.mapledurham.co.uk

OXFORD
To be so close to the ancient 'city of dreaming spires' and not actually visit it would be a crime. With its mix of ancient and modern in a bustling cosmopolitan environment, there truly is something for everyone here.

Oxford Tourist Information Centre, 15–16 Broad Street, Oxford, Oxfordshire OX1 3AS
01865 726 871
www.oxfordcity.co.uk

Activity

BOATING ON THE THAMES
Get afloat on the mighty River Thames. Hobbs of Henley have a fleet of self-drive motor launches, available by the hour or day, for up to 12 people. There's also a fleet of Edwardian-style launches, complete with chauffeur, if required – ideal for the Henley Regatta. You could even hire a rowing boat.

Hobbs of Henley
Station Road, Henley on Thames, Oxfordshire RG9 1AZ
01491 572035
www.hobbs-of-henley.com

HORSE RACING AT NEWBURY
One of the finest sporting venues in the UK, with an average of 30 flat and National Hunt race days per year. Highlights include the prestigious Hennessy Cognac Gold Cup over the jumps, and the Juddmonte Lockinge Stakes on the flat. Within the venue, there's an 18-hole (par 71) golf course, with practice facilities, and a 20-bay floodlit driving range.

Newbury Racecourse, Newbury, Berkshire RG14 7NZ
01635 40015
www.newbury-racecourse.co.uk

WALK THE THAMES PATH
Follow England's best-known river for 184 miles (294km) as it meanders through peaceful water meadows rich in wildlife, historic towns and many lovely villages, and on through the bustle of the City of London. Reliably gentle underfoot, the Thames Path is perfect for an afternoon's stroll, a weekend break or an even longer trek.

01865 810224
www.nationaltrail.co.uk/thamespath

The Walk - On the Wilde Side of Reading

A canal-side trail past Reading Gaol, where Oscar Wilde served time.

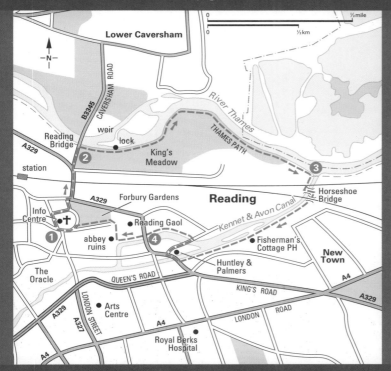

Walk Details

LENGTH: 3 miles (4.8km)

TIME: 1hr 15min

ASCENT: Negligible

PATHS: Pavements, river and canal tow path, no stiles

SUGGESTED MAP: aqua3 OS Explorer 159 Reading, Wokingham & Pangbourne. A good street map of Reading

GRID REFERENCE: SU 716735

PARKING: Reading Station, Chatham Street, Garrard Street, Hexagon

① Start the walk by the statue of Queen Victoria and, with your back to the Town Hall, turn right, passing the tourist information centre and the museum. Cross Valpy Street and turn right into Forbury Road. Walk to the roundabout, with the Rising Sun pub on the corner, and turn left towards the railway bridge. Pass beneath the railway line and cross the road at the pedestrian lights. Avoid King's Meadow Road and make for Reading Bridge.

② Take the steps on the right just before the bridge and join the Thames Path, heading downstream with the river on the left. Pass Caversham Lock as the sound of traffic begins to fade and your surroundings become leafier.

Skirt King's Meadow, with smart apartment buildings and lines of houses on the opposite bank. Pass the boat yard and continue under the tree branches. Eventually reach Kennet Mouth and here a distinctive Sustrans waymark directs you over the bridge (in direction of Bristol!).

③ Cross Horseshoe Bridge and turn right on the far side, heading for central Reading. Pass beneath Brunel's railway bridge, continue to Fisherman's Cottage and Blakes Lock, and leave the canal tow path at the next bridge. Turn right along King's Road, passing the listed façade of Huntley and Palmer's biscuit factory, then turn immediately right and cross the bridge built by Reading Gas

Company (1880). Join the tow path and keep walking, with the vast hulk of the Prudential building over on the left bank.

④ Pass under King's Road, keep to the right and follow Chestnut Walk. Reading Gaol is on the right. Walk to the ruins of Reading Abbey and turn right. Keep beside the gaol and enter Forbury Gardens through the flint arch. Keep to the left edge, with the statue of the lion on the right. Look for the abbey gateway on the left, with Reading Crown Court adjacent, and exit at Victoria Gate. Walk ahead to the outer gate of Reading Abbey, pass the Church of St Laurence-in-Reading on the right and return to the tourist information centre and the statue.

✳ Sunset on the River Thames, Reading, Berkshire

The Black Boys Inn

Berkshire

The Essentials

Time at the Bar!
Bar & Food 12-1.45pm, 7-8.45pm
Closed Sun

What's the Damage?
Main courses from £11.50

Bitter Experience:
No real ales

Sticky Fingers:
Children over 12 years welcome

Muddy Paws:
No dogs

Zzzzz:
8 rooms, £75-£95

Anything Else?
Terrace, garden, car park

The Inn

The pastel-coloured roadside building may look like a pub from the outside, especially with the words Brakspear writ large on the façade, but new owners and new ideas have seen this country pub transformed for the better. Plenty of money has been spent on revamping the interior, and the result is certainly swish, with discreet, heritage-style colours, soft lighting, varnished floorboards and well-padded chairs. And there's a talented chef in the kitchen. Indeed, a pub that operates as a restaurant and takes its food seriously is a fair assessment of this 16th-century building.

Should you wish to stay the night, eight attractive bedrooms are to be found in an annexe a few steps from the entrance. Light and spacious, with contemporary styling and gorgeous views across the Chiltern hills, they come with comfortable beds, and baths or power showers (with water from the inn's own well) in compact modern bathrooms, while rooms on the first floor (reached via an iron staircase) have wonderful high, beamed ceilings. In addition to all this, there's a library in the bar for the bedrooms' DVD players, and internet connection.

The Food

The restaurant seems to have settled into an easy familiarity within its smart surroundings, offering well-spaced tables, comfortable chairs and gentle lighting to create a calm environment in which to study Simon Bonwick's menus. These have some appealing ideas: foie gras with prune and armagnac chutney and toasted brioche, for example, or a main course sautéed calf's sweetbread with petit choucroute and grain mustard. First-class materials underpin the operation, whether it's fresh, hand-picked Salcombe crab (with lime and red pepper gelée), roquefort cheese with pear vinaigrette, or baked rack of local pig teamed with paisley pudding, black mustard seed and apple and ginger.

The cooking demonstrates a knowing facility with contemporary styles, but it is the fact that flavours and textures are intelligently considered that proves ultimately satisfying. Date and pecan sticky toffee pudding has a traditional feel at dessert stage, but there's autumn berry and marzipan fritter with a vanilla mousse and berry soup for the more adventurous. For the quality of the cooking, prices are reasonable.

What To Do

Shop

CHILTERN VALLEY WINERY & BREWERY

Set in an area of outstanding natural beauty, this is home to award-winning wines and farm-brewed, full-mash real ales.

Old Luxters Vineyard, Hambleden, Henley on Thames, Oxfordshire RG9 6JW
01491 638330
www.chilternvalley.co.uk

THE HERB FARM

The Herb Farm sells many unusual herbs, 40 varieties of lavender, scented geraniums, lemon verbena and bay trees. You'll find inspiration in the delightful gardens, where there are David Austin roses and a beech maze.

Peppard Road, Sonning Common, Reading, Berkshire RG4 9NJ
0118 972 4220
www.herbfarm.co.uk

MAIDENHEAD FARMERS' MARKET

All the best of the region can be bought at Berkshire's longest-running farmers' market, with up to 30 stallholders selling eggs, cheese, bread, meat and more.

Grove Road Car Park, Maidenhead, Berkshire
www.greenlink-berkshire.org.uk

STANLEY SPENCER GALLERY

This gallery, a former Methodist chapel where Spencer was taken as a child to worship, is devoted exclusively to the work of the great master. It is situated in the village where Spencer was born and lived for most of his life.

The Kings Hall, High Steet, Cookham, Berkshire SL6 9SJ
01628 471885
www.stanleyspencer.org.uk

Visit

CLIVEDEN

Infamously associated with the 'Profumo Affair', Cliveden was one of the haunts of the rich and famous. Enjoy the magnificent formal gardens overlooking the Thames, the stunning parterre and Italianate mansion, and the magical walks through the woods. Outdoor theatre has come to Cliveden, with productions ranging from murder mysteries to Shakespeare.

Taplow, Maidenhead, Buckinghamshire SL6 0JA
01628 605069
www.nationaltrust.org.uk

HUGHENDEN MANOR

Have a fascinating glimpse into the life of Benjamin Disraeli who lived here until his death in 1881. Inside the handsome house is a collection of memorabilia, personal belongings, furnishings and paintings. There are stunning views over the Chilterns, and gardens designed by his wife Mary Anne.

High Wycombe, Buckinghamshire HP14 4LA
01494 755573
www.nationaltrust.org.uk

SAVILL GARDEN

One of the country's greatest ornamental gardens, Savill Garden is to be found within Windsor Great Park. There are 35 acres of contemporary and classically designed gardens and exotic woodland, with a wonderful display of colour all year round. Leith's restaurant in the iconic, leaf-shaped visitor centre is unmissable.

Windsor Great Park, Windsor, Berkshire SL4 2HT
01784 435544
www.theroyallandscape.co.uk

STONOR PARK

One of the oldest manor houses in the country, Stonor has been the home of the Camoys for over 800 years, and is in a stunning setting in a beautiful Chiltern valley, surrounded by a deer park. The house contains a remarkable collection of rare European and American sculpture, old masters and stained glass. In the grounds is a walled Italianate garden, and the views from the kitchen garden are spectacular. The cafe is a good place for lunch.

Stonor, Henley on Thames, Oxfordshire RG9 6HF
01491 638587
www.stonor.com

Activity

BOATING ON THE THAMES

Hobbs is a long-established, family-run business – hire a motor launch for an hour or two, or treat yourself to a chauffeur-driven Edwardian launch trip up the river. There are occasional popular jazz and wildlife cruises, too.

Hobbs of Henley, Station Road, Henley on Thames, Oxfordshire RG9 1AZ
01491 572035
www.hobbs-of-henley.com

GOLF

Something of a hidden gem, Temple Golf Club is beautifully situated in stunning landscape, with panoramic views over the Thames. This long established, par 70 undulating course is challenging and enjoyable.

Temple Golf Club, Henley Road, Hurley, Berkshire SL6 5LH
01628 824795
www.templegolfclub.co.uk

The Walk - Wargrave To Bowsey Hill

A stroll that takes you to the top of peaceful Bowsey Hill.

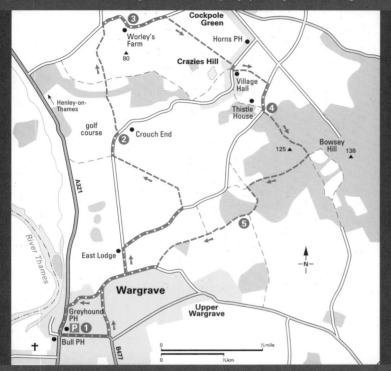

Walk Details

LENGTH: 6 miles (9.7km)

TIME: 2hrs 15min

ASCENT: 248ft (76m)

PATHS: Stretches of road, field and woodland paths, 13 stiles

SUGGESTED MAP: aqua3 OS Explorer 171 Chiltern Hills West

GRID REFERENCE: SU 786785

PARKING: Public car park in School Lane, just off A321

❶ Turn left. Walk along School Lane, (B477). On 1st bend, bear left into Dark Lane, head up the hill; turn right at the T-junction. Follow road; turn left ('Crazies Hill'). Bear right by East Lodge, follow the lane to the bend; bear left over the stile to join the waymarked path. Keep alongside the fence, and across the fields towards the trees. Cross stile; turn right at the road, veering left opposite the house, 'Crouch End'.

❷ Keep close to the left boundary of the field; look for the stile in bottom corner. Descend steeply to 2 stiles and bridleway beyond. Cross the stile almost opposite; climb hillside. Look for the stile further up the slope and keep ahead on higher ground, following the path alongside fence. Descend to kissing gate at road; turn immediately right. Head uphill, passing Worley's Farm.

❸ Take the next waymarked path on the right, just before the row of trees, and aim a little to the left as you cross the field, lining up with white house in distance. Head towards stile in hedge and maintain direction, keeping to left of house. Look for stile; follow enclosed path to road. Turn right, then left beside village hall; after a few paces, bear left by Old Clubhouse. Follow path by paddock to a stile by road. Bear right, past entrance to Thistle House and bridleway into trees on right.

❹ Continue for several paces to the stile on the left. Join woodland path (watch for white arrows on tree trunks) eventually reaching the waymarked junction. Turn right here, avoid the path on the right and keep going to the next waymarked junction, on the edge of the wood. Bear left; walk down to a flight of steps and a footbridge. Make for the woodland perimeter; turn right along the field edge.

❺ Cross the bridleway via 2 stiles. Proceed along the woodland edge. Look for the hedge gap on the right; cross into adjoining field; maintain direction. Make for kissing gate and footbridge in field corner. Follow the path across the field, heading towards the trees. Make for the kissing gate leading out to road. Turn right. Follow it to A321, turn left. Walk to School Lane.

The White Horse
West Sussex

The Inn

The low, wisteria-clad inn dates from 1768, and its glorious Sussex Downs setting close to Chichester made it a good staging post for horses when travelling over the Downs. Now it's the perfect place for foodies and wine buffs to be fed and watered in style. Charles Burton dreamt of owning this fine old inn when he worked here as a waiter in the 1970s. He realised that dream in 1998 and has since developed the impressive rooms. There's a simplified, modern look in the wood-floored bar, with its crackling fire, relaxing sofas and floor-to-ceiling wine rack, which leads through to the smart, uncluttered dining rooms with well-spaced tables covered in pristine white cloths and fresh flowers.

Named after a premier wine or champagne (available for tasting in the restaurant), the nine contemporary rooms are light and airy with rugs on polished boards, king-size beds and plasma screens, while bathrooms boast power showers, bathrobes and posh smellies. Breakfast is another treat – delivered to your room in a country hamper filled with hot pastries, fruit, preserves, fresh orange juice and coffee.

The Essentials

Time at the Bar!
11am-3pm, 6-11pm. Closed Sun evening & all Mon
Food: 12-2pm, 7-10pm

What's the Damage?
Main courses from £14.95

Bitter Experience:
Ballard's Best

Sticky Fingers:
Children welcome; smaller portions

Muddy Paws:
Dogs allowed in the bar

Zzzzz:
9 rooms, £95-£160; single £75-£95

Anything Else?
Garden, car park

The White Horse, High Street, Chilgrove, Chichester, West Sussex PO18 9JX

The Food

Designed as a place to relax, the bar offers a glass of magnificent wine and something light and delicious from the lunchtime menu, perhaps Italian-style open sandwiches or hand-picked Selsey crab. Delve seriously into the wine list at dinner to accompany some ambitious dishes from the restaurant menu (also served in the bar), which may list warm salad of black pudding with scallops and orange sauce, or red pepper-filled crab with a creamed mussel sauce for starters.

For the main course, go for the lamb hotpot, the Rother Valley organic beef fillet served with green peppercorn sauce, the calves' liver and bacon with shallot gravy, or the fishy option, perhaps sea bass with smoked salmon mousse with a scallop sauce. Leave room for warm chocolate tart with orange ice cream, raspberry soufflé or a classic sticky toffee pudding served with clotted cream. A choice of wine by the glass is recommended with every dish, so indulge yourself and explore the legendary global list of wines.

What To Do

Shop

GOODWOOD HOUSE

As well as offering horse racing and motor sports, Goodwood has produced clothing and merchandise that reflect the Earl of March's passion for style and design. There are separate ranges for both motor sports and horse racing, using the finest materials and the best of British craftsmanship.

Goodwood, Chichester,
West Sussex PO18 0PX
01243 755000
www.goodwood.co.uk

PETERSFIELD MARKET

A twice-weekly market is held every Wednesday and Saturday throughout the year in The Square, around the magnificent equestrian statue of William III. The ancient town of Petersfield, originally built as a Norman 'new town' at the end of the 11th century, is a charming and thriving country market town situated amid the gentle slopes of the South Downs.

The Square, Petersfield, Hampshire

SELBORNE POTTERY

Established in 1985 by Robert Goldsmith. All the work produced here is hand-thrown and turned stoneware – no machines or moulds are used, and the traditional techniques have taken many years to perfect. Combined with high-temperature stoneware glazes, fine brushwork, wax resist and glaze trailing, the finished pots with rich copper red and cobalt blue glazes are both functional and decorative with a contemporary look.

Selborne, Alton, Hampshire GU34 3JQ
01420 511413
http://web.onetel.net.uk/~selbornepottery

Visit

FISHBOURNE ROMAN PALACE

The Romans built some superb buildings to remind them of home. Fishbourne Roman Palace was discovered by accident during the digging of a water mains trench in 1960. This led to nine seasons of excavations that showed the site had developed from a military base at the time of the Roman invasion in AD43 to a sumptuous palace by the end of the first century.

Salthill Road, Fishbourne, Chichester,
West Sussex PO19 3QS
01243 785859
www.sussexpast.co.uk/property/site

PETWORTH HOUSE & PARK

Set in a Capability Brown-landscaped deer park, this vast 17th-century mansion is home to the National Trust's finest art collection, with works by Turner, Van Dyck, Reynolds and Blake. Also includes intricate wooden carvings, fine furniture and sculpture, and fascinating servants' quarters.

Petworth, West Sussex GU28 0AE
01798 342207
www.nationaltrust.org.uk

WEALD & DOWNLAND OPEN AIR MUSEUM

Wander through architectural history dating from the 13th to the 19th century. Here, in 50 acres of beautiful Sussex countryside, over 40 buildings have been rescued, conserved and rebuilt to their original design, many with gardens. There are also farm animals, woodland walks and a lake.

Town Lane, Singleton, Chichester,
West Sussex PO18 0EU
01243 811363
www.wealddown.co.uk

Activity

CYCLING

In all directions, there are views, woods, lanes, open countryside and great country pubs for lunch. There is a safe family ride along the Centurion Way cycle path, or ride off-road around the tracks on the beautiful West Dean Estate. Or head to the top of the Trundle overlooking Goodwood Racecourse, with views to the coast.

Shed End Bikes
108 West Dean, Chichester,
West Sussex PO18 0RX
01243 811766
www.shedendbikes.co.uk

MOTOR & HORSE RACING

If motor racing is your thing, then come for the Festival of Speed or the Goodwood Revival. Horses have raced at Goodwood for over 200 years, and Glorious Goodwood is the culmination of the summer season. A historic golf course, trial flying lessons and shooting are also here to tempt you, set in 12,000 acres.

Goodwood, Chichester,
West Sussex PO18 0PX
01243 755000
www.goodwood.co.uk

WALKING THE SOUTH DOWNS WAY

Experience some of our finest countryside between Winchester, first capital of England, and the white chalk cliffs of Eastbourne. If you are interested in great views, attractive wildlife, visible prehistory and pretty villages, or if you just fancy a challenge, the South Downs Way awaits you.

Andy Gattiker
South Downs Way National Trail Officer
01243 558716
www.nationaltrail.co.uk/southdowns

The Walk - *Views and Yews at Kingley Vale*

Discover an ancient forest teeming with wildlife high up on the South Downs.

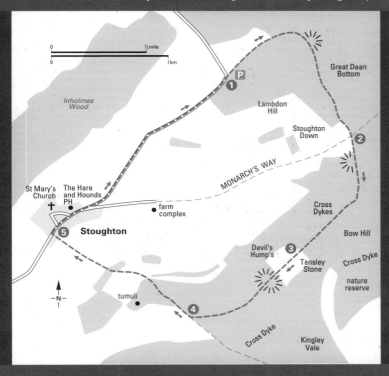

Walk Details

LENGTH: 5 miles (8km)

TIME: 2hrs

ASCENT: 440ft (134m)

PATHS: Mostly woodland paths and downland tracks

SUGGESTED MAP: aqua3 OS Explorer 120 Chichester, South Harting & Selsey

GRID REFERENCE: SU 814215

PARKING: Free car park at Stoughton Down

❶ From the car park make for the bridleway near the exit and follow it away from the road, skirting dense beech woodland. There are striking views on the left over pastoral, well-wooded countryside. Keep right at the fork and follow the stony path as it curves to the right. Veer right at the next waymarked fork and begin a gradual ascent beneath the boughs of beech trees.

❷ Eventually break cover from the trees at a major junction of waymarked tracks. Go straight on, looking to the right all the way for some spectacular views. Continue to the next bridleway sign at a fork and join the path running parallel to the track. Cut between the trees and keep going until you reach the gap on the right. Keep to the waymarked path as it runs down the slope. Rejoin the enclosed track, turning left to follow the track as it runs up the slope towards Bow Hill.

❸ On reaching Devil's Humps, veer off the path to enjoy magnificent vistas across downland countryside. Immediately below are the trees of Kingley Vale. This was a wartime artillery range but Kingley Vale became a nature reserve in 1952 and today it is managed by Natural England. Head along the footpath in a westerly direction, with the nature reserve on the left. Continue between the carpets of bracken and the lines of beech trees.

❹ Turn right at the next main junction and follow the bridle track along the field edge. On the left you will see glimpses of Chichester Harbour, with its complex network of watery channels and sprawling mudflats. Pass by several ancient burial tumuli before descending through an area of beech woodland. Keep going until you reach the road. Turn right and walk through the pleasant village of Stoughton.

❺ Pass the entrance to St Mary's Church on the left, followed by the Hare and Hounds pub. Continue walking through the village and on your right you will see Monarch's Way. Follow the road out of Stoughton, all the way to the lefthand bend where you will see the entrance to the car park on Stoughton Down on the right.

The Crab & Lobster

West Sussex

The Inn

This gloriously located pub, south of Chichester, is tucked away on the banks of Pagham Harbour. The new-look 'Crab' is a stunning south coast hideaway, perfect for Goodwood race-goers, walkers exploring the South Downs and well-heeled 'twitchers' searching for wintering waders on the marshes. Expect a contemporary feel in the opened-up bar, with original flagstones, crackling log fires, deep leather chairs in the bar and high-backed upholstered chairs around darkwood tables in the cosy dining area.

Four swish new bedrooms ooze style and comfort, and you won't be disappointed with the soothing heritage colours, the plasma screens, the Egyptian cotton sheets on king-size beds, or the power showers and posh L'Occitane smellies in the expensively tiled bathrooms. Book the Loft Suite for the hand-made bed, the squashy sofa, the plank-floored bathroom with walk-in double shower, and the marsh views – telescope provided. Breakfast on home-made muesli, local sausage, bacon and black pudding, and then explore the marshland paths.

The Essentials

Time at the Bar!
11am-11pm
Food: 12-2.15pm, 6-9.30pm

What's the Damage?
Main courses from £11.50

Bitter Experience:
Harvey's Sussex

Sticky Fingers:
Children welcome; smaller portions available

Muddy Paws:
No dogs

Zzzzz:
4 rooms, £120-£140

Anything Else?
Terrace, small garden, car park

The Food

Local produce is the mainstay of the innovative modern menu and, as befits its seaside location and name, fresh fish and seafood dominate. Crab and lobster are landed on Selsey beach, fish is delivered daily from south coast ports, while organic lamb is reared on neighbouring fields, and both the Hereford beef and Old Spot pork come from local farms. This translates to starters of Golden Cross goats' cheese baked with local vine tomatoes, and seared scallops wrapped in bacon with wilted spinach and anchovy dressing.

Main courses may take in lamb cutlets with roasted garlic and thyme jus, chargrilled beef fillet with hand-cut chips and peppercorn sauce, and baked whole crab gratin with a warm potato and watercress salad. Open sandwiches, perhaps warm sirloin of beef with poached oyster and roasted vine tomato, are served at lunchtime only. Try the warm chocolate brownie with coffee ice cream for pudding.

What To Do

Shop

ARUNDEL FARMERS' MARKET

Buy local meat, cakes, wines and award-winning bread from the local Slindon Bakery at this charming market in a beautiful setting in the ancient and historic town.

The Square, Arundel,
West Sussex BN18 9AG
01903 844772

EAST BEACH CAFÉ

Not strictly a shop, but an unmissable place to buy lunch! Architect Thomas Heatherwick's eye-catching, contemporary building is right on the beach so you can be beside the seaside and eat spectacularly well.

East Beach, Littlehampton,
West Sussex BN17 5NZ
01903 731903
www.eastbeachcafe.co.uk

MONTEZUMA CHOCOLATE

An innovative company with a taste for ethical trading, Montezuma is one of Britain's best chocolate shops, selling chilli-, peppermint-, nutmeg- and cinnamon-flavoured bars and exotic truffles.

29 East Street, Chichester,
West Sussex PO19 1HS
01243 537385
www.montezumas.co.uk

PAUL COOPER GALLERY

Specialising in original paintings and signed prints by the leading British and American artists, this delightful gallery is one of several interesting shops to be found in the tiny coastal village of Rustington.

162 The Street, Rustington,
West Sussex BN16 3DA
01903 775550
www.paulcooper.eclipse.co.uk

Visit

CASS SCULPTURE PARK

The work of over 120 contemporary British artists in 26 acres of beautiful parkland with sea views.

Cass Sculpture Foundation, Goodwood,
West Sussex PO18 0QP
01243 538449
www.sculpture.org.uk

DENMANS GARDEN

A tamed wilderness punctuated with interesting secret corners and statues. The walled garden is delightful, and there's a good cafe and well-stocked plant shop.

Denmans Lane, Fontwell,
West Sussex BN18 0SU
01243 542808
www.denmans-garden.co.uk

GOODWOOD HOUSE

This great country house is home to some very important works of art, with paintings by Canaletto, Stubbs, Reynolds and Van Dyck. Magnificent French furniture, Sèvres china and restored tapestries.

Goodwood, Chichester,
West Sussex PO18 0PX
01243 755000
www.goodwood.co.uk

UPPARK HOUSE & GARDENS

A fine, late 17th-century house, high on the South Downs, with sweeping panoramic views to the sea. The elegant Georgian interior houses a renowned Grand Tour collection and an 18th-century dolls' house with all its contents. Don't miss the Victorian kitchen. H G Wells's mother was housekeeper.

South Harting, Petersfield,
West Sussex GU31 5QR
01730 825857
www.nationaltrust.org.uk

Activity

HORSE RACING AT GOODWOOD

The Duke of Richmond brought racing here in 1802 and, 200 years on, Goodwood is one of the best racecourses in the world. On the Sussex Downs, it's a breathtaking backdrop for high-class flat racing.

Goodwood, Chichester,
West Sussex PO18 0PX
01243 755000
www.goodwood.co.uk

HORSE RIDING ON THE DOWNS

Ride along the rolling hills in this area of outstanding natural beauty, with dense groves of ancient yews. Spectacular views with glimpses of hidden downland villages.

Willowbrook Riding Centre
Hambrook Hill South, Hambrook,
Chichester, West Sussex PO18 8UJ
01243 572683
www.willowbrook-stables.co.uk

KITE SURFING

Not for the fainthearted! Take off and land on the beach, and let the boat pull you out over the sea for a unique view of the south coast.

Zero Gravity
222 The Sea Front, Hayling Island,
Hampshire PO11 0AU
02392 460555
www.kitesurflessons.co.uk

STAR GAZING

See shooting stars, the planets, the Northern Lights, remote galaxies and magnificent moons from the largest planetarium in the country.

S. Downs Planetarium & Science Centre
Sir Patrick Moore Building, Kingsham Farm, Kingsham Road, Chichester,
West Sussex PO19 8RP
01243 774400
www.southdowns.org.uk

The Walk - Sails and Trails at West Itchenor

A waterside walk that takes in Chichester Harbour's wildlife and yachting activity.

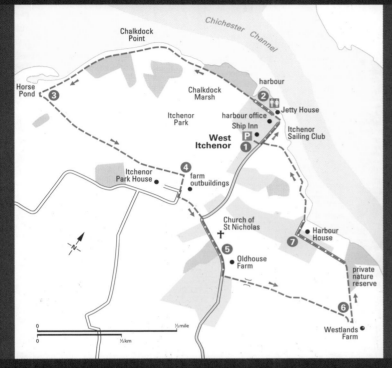

Walk Details

LENGTH: 3.5 miles (5.7km)

TIME: 1hr 30min

ASCENT: Negligible

PATHS: Shoreline, field tracks and paths, 1 stile

SUGGESTED MAP: aqua3 OS Explorer 120 Chichester, South Harting & Selsey

GRID REFERENCE: SU 797013

PARKING: Large pay-and-display car park in West Itchenor

❶ From the car park walk out to the road. Bear left, heading towards the harbour front. Pass the Ship Inn and head towards the water's edge. Look for the harbour office and the toilets and follow the footpath along to the left of Jetty House.

❷ Cut between the hedging and fencing to reach the boat-yard then continue ahead on the clear country path. Keep left at the next junction; shortly the path breaks cover to run hard by the harbour and its expanses of mud flats. Cross Chalkdock Marsh and continue on the waterside path.

❸ Keep going until you reach the footpath sign. Turn left, by the sturdy old oak tree, and follow the path away from the harbour edge,

keeping to the right-hand boundary of the field. Cross the stile to join the track on the bend and continue ahead, still maintaining the same direction. Pass Itchenor Park House on the right and approach some farm outbuildings.

❹ Turn right by a brick-and-flint farm outbuilding and follow the path, soon merging with the concrete track. Walk ahead to the next junction and turn left by the white gate, down to the road. Bear right here, pass the speed restriction sign and soon you reach the little Church of St Nicholas.

❺ Follow the road along to Oldhouse Farm then turn left at the footpath sign to cross the footbridge. Keep to the right of

several barns and follow the path straight ahead across the field. Pass the line of trees and keep alongside a ditch on the right into the next field. The path follows the hedge line, making for field corner. Ahead are buildings of Westlands Farm.

❻ Turn sharp left by the footpath sign and follow the path across the field. Skirt woodland, part of a private nature reserve, and veer left at entrance to Spinney. Follow residential drive to Harbour House.

❼ Turn right just beyond it and follow the path along the harbour edge. Keep going along here until you reach Itchenor Sailing Club. Bear left and walk up the drive to the road. Opposite is the Ship Inn. Turn left to return to the car park.

· S · RICHARD'S WALK ·

The Royal Oak

West Sussex

The Inn

With Goodwood Racecourse just up the hill and the cathedral city of Chichester only about two miles (3km) away, pub entrepreneur Nick Sutherland was destined to succeed when he bought this tiny 200-year-old village inn. Within a year he had extended the dining area and converted the rear barn and cottage into bedrooms, and the once sleepy local morphed into a thriving and very stylish gastropub-with-rooms. From the pretty raised terrace, step into the open-plan bar and dining area to find a buzzy atmosphere and a rustic chic feel, with crackling log fires, fat cream candles on scrubbed tables, leather sofas, and local ales tapped from the cask.

Money has been lavished on the bedrooms, so expect a contemporary look and great attention to detail, with big comfy beds, leather chairs, magazines and luxurious bathrooms, plus plasma screens, CD/DVD players and PlayStations. Two smart cottages across the road are let out as B&Bs during the week, with self-catering packages available at weekends. So why not book a chef to cook a private dinner for you?

The Royal Oak, Pook Lane, East Lavant, Chichester, West Sussex PO18 0AX

The Essentials

Time at the Bar!
12-11pm
Food: 12-2.30pm, 6-9.30pm

What's the Damage?
Main courses from £11

Bitter Experience:
Harvey's Sussex Best, Ballard's
Best, Arundel Gold, guest ale

Sticky Fingers:
Children welcome, children's menu

Muddy Paws:
Dogs welcome in the bar

Zzzzz:
8 rooms, £110-£195

Anything Else?
Terrace, garden, car park

The Food

The food draws people from all over, the modern British menu offering classy renditions of pub classics, plus more obvious restaurant dishes such as seared scallop and king prawn salad with lime and shallot dressing, or confit duck leg with red wine and Puy lentil sauce. In general, main courses strike a more robust, traditional note, say fresh haddock cooked in deliciously light beer batter and served with minted pea puree and chips, salmon fishcake with parsley and caper sauce, and fillet steak served with roasted tomatoes, field mushrooms and a peppercorn sauce. You'll also find lunchtime sandwiches, and home-made comfort puddings, perhaps mulled wine trifle, warm orange bread and butter pudding with Marsala custard, and a classic crème brûlée.

Everything is prepared from quality raw ingredients, with the London markets of Billingsgate, Smithfield and Covent Garden the source of much of the produce, although crab comes from Selsey and the pork is reared in Sussex. Local Ballard's and Harvey's ales and some top-notch French classics feature on the good-value wine list.

What To Do

Shop

ADSDEAN FARM SHOP

Foodies will want to take home free-range home-produced pork and beef, lamb from the farm next door, home-cured meats and seasonal game such as pheasant, partridge and venison – sourced from regular shoots on the farm.

Funtington, Chichester,
West Sussex PO18 9DN
01243 575212
www.adsdeanfarm.co.uk

CHICHESTER

A market cross stands at the meeting of West, North, East and South Streets in this historic cathedral city, each of which is packed with interesting shops, many privately owned. There is a good mixture of stylish boutiques and brand chain stores within Chichester's ancient streets – designer fashion labels, organic luxury chocolates and French pastries are just some of the quality commodities that await the 'professional shopper'. A good choice of upmarket restaurants, organic cafes and gastropubs enhances the experience.

01243 534677
www.chichester.gov.uk

WINE & FOOD TRAIL

Uncover some of southern England's best-kept culinary secrets on this tour of sites specialising in local and regional produce. Use the Wine Trail map to plot your route and combine a visit to a vineyard with a trip to a farmers market or a cheese producer.

01444 259265
www.atasteofsussex.co.uk
www.buylocalfood.co.uk

Visit

ARUNDEL CASTLE

There has been a fortification here since the 11th century, though most of the present building is Victorian. Today the castle remains the ancestral home of the Dukes of Norfolk. Within its great battlemented walls you'll find fine furniture dating from the 16th century, tapestries, clocks and portraits by prestigious artists such as Van Dyck and Gainsborough, among others.

01903 883136
www.arundelcastle.org

LANCING COLLEGE CHAPEL

This Gothic chapel stands high on the South Downs and can be seen for miles around. Founded in 1868 and dedicated in 1911, the nave is an incredible 90ft (27.5m) to the apex of the vault. The newly installed stained-glass window is dedicated to the memory of Bishop Trevor Huddleston, a pupil at Lancing in the late 1920s.

Lancing, West Sussex BN15 0RW
01273 465949
www.lancingcollege.co.uk

WEST DEAN GARDENS

Features of these fabulous historic gardens, once owned by the poet Edward James and laid out along classic 19th-century lines, include a 300ft (91m) pergola, an arboretum, a restored walled kitchen garden with 13 glasshouses, plus a gallery and a visitor centre. Regular events held throughout the year include a popular Chilli Festival.

West Dean, Chichester,
West Sussex PO18 0QZ
01243 818210
www.westdean.org.uk

Activity

BOAT TOUR

Chichester's vast natural harbour has 50 miles (80km) of shoreline and 17 miles (27km) of navigable channel, making it great for a leisurely boat trip, especially as the harbour is a haven for wildlife.

Solar Boat Tours, Itchenor, Chichester,
West Sussex PO20 7AW
01243 513275
www.conservancy.co.uk

**RACING AT GOODWOOD
& FONTWELL**

For racegoers the place to be is Goodwood. One of the south's loveliest and most famous racecourses rises and falls around a natural amphitheatre, with the horses dashing along the ridge to create one of the greatest spectacles in the racing world. For one week every summer it becomes Glorious Goodwood, when thousands of punters come to one of the most colourful events of the sporting and social calendar. Regular meetings are also held at Fontwell Racecourse a few miles east along the coast.

Goodwood Racecourse
01243 755000
www.goodwood.co.uk
Fontwell Racecourse
01243 543335
www.fontwellpark.co.uk

SEA FISHING

Head out beyond Chichester Harbour for some serious sea fishing – half- or full-day trips, or an evening outing for mackerel. Rods and bait are supplied.

Something Fishy Charters, 12 The Parade,
East Wittering, West Sussex PO20 8BN
01243 671153

The Walk - *Espying the Spire at Chichester*

Enjoy a walk around the ancient treasures of a cathedral city.

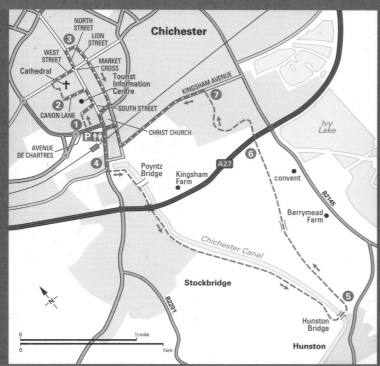

Walk Details

LENGTH: 4.5 miles (7.2km)

TIME: 2hrs

ASCENT: Negligible

PATHS: Urban walkways, tow path and field paths, 4 stiles

SUGGESTED MAP: aqua3 OS Explorer 120 Chichester, South Harting & Selsey

GRID REFERENCE: SZ 857044

PARKING: Fee-paying car park in Avenue de Chartres

❶ Leave the car park. Cross the footbridge over Avenue de Chartres. Head towards the city centre. Turn right at city map and left into South Street. Bear left into Canon Lane, just beyond the tourist information centre. Turn right into St Richard's Walk then approach the cathedral.
❷ Swing left at cloisters and left again (keep stone wall left). Make for West Door. Pass the Bell Tower to reach West Street; bear right. Opposite is pub. Proceed on West Street. At Market Cross, turn left into North Street. Bear right beyond Council House into Lion Street.
❸ Walk to St Martin's Square (opposite is St Mary's Hospital). Turn right; proceed to East Street (Corn Exchange on left.) Go over into North Pallant. Walk to Pallant House. Keep ahead into South Pallant. Follow the road round to the right, passing Christ Church on your left. Turn left at the next junction, head for the traffic lights; continue south into Southgate.
❹ Cross railway; then swing left to reach canal basin. Follow tow path to Poyntz Bridge; continue to the next bridge, carrying A27. Continue over next footbridge and follow path to road. Confusingly, the bridge is labelled Poyntz Bridge on OS maps.
❺ Bear left briefly to the stile by the car park entrance. Cross into field. Keep field boundary on immediate right and make for footbridge and stile. Continue ahead, with trees and bushes on left. Make for stile in field corner; cross the next field, maintaining direction. Aim for the stile in the wooded corner and just beyond it is the busy A27.
❻ Cross with extreme care over to the footpath opposite. Turn right at the junction; follow the tarmac path to the recreation ground. Cross to far side of the green, keeping the cathedral spire straight ahead. Look for Cherry Orchard Road, with post-box and telephone box on corner.
❼ Bear left at the crossroads into Kingsham Avenue; follow avenue into Kingsham Road. Turn right at T-junction, pass bus station and, on reaching the one-way system, cross at the lights. Bear right into Southgate, then left into Avenue de Chartres. The car park is on the left.

The Halfway Bridge Inn

West Sussex

The Inn

Interested in following the polo set at Cowdray Park or attending the races at Goodwood? Then this rambling, red-brick 18th-century coaching inn right beside the A272 is the place to stay. Six stunning rooms, four of which are suites, are located in a magnificent converted Sussex barn, just staggering distance from the pub. Think quality, a contemporary stylish feel and attention to detail, with big comfy beds, leather chairs, superb fabrics, excellent lighting, luxurious bathrooms kitted out with power showers and top toiletries, and up-to-the-minute 'toys for the boys' – plasma screens, CD/DVD players and Game Boys – to keep you amused.

Taste and style extend to the pub and the series of cosy, interconnecting rooms that radiate out from the central bar. Modern colours and furnishings combine well with the traditional old beams, wooden floors, and no fewer than five log fires (one in an old kitchen range) to create a casual and relaxed atmosphere for drinking or an intimate dinner. There are tables on the lawn and a flower-festooned rear terrace for those days when the weather is right for alfresco dining.

The Food

Traditional pub dishes are given a uniquely modern twist and everything is freshly prepared from quality raw ingredients. London is the source of much of the quality produce – Billingsgate Market for fish, Smithfield Market for meat and Covent Garden for exotic vegetables – although the menu does champion Selsey crab, Sussex pork, lamb from the Goodwood Estate, and locally grown soft fruits and vegetables.

After an appetiser of scallops with Puy lentils and Provençale sauce, tuck into steak and kidney suet pudding with braised red cabbage, whole lemon sole served with red chilli butter, or opt for rack of Sussex lamb with redcurrant and mint jus. If you have room, try the warm chocolate fondant with home-made chocolate and thyme ice cream, or a classic baked rice pudding with butterscotch sauce.

Light lunches in the bar take in seafood bisque and hearty sandwiches, perhaps crab or roast beef with horseradish. Expect to find local Arundel Gold and Harvey's Sussex Bitter on hand pump and a select list of wines offering 15 by the glass, including champagne.

The Essentials

Time at the Bar!
Food: 12-2.30pm, 6.30-9.30pm

What's the Damage?
Main courses from £10.95

Bitter Experience:
Skinner's Betty Stogs,
Ballard's Best

Sticky Fingers:
Children welcome, half portions
of main menu available

Muddy Paws:
Dogs welcome in the bar and garden

Zzzzz:
6 rooms, £120-£160

Anything Else?
Terrace, garden, car park

What To Do

Shop

RICHARD GARDNER ANTIQUES

Over the years Petworth has become a mecca for antiques and fine arts, attracting visitors from far and wide. Among the town's many businesses is the award-winning Richard Gardner Antiques where six large showrooms display a wide range of stock, including bronzes and glass, furniture, porcelain, sculpture, silver, Chinese pottery, Staffordshire figures and more.

Market Square, Petworth,
West Sussex GU28 0AN
01798 343411
www.richardgardnerantiques.co.uk

SPRIGGS FLORIST

One of the country's leading florists, Spriggs's stock of unusual plants and flowers is delivered direct from the Dutch flower markets. Quirky containers and a range of glassware and candelabras are available, and a choice of superb silk orchid plants can be despatched by post.

Lancaster House, Golden Square, Petworth,
West Sussex GU28 0AP
01798 343372

Visit

BIGNOR ROMAN VILLA

Rediscovered in 1811, this Roman house was built on the grand scale. It is one of the largest known villas of its kind and has the longest mosaic in Britain (82ft/25m) surviving in its original position.

Bignor, Pulborough,
West Sussex RJ20 1PH
01798 869259
www.bignorromanvilla.co.uk

NUTBOURNE VINEYARDS

Wander through the vineyards, learn how grapes are grown in this often chilly and inhospitable country, and then visit the historic windmill to taste and buy some of the award-winning wines.

Gay Street, Nutbourne, Pulborough,
West Sussex RH20 2HH
01798 815196
www.nutbournevineyards.com

PARHAM HOUSE & GARDENS

This magnificent Elizabethan mansion is one of the great treasures of Sussex, recalling the days of lavish weekend house parties, servants living a separate life below stairs and the days of gracious living. The wonderful setting, deer park and views of the South Downs enhance Parham's beauty and little has changed here since Tudor times. The house has been open to the public since 1948.

Storrington, Pulborough,
West Sussex RH20 4HS
01903 744888
www.parhaminsussex.co.uk

PETWORTH COTTAGE MUSEUM

The Petworth Cottage Museum provides a glimpse of rural life around 1910. It has a scullery with a stone sink and 'copper' for washing clothes and boiling water; the bedroom includes an iron bedstead, a washstand and a hand-made bedspread. Care has been taken in the garden to choose plants that would be found in this setting during the Edwardian era.

346 High Street, Petworth,
West Sussex GU28 0AU
01798 342100
www.petworthcottagemuseum.co.uk

Activity

BALLOONING

For that once-in-a-lifetime flying experience, take to the air and soar across the Sussex countryside in a hot-air balloon. The take-off point is north of Petworth.

01428 707307
www.hotair.co.uk

BIRDWATCHING

Bring your binoculars and explore the nature trail that winds through the RSPB reserve at Wiggonholt to viewing hides overlooking the watermeadows in the Arun Valley.

Wiggonholt, Pulborough,
West Sussex RH20 2EL
01798 875851
www.rspb.org.uk

BOAT TRIP

Enjoy a boat trip on the tranquil, tree-lined Chichester Ship Canal, an inland waterway between London and Portsmouth until 1855. It was designed by John Rennie and opened in 1822.

Canal Basin, Canal Wharf, Chichester
West Sussex PO19 8FR
01243 771363
www.chichestercanal.org.uk

COWDRAY PARK

Built by the Earl of Southampton in the early years of the 16th century, Cowdray House was one of the great palaces of Tudor England. Sadly, it was destroyed by fire in 1793 and today is no more than a romantic ruin. Its setting, however, is truly splendid and the adjoining park is used for sporting activities.

The Estate Office, Cowdray Park, Midhurst,
West Sussex GU29 0AQ
0845 056 0553
www.cowdray.co.uk

The Walk - Tennyson Country at Black Down

Follow in the footsteps of Alfred, Lord Tennyson on this gloriously wooded, high-level walk.

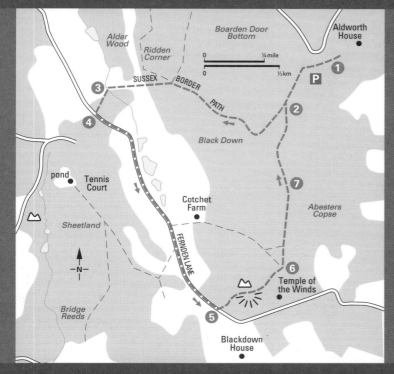

Walk Details

LENGTH: 4.5 miles (7.2km)

TIME: 2hrs

ASCENT: 315ft (95m)

PATHS: Woodland paths and tracks, some minor roads

SUGGESTED MAP: aqua3 OS Explorer 133 Haslemere & Petersfield

GRID REFERENCE: SU 922306

PARKING: Free car park off Tennyson's Lane, near Aldworth House to the south-east of Haslemere

❶ Turn left out of the Tennyson's Lane car park and then left again to join the Sussex Border Path. Keep left at the junction and swing right at the fork.

❷ Follow the long-distance border trail to the triangular green and veer right here. Keep left at the fork, still on the Sussex Border Path, and pass over the crossroads. Veer left just beyond it at the fork and drop down to the rhododendron bushes. Turn sharp left here and follow the path through the tunnel of trees.

❸ Bear left at the drive and when, after a few paces, the drive curves to the right, keep ahead through trees to join the road.

❹ Turn left towards the entrance to Sheetland. Avoid the turning and follow the lane for about 1 mile (1.6km), passing the entrance to Cotchet Farm on your left. Continue along Fernden Lane.

❺ Make for the signposted bridleway on the left and after a few paces you will reach the National Trust sign ('Black Down'). Keep left here and follow the sunken path as it climbs between the trees, quite steeply in places. On higher ground, follow the path as it winds pleasantly along between the bracken and silver birch. Walk along to the seat, which takes advantage of the magnificent view, partly obscured by trees. Keep the seat and the view on your right and walk along to the seat at what is known as the Temple of the Winds.

❻ Do not retrace your steps but instead take the path running up behind the seat to the junction. Don't turn left at this point; instead head north on the bridleway. Avoid the path you will see running off sharp right and the flight of steps and veer left or right at the waymarked fork. Both paths soon merge again.

❼ Continue ahead and veer right at the next fork. Keep ahead at the next junction, now following part of the Sussex Border Path again. Alfred, Lord Tennyson would have found inspiration for his writing in this countryside near his home at Aldworth. Veer to the right at the fork, still following the long-distance trail, and head back to the road by the car park entrance.

The Bull

East Sussex

The Essentials

Time at the Bar!
11am–11pm
Food: Mon-Fri 12-2.30pm, 7-9.30pm;
Sat 12-3pm, 7-9.30pm; Sun 12-6pm

What's the Damage?
Main courses from £9.50

Bitter Experience:
Harvey's Sussex, Timothy Taylor
Landlord, guest ale

Sticky Fingers:
Children welcome; children's menu

Muddy Paws:
Dogs welcome in the bar

Zzzzz:
4 rooms, £80-£100

Anything Else?
Terrace, garden, car park

The Inn

Ditchling Beacon is a key landmark for walkers and cyclists tackling the famous South Downs, which tower above the village. And the 16th-century Bull, a former coaching inn, is the place to head for following a day on the Downs. It's been restored with passion (and a contemporary touch) by Dominic Worrall, yet still retains its historic charm and character. Head for the bar and you'll find feature fireplaces with glowing log fires, sagging ceiling timbers, bare floorboards and a mix of simple benches, carved settles and farmhouse chairs at big scrubbed tables. Quirky *objets d'art*, modern art on the walls and vases of lilies on the bar add a touch of class.

There are four individually decorated bedrooms, all named after their principal colour. Ruby, for example, as you might guess, has bright red walls, plus white-painted timbers, Thai silk curtains, a plasma TV/DVD player, a big leather sleigh bed with Egyptian cotton sheets and a claw-foot bath in the fully tiled bathroom. Welcome extras include fresh flowers, fat cream candles and digital radios.

The Food

Local is the watchword when it comes to food and drink. You'll find top-notch ales from Harvey's (Lewes) and Welton's (Horsham) breweries on hand pump, and very quaffable fizz from Ridge View Vineyard up the road. Menus change daily and make good use of lamb from Foxhole Farm on the edge of the village, seasonal game, including venison, from the Balcombe Estate, Sussex pork and beef, south coast fish, and asparagus from nearby Little Horsted Farm. This translates to classic mains like roasted sausages with mash and onion gravy, haddock in Harvey's ale batter with hand-cut chips and mushy peas, and beef fillet with chips and black pepper jus.

More contemporary dishes run to whole roasted lemon sole with crushed olive new potatoes and lemon caper butter, and loin of pork with apricot crumble, sage mash and mustard sauce. Precede these with king prawn open ravioli with rocket and pesto, or vegetable and mozzarella terrine, and finish with Sussex pond pudding with lemon and lime anglaise or a plate of local cheeses. For a snack, share a camembert, roasted in its box and served with grape chutney and crusty bread.

What To Do

Shop

ABODE
Stylish and well-designed contemporary, vintage and antique home furnishings and accessories sourced from both local and international designers.

32 Kensington Gardens, Brighton, East Sussex BN1 4AL
01273 621116 www.abodeliving.co.uk

ANANDA
Reclaimed hardwood furniture in colonial and contemporary styles imported from Java – home accessories, kilims and folk art.

24 Bond Street, Brighton, East Sussex BN1 1RD
01273 725307 www.ananda.co.uk

BILL'S PRODUCE STORE
Unique cafe and shop specialising in fresh organic fruit and vegetables, flowers and plants and a mind-boggling array of goodies in an amazing deli section.

56 Cliffe High Street, Lewes, East Sussex BN7 2AN
01273 476918

BONNE BOUCHE CHOCOLATES
If you love hand-made, high-quality chocolates, then don't miss this shop tucked down an alleyway.

3 St Martins Lane, Lewes, East Sussex BN7 1UD
01272 472043

BOW WINDOWS BOOKSHOP
Bookworms will find it hard to leave the creaking shelves of Bow Windows Bookshop where the stacks of old fine and rare books on all subjects never fail to enthrall.

175 High Street, Lewes, East Sussex BN7 1YE
01273 480780 www.bowwindows.com

PARTERRE
Parterre on the High Street sells upmarket garden-related products ranging from Amazonas hammocks and Roger Lascelles clocks to Muck Boots and stylish Fermob garden furniture from France.

170 High Street, Lewes, East Sussex BN7 1YE
01273 476305
www.parterredesign.co.uk

Visit

CHARLESTON FARMHOUSE
Set in the midst of rolling countryside, 17th-century Charleston Farmhouse is inextricably linked with the bohemian world of the artists Vanessa Bell and Duncan Grant. The house was also a meeting place for other unconventional members of the Bloomsbury Group, including Virginia Woolf and EM Forster. Decorated furniture and murals.

Charleston, Firle, Lewes East Sussex BN8 6LL
01323 811626
www.charleston.org.uk

DITCHLING MUSEUM
Situated in the old school, Ditchling's museum celebrates rural life through the decades. Tools, country crafts and costumes are displayed and, among many famous artists celebrated here, are the calligrapher Edward Johnston, who created the typeface and logo for the London Underground, and the cartoonist Rowland Emett.

Ditchling Museum, Church Lane, Ditchling, East Sussex BN6 8TB
01273 844744
www.ditchling-museum.com

ROYAL PAVILION
Don't miss this former seaside residence of King George IV, 'the most extraordinary palace in Europe', with its myriad domes and minarets. View the music room, the banqueting room and royal bedrooms, then stroll through the restored Regency gardens.

4/5 Pavilion Buildings, Brighton, East Sussex BN1 1EE
01273 292820
www.royalpavilion.co.uk

Activity

PARAGLIDING & HANG GLIDING
Wheel effortlessly like a bird high above the Sussex countryside following a day (or longer) course at exclusive training sites on the South Downs with one of the experienced team from the Sussex Hang Gliding and Paragliding School.

Tollgate, Lewes, East Sussex BN8 6JZ
01273 858170
www.sussexhgpg.co.uk

HORSE RIDING
Trot or canter along the South Downs Way and savour the views across the Weald on horseback during a half- or full-day's hack.

Ditchling Common Stud, Burgess Hill, West Sussex RH15 0SE
01444 871900
www.ditchlingcommonstud.co.uk

The Walk - Delightful Downs at Ditchling

A gloriously wooded, high-level walk exploring the South Downs.

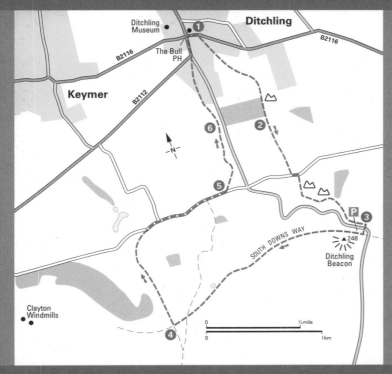

Walk Details

LENGTH: 5.5 miles (8.8km)

TIME: 2hrs 30min

ASCENT: 600ft (183m)

PATHS: Field paths, bridleways and a stretch of road, 11 stiles

SUGGESTED MAP: aqua3 OS Explorer 122 South Downs Way – Steyning to Newhaven

GRID REFERENCE: TQ 326152

PARKING: Free car park at rear of village hall in Ditchling

① Turn right out of the car park; follow the B2116. Pass Charlton Gardens; bear right, joining path ('Downs'). Cross 3 pastures via 5 stiles; follow the broad path through woodland. Keep right at the fork by the bridleway waymark post; pass by the house. Keep ahead alongside the beech hedge where the concrete track runs off right.
② Pass Claycroft House. Follow the path between the trees and houses. At the road, turn left and proceed to the bridleway on the right, pointing towards South Downs Way. Follow path, swing left at the junction; climb the steep escarpment. Keep view of Weald on left and, further up, path runs by road. Look for South Downs Way sign ahead. Turn right.

③ Pass by the car park and over Ditchling Beacon. Go through the gate. Look for trig point left. Head west along South Downs Way, pass the dew pond. Make for the junction of paths. Keymer is signed to the right and Brighton to the left.
④ Follow the path north towards Keymer, soon descending quite steeply. Keep right at the fork, making for gate out to lane. Bear left to the junction, then turn right past turning for Keymer on the left. Walk towards Ditchling; join Sussex Border Path at next stile on the left.
⑤ Cross the field to the stile; enter woodland. Follow the path through the trees, then go straight over the drive and alongside barns and loose boxes. Cross grass to line of trees,

curve right and briefly follow track to several stiles and a footbridge. The path makes its way across the elongated field towards the trees.
⑥ Cross stile, avoiding another stile leading out to road; continue across pasture, keeping to left of houses. Make for far left corner of field; look for opening in hedgerow. Follow path round to right, alongside row of houses. Cross stile on right and follow path to road. Bear left by the grassy roundabout. Take path to right of sign for Neville Bungalows. Cut between the trees, hedges and fences, following the narrow path to road. Bear right towards Haywards Heath and Lindfield and walk back to the centre of Ditchling, turning right into Lewes Road for car park.

The Griffin Inn

East Sussex

The Inn

Fronting sleepy Fletching's attractive high street, the Griffin is a civilised 400-year-old inn that's everything a village local should be, and more. Much of its success is due to the enthusiasm of the Pullan family, who have been at the helm for over 27 years. Inside, you'll find a classic old-style country pub, full of oak beams and panelling, blazing log fires and a motley collection of old furnishings. On warm summer evenings, the sheltered rear patio, replete with posh brollies and teak tables topped with linen cloths, makes a welcome extension to the comfortable restaurant. Beyond, the landscaped garden affords stunning views to the distant South Downs, the perfect spot for alfresco sipping and the venue for Sunday jazz and the inn's famous spit roasts.

The bedrooms all ooze charm and character, with timbers, beams and feature fireplaces, and rooms in Griffin House next door are kitted out with antique French painted furniture. You'll find crisp Egyptian cotton sheets, flat-screen TVs/DVD players and smart tiled bathrooms, with double-ended baths, huge storm showers, Molton Brown smellies and fluffy bathrobes.

The Essentials

Time at the Bar!
12pm-12am
Food: Daily 12-2.30pm, 7-9.30pm
(bar food Sun only)

What's the Damage?
Main courses from £13

Bitter Experience:
Harvey's Sussex Best,
King's Horsham Best, Welton's Ales

Sticky Fingers:
Children welcome; children's menu

Muddy Paws:
Dogs welcome

Zzzzz:
13 rooms, £80-£130

Anything Else?
Patio, garden, car park

The Food

Excellent cooking lures foodies from afar, with a twice-daily changing chalkboard in the bar and a short, more imaginative menu in the restaurant. The repertoire draws on local, mostly organic, suppliers, notably meat from Fletching farms, fish from Rye day boats, and vegetables supplied from the inn's own market garden on the edge of the village. From an eclectic line-up of dishes in the bar, choose from sweet potato and chilli soup or scallops with crispy pancetta and tomato and coriander salsa, then venison cobbler, Rye Bay cod in Harvey's batter with home-made tartare sauce and chips, or wild boar sausages on chorizo and chickpea stew. Find room for warm chocolate brioche bread and butter pudding if you can.

You have to book a table in the restaurant to sample the likes of carpaccio of organic veal with pickled porcini, beef fillet with garlic jus or rump of Romney Marsh lamb with lentil and pumpkin risotto, and certainly for Thursday's 'fishtastic' menu. The impressive wine list runs to 100 bins from select suppliers, with 15 wines offered by the glass, while ale drinkers will not be disappointed with the locally-brewed Harvey's and King's beers on tap.

What To Do

Shop

BOATHOUSE ORGANIC FARM SHOP

In the heart of the Ouse Valley, just north of Lewes, this thriving farm shop sells organic beef, lamb and mutton reared on the farm, as well as other meats from local farmers and a full range of organic fruit, vegetables, groceries and dairy produce. You'll also find home-cooked ready meals prepared with ingredients from Boathouse Farm.

The Orchards, Uckfield Road, Clay Hill, Lewes, East Sussex BN8 5RX

01273 814188

www.boathouseorganicfarmshop.co.uk

BRIGHTON

Churchill Square is Brighton's premier shopping destination. In the heart of the city, it offers more than 80 leading high street stores all under one roof. The spacious, innovative design of the centre appeals to shoppers, and it's perfect for casual browsing, too. The famous Lanes are the place for more quirky purchases.

www.churchillsquare.com

CAMELIA BOTNAR HOMES & GARDENS

Visit this local independent craft and garden centre north of Henfield and discover a fascinating assortment of award-winning artistic ironwork, studio ceramics and bespoke oak, pine, beech and maple furniture, all produced in nearby workshops. There is also a vast range of shrubs, herbs, herbaceous plants, trees and seasonal bedding.

Littleworth Lane, Cowfold, West Sussex RH13 8NA

01403 864773

www.cameliabotnar.com

Visit

MICHELHAM PRIORY

Explore the Tudor mansion that evolved from a former Augustinian Priory and discover its glorious gardens on an absorbing tour packed with facts and fine detail. Surrounding the priory is England's longest water-filled medieval moat, and in the grounds are physic, cloister and kitchen gardens, an orchard, a nature and sculpture trail, moat walk and rope museum.

Upper Dicker, Hailsham, East Sussex BN27 3QS

01323 844224

www.sussexpast.co.uk

SHEFFIELD PARK GARDEN

You get a glimpse of this fabulous place from the Griffin's beer garden, so why not explore it? Laid out in the 18th century by Capability Brown and further developed in the early 20th century, it features four lakes and, in spring, there are dramatic shows of daffodils and bluebells. Visit in autumn for the stunning trees and shrubs.

Sheffield Park, Uckfield, East Sussex TN22 3QX

01825 790231

www.nationaltrust.org.uk

WAKEHURST PLACE

This is Kew's 'country garden', with plants from all corners of the world. Here, where the emphasis is on mixing botanical science with horticulture, you can amble among walled gardens and water gardens, discover a wetland conservation area and explore woodland.

Ardingly, Haywards Heath, West Sussex RH17 6TN

01444 894067

www.kew.org

Activity

GOLF

Its title may be grand but novices should not be put off; this prestigious golfing hotel and spa welcomes golfers of any handicap on the lush fairways and neatly trimmed greens of the two spectacular championship courses.

East Sussex National Golf Resort, Little Horsted, Uckfield, East Sussex TN22 5ES

01825 880088

www.eastsussexnational.co.uk

HORSE RACING AT PLUMPTON

Think of horse racing in East Sussex and you immediately think of Plumpton – this is the place to go to enjoy the sport of kings. Superbly situated below the South Downs, the racecourse is one of the smaller jump courses in the country and never fails to draw large crowds from far and wide.

Plumpton Racecourse, Plumpton, East Sussex BN7 3AL

01273 890383

www.plumptonracecourse.co.uk

STEAM TRAIN RIDE

Relive the great days of railway travel by taking a nostalgic trip on the old-fashioned Bluebell Railway. The lovely old trains steam through the heart of the Sussex countryside between Sheffield Park and Kingscote. At Horsted Keynes station, you can see how the Steam Preservation Society has expertly re-created the look and feel of a sleepy country station in the years before World War II.

Bluebell Railway

Sheffield Park Station, Haywards Heath, East Sussex TN22 3QL

01825 720800

www.bluebell-railway.co.uk

The Walk - Visiting Winnie-the-Pooh

Exploring the haunts of AA Milne's creation in Ashdown Forest.

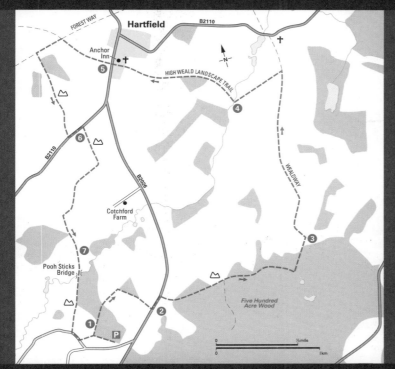

Walk Details

LENGTH: 7 miles (11.3km)

TIME: 3hrs

ASCENT: 170ft (55m)

PATHS: Paths and tracks across farmland and woodland, 20 stiles

SUGGESTED MAP: aqua3 OS Explorer 135 Ashdown Forest

GRID REFERENCE: TQ 472332

PARKING: Pooh free car park, off B2026 south of Hartfield

❶ Follow the path ('Pooh Bridge'), take 3rd turning on right; descend to stile. Cross tree-ringed field to stile near the corner, follow the woodland path to another stile; head diagonally right across field to 4th stile by gate. Cross drive to 5th stile and gate, then aim right to another gate. Go forward to stile and road.

❷ Turn left, then right opposite The Paddocks; follow path through Five Hundred Acre Wood to reach Wealdway. Proceed, passing Kovacs Lodge. Climb quite steeply; make a wide sweep to the left. Follow the track round to right to fork, veer left and approach the private drive sign.

❸ Take righthand path and skirt the farm. Rejoin the drive and keep right, following Wealdway as it cuts across farmland. Pass turning to Buckhurst then bear left over stile to follow High Weald Landscape Trail. Cross field to gate and stile; cut through wood to brick bridge.

❹ Turn right; follow the fence, passing paddocks. Veer right via a gateway in the field corner; make for the next field. Head diagonally left across farmland to a stile. Keep to righthand edge of the field to the stile, then cross the footbridge and continue by the field edge. Turn left at the stile and enter Hartfield.

❺ Bear right at the B2026, then left. Cross the stile in field corner and go over the next stile to Forest Way. Turn left; follow the old trackbed until the gate on the left. Cross pasture to the gate; follow woodland

bridleway. Emerging from the trees, continue to Culvers Farm.

❻ Make for the road then turn left. Walk to 1st righthand footpath ('Pooh Bridge'). Cross the stile; follow track ahead to 3 stiles before crossing field. Follow waymarks and make for stile in corner. Cross drive to another stile; head diagonally down the field to a stile in corner. Continue on path, heading for the next stile. Follow the lane south.

❼ When it sweeps left towards Cotchford Farm, proceed on the bridleway to Pooh Bridge; follow track as it climbs by woodland and paddocks. Turn left at the road and when it bends around to the right, go ahead into trees. Follow footpath through wood, back to the start.

The George Inn

East Sussex

The George Inn, High Street, Alfriston, East Sussex BN26 5SY

The Essentials

Time at the Bar!
12-11pm
Food: 12-2.30pm, 7-10pm

What's the Damage?
Main courses from £10.50

Bitter Experience:
Greene King IPA, Abbot Ale
& Old Speckled Hen

Sticky Fingers:
Children welcome

Muddy Paws:
Dogs allowed in the bar

Zzzzz:
6 rooms, £90-£130; single £60

Anything Else?
Garden, terrace

The Inn

A magical Sussex village situated at the foot of the South Downs beside the Cuckmere River is the setting for this striking Grade II listed stone and half-timbered inn. First licensed in 1397, it creaks with age and oozes historic charm, from its head-cracking oak beams and thick standing timbers to the ancient plank floors and vast inglenook fireplace in the classic, hop-adorned bar. Order a pint of Abbot Ale and relax with the newspapers on a cushioned settle by the fire in winter, or head out into the peaceful, stone-walled garden in summer – a path leads directly to the peaceful village green and fine church.

Refurbished rooms retain the inn's original features, so expect wonky floors, timbered walls, vaulted ceilings and leaded windows in the oldest rooms. There are big sleigh beds and feature fireplaces, bespoke furniture, TVs and DVD players, and modern ensuite bathrooms. For atmosphere, book the Bob Hall room, with its inglenook fireplace, lofty beamed ceiling and 15th-century wall mural. Rear rooms have views of the South Downs. Bike hire can be arranged, picnics prepared for walkers, and hampers made up for those heading for Glyndebourne.

The Food

Follow a brisk morning's walk on the Downs with lunch in the bar. Share one of the rustic boards – salami, baked mustard ham and chorizo served with breads, warm olive oil, balsamic vinegar and roasted garlic – or go for the brie and bacon sandwich, served with either chips or a small bowl of soup. If you have worked up an appetite, try the hearty and warming steak, mushroom and Guinness suet pudding, or perhaps the pork and leek sausages on a mound of mash with red onion gravy.

Cooking style moves up a notch or two in the evenings, the chalkboard listing such starters as salt and pepper sardines with tomato and red onion, or sautéed crevettes and chorizo in hot chilli oil. Main course options may include confit of pork belly with red cabbage and apple, rack of local lamb with tomato and olive sauce, and sea bass poached in white wine, ginger, lime and coriander. Leave room for the banana and Baileys bread and butter pudding with hot custard, or alternatively round off with The George's 'cracking' cheese board.

What To Do

Shop

BILL'S PRODUCE STORE

This is a charmingly haphazard foodie heaven, offering fresh, locally-sourced produce and deli-style goods. Share a table for the best lunch around, and take home lovely goodies from the shop.

56 Cliffe High Street, Lewes,
East Sussex BN7 2AN
01273 476918
www.billsproducestore.co.uk

BREAKY BOTTOM VINEYARD

Peter Hall has been making award-winning wines since 1974 at Breaky Bottom, which nestles in a sleepy fold of the South Downs. He also makes delicious cassis from his own blackcurrants.

Rodmell, Lewes, East Sussex BN7 3EX
01273 476427
www.breakybottom.co.uk

DOWNSVIEW BUTCHERS

Downsview Butchers produce great-tasting lamb and beef from their organic farm, along with pork, poultry, game, rabbits, geese and guinea fowl. You can also buy from them at East Dean Farmers' Market at Beachy Head every Wednesday.

Freshwater Square, Willingdon, Eastbourne,
East Sussex BN22 0PR
01323 505009

TRENCHERMAN & TURNER

There are some fantastic local cheeses at this deli, including 'Scrumpy Sussex', made with local cider. You'll also find award-winning wines, organic ham, bacon and local free-range eggs, as well as jams, mustards and chutneys.

52 Grove Road, Little Chelsea, Eastbourne,
East Sussex BN21 4UD
01323 737535

Visit

ALFRISTON CLERGY HOUSE

In 1896, this 14th-century thatched 'hall house' was the first building bought by the National Trust – for £10. It has a chalk and sour milk floor and a pretty cottage garden.

The Tye, Alfriston, Polegate,
East Sussex BN26 5TL
01323 870001
www.nationaltrust.org.uk

CHARLESTON

In 1916, artists Vanessa Bell and Duncan Grant moved to Charleston, and began to transform the house with murals inspired by Italian fresco painting. Over the next 50 years, they formed the Bloomsbury Group with Virginia Woolf, Lytton Strachey and E M Forster. The house and gardens give a fascinating insight into their lives.

Charleston, Firle, Lewes,
East Sussex BN8 6LL
01323 811626
www.charleston.org.uk

HERSTMONCEUX CASTLE

This magnificent moated castle is set in beautiful parkland – stroll through rose and rhododendron gardens and past the lily-covered lakes to the 1930s folly.

Hailsham, East Sussex BN27 1RN
01323 833816
www.herstmonceux-castle.com

MICHELHAM PRIORY

This beautiful house, nestling deep in the countryside, dates back to 1229, and has the longest water-filled medieval moat in the country.

Upper Dicker, Hailsham,
East Sussex BN27 3QS
01323 844224
www.sussexpast.co.uk

Activity

CYCLING THE SOUTH DOWNS

The pretty village of East Dean at Beachy Head has lots of interest. A good way to explore the area is on two wheels – there's a traffic-free cycle route through forests to the Seven Sisters cliffs, with outstanding views of Beachy Head.

Cuckmere Cycle Company
Seven Sisters Country Park, Exceat,
Seaford, East Sussex BN25 4AD
01323 870310
www.cuckmere-cycle.co.uk

FLYING

Enjoy the golden age of flying in the art deco seats of a vintage Dragon Rapide biplane or in a Tiger Moth. Buzz up the Sussex coastline past the Brighton Pavilion.

Delta Aviation
Shoreham Airport, Shoreham by Sea,
West Sussex BN43 5FF
01223 874346
www.deltaaviation.co.uk

HORSE RACING AT PLUMPTON

Plumpton is one of the smallest and most successful jump courses in the country, with a spectacular backdrop of the Sussex Downs.

Plumpton Racecourse, Plumpton,
East Sussex BN7 3AL
01273 890383
www.plumptonracecourse.co.uk

OPERA AT GLYNDBOURNE

Glyndbourne holds a unique place in the world of opera. Set in glorious Sussex countryside, it is a sublime spot for enjoying both the music and the surroundings – dig out your best bib and tucker, and take a picnic.

Lewes, East Sussex BN8 5UU
01273 812321
www.glyndbourne.com

The Walk - *The Long Man at Wilmington*

Visit the legendary chalk figure, which still puzzles archaeologists and historians.

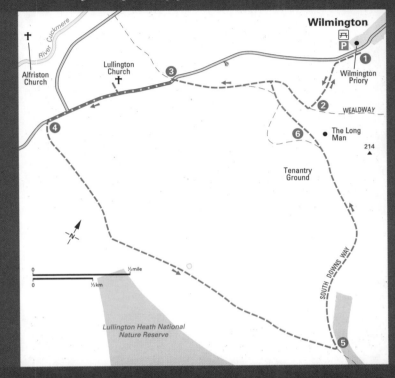

Walk Details

LENGTH: 6.25 miles (10.1km)

TIME: 2hrs 30min

ASCENT: 465ft (152m)

PATHS: Downland paths and tracks, stretch of country road, 1 stile

SUGGESTED MAP: aqua3 OS Explorer 123 South Downs Way – Newhaven to Eastbourne

GRID REFERENCE: TQ 543041

PARKING: Long-stay car park at Wilmington

❶ Make for the car park exit; follow the path parallel to the road, heading towards the Long Man. Bear left at the next gate and take Wealdway to the chalk figure. Climb quite steeply, curving to the right. Go through the gate, avoid the Wealdway arrow and keep ahead towards the escarpment, veering right just below the Long Man.
❷ Go through the next gate, cross the track. Bear left at the fence. After a few paces, reach the gate and sign for the South Downs Way. Pass the small reservoir; follow the track to the road.
❸ Turn left then walk to the signpost ('Lullington church'), following the path that runs beside the cottages. After visiting the

church, retrace your steps to road. Turn right. Head down the lane, looking out for Alfriston church on the right. Pass the turning to the village on the right and continue ahead towards Seaford. Look for the post box and then swing left, signposted 'Jevington'.
❹ Follow the bridleway as it climbs steadily between tracts of remote downland. Keep left at the next main junction and there is a moderate climb. Avoid a bridle track branching off to the left and proceed towards Jevington. Lullington Heath National Nature Reserve is on your right now. Pass the bridleway to Charleston Bottom on the right and keep on the track as it climbs quite steeply. Pass a 2nd sign and map for

the nature reserve and make for the junction with the South Downs Way.
❺ Turn left and then follow the enclosed path to the gate. Go straight ahead alongside woodland and pass through the 2nd gate. The path begins a gradual curve to the left and eventually passes along a rim of dry valley, Tenantry Ground. Keep the fence on your left and look for the gate ahead. Swing right as you approach the gate to reach the stile then follow the path alongside the fence, crossing top of Long Man.
❻ To your right, you can just make out the chalk figure down below. Continue, keeping the fence on your right, and descend to the gate. Turn right here and retrace your steps to the car park at Wilmington.

The George in Rye

East Sussex

The George in Rye, 98 High Street, Rye, East Sussex TN31 7JT

The Inn

For Alex and Katie Clarke, bringing this down-at-heel 16th-century coaching inn in the centre of Rye back to life was a labour of love. And locals and visitors adore it. Since its launch in the autumn of 2006, they have adopted its stunning interior and smart courtyard with enthusiasm. At its heart is the George Tap, a classic pub, complete with heavy ships' timbers in the ceiling, a roaring winter fire and lots of nooks and crannies. Harvey's Sussex Ale and Biddenden cider are on draught, and eight wines from vineyards in Kent and Sussex feature on the short modern wine list.

Along rambling corridors and under steeply pitched roofs, urban cool bedrooms come in all shapes and sizes, from intimate standard rooms to lavish junior suites, and while the beds themselves may be either antique or modern, they are all made up with Italian Frette linen sheets. Tivoli clock radios, flat-screen TVs, power showers (if it's not a roll-top bath) and Aveda smellies are all standard issue.

The Food

The George Tap gives on to a casual, good-looking dining room and both share an unfussy day menu of chicken liver pâté, potted shrimps, club sandwiches, home-made beef burger or grilled rib-eye steak with chunky chips, and Rye Bay scallops with chilli and herb butter. Breakfast and afternoon tea are further pluses. But the restaurant moves up a gear in the evening with a menu that criss-crosses the Mediterranean, picking up chorizo, tabbouleh and Turkish flatbread along the way. Pear, apple and beetroot salad with lemon dressing is a zingy wake-up call, or there could be chargrilled sardines with aioli and local leaf salad.

The main course roast pork loin with warm potato salad and braised spinach is meltingly tender comfort food, while, in contrast, roasted sea bass with saffron fondant potato and braised leeks is a classic combination of textures and flavours. The dessert menu may be short, but it includes an outstanding chocolate, almond and armagnac cake, a fine tarte au citron and a good plate of tasty English cheeses.

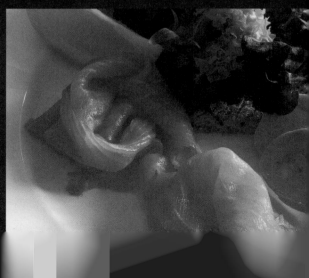

The Essentials

Time at the Bar!
11am-11pm
Food: 12-3pm, 6.30-10pm

What's the Damage?
Main courses from £12

Bitter Experience:
Harvey's Best, Copper Ale, Rother
Valley Level Best, Greene King Old
Speckled Hen

Sticky Fingers:
Children welcome

Muddy Paws:
Dogs welcome in the bar

Zzzzz:
24 rooms, £125-£225

Anything Else?
Terrace, no car park

What To Do

Shop

GLASS ETC

Apart from a wealth of decorative and functional glass products, Glass Etc in Rope Walk sells a range of antique and retro furniture, and deals in architectural ironmongery and kitchenalia. Throughout the rest of Rye's quaint old streets you'll find antiquarian bookshops, retail outlets specialising in sporting equipment, jewellers and shops offering fresh local produce.

18-22 Rope Walk, Rye,
East Sussex TN31 7NA
01797 226600
www.visitrye.co.uk

STORMONT STUDIO

The Stormont Studio holds a collection of more than 400 works of art by nationally and regionally important artists including Whistler, Bell, Burra, Grant, Epstein and Hitchens. For exhibitions of contemporary paintings, prints, photography, ceramics, sculpture and textiles, visit Rye Art Gallery where you can browse and buy.

Ockman Lane, Rye, East Sussex TN31 7JY
01797 222433

Rye Art Gallery

Easton Rooms, 107 High Street, Rye,
East Sussex TN31 7JE
01797 222433
www.ryeartgallery.co.uk

Visit

BODIAM CASTLE

One of the most evocative castles in Britain, moated Bodiam was built in 1385, as both a defence and comfortable home. The exterior is virtually complete and the ramparts rise dramatically out of the moat.

Bodiam, Robertsbridge,
East Sussex TN32 5UA
01580 830436
www.nationaltrust.org

CHAPEL DOWN WINERY

Discover England's leading wine producer and enjoy a range of tours and tastings to learn about the history of English wine. Wander around the vineyards and herb garden, take lunch on the bistro terrace and visit the Wine and Fine Food Store to buy some wine and quality English produce to take home – cheeses, smoked meats, chutneys, pies and much more.

Tenterden Vineyard, Smallhythe,
Kent TN30 7NG
01580 752501
www.englishwinesgroup.com

GREAT DIXTER

This was the home of gardening writer Christopher Lloyd who, over many years, transformed the garden into a plantsman's dream. With its medieval buildings, natural ponds and striking yew topiary, Great Dixter is one of the most exciting, colourful and constantly changing gardens of modern times. The house is equally fascinating, with its magnificent great hall, the largest surviving example of a timber-framed hall in Britain.

Northiam, Rye, East Sussex TN31 6PH
01797 252878
www.greatdixter.co.uk

Activity

BIGGEST LITTLE RAILWAY IN THE WORLD

Visit one of Kent's favourite tourist attractions and take a ride on the world-famous Romney, Hythe and Dymchurch Railway. The line skirts atmospheric Romney Marsh, which has been a haunt of artists and writers for centuries. Evoking the great days of steam travel, the RHDR offers daily services from Easter until the end of September.

RHDR, New Romney Station, New Romney,
Kent TN28 8PL
01797 362353
www.rhdr.org.uk

BIRDWATCHING

Explore the seashore, saltmarsh, shingle and gravel pits of Rye Harbour Nature Reserve via a network of level footpaths and discover the birdlife – four hides offer the chance to see summer and winter migrants at close quarters.

Rye Harbour Nature Reserve,
East Sussex TN36 4LU
www.naturereserve.ryeharbour.org

THE 1066 COUNTRY WALK

Follow in William the Conqueror's footsteps through 31 miles (50km) of glorious Sussex countryside from Rye to Pevensey. The perfect way to learn about the Norman invasion.

Rye Tourist Information Centre, Strand Quay, Rye, East Sussex TN31 7AY
01797 226696
www.1066country.com

The Walk - *Wide Skies and Lonely Seas at Rye*

This remote coastal walk offers excellent opportunities for birdwatching.

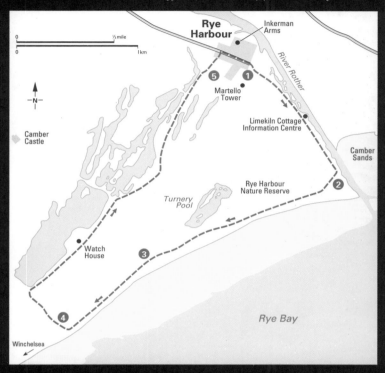

Walk Details

LENGTH: 4.5 miles (7.2km)

TIME: 2hrs

ASCENT: Negligible

PATHS: Level paths and good, clear tracks, no stiles

SUGGESTED MAP: aqua3 OS Explorer 125 Romney Marsh, Rye & Winchelsea

GRID REFERENCE: TQ 942190

PARKING: Spacious free car park at Rye Harbour

❶ Keep the Martello Tower and the entrance to the holiday village on your right and enter Rye Harbour Local Nature Reserve. In late May and June the shingle here is transformed by a colourful array of flowers. Salt marsh, vegetation along the river's edge and grazing marsh add to the variety and the old gravel pits now represent an important site for nesting terns, gulls, ducks and waders. The Rother can be seen on the left, running parallel to the path. Head for Limekiln Cottage Information Centre and continue on the firm path, with the Rother still visible on the left. Camber Sands (a popular holiday destination) nudges into view beyond the river mouth.

❷ Follow the path to the beach, then retrace your steps to the point where the permissive path runs off to the left, cutting between the wildlife sanctuary areas where access is not allowed. Pass the entrance to the Guy Crittall hide on the right. From here enjoy superb views over Turnery Pool. Continue west on the clear path as it gradually edges nearer the shore.

❸ Ahead now is the outline of the old abandoned lifeboat house and, away to the right in the distance, the unmistakable profile of Camber Castle. Keep going on the clear path until you reach the waymarked footpath on the right, running towards the line of houses on eastern edge of Winchelsea.

❹ Take this footpath and head inland, passing the small pond on the right. Glancing back, an old lifeboat house can be seen. Turn right at the next junction, pass by the Watch House and continue on the track as it runs alongside several lakes. Pass to the left of some dilapidated farm outbuildings and keep going along the track. Lakes are still seen on the lefthand side, dotted with trees, and silent fishermen can often be seen along here. Begin the approach to Rye Harbour; on the left is church spire.

❺ On reaching the road in centre of village, turn left to visit the parish church before heading back along the main street. Pass Inkerman Arms and return to the car park.

The Swan Inn
Surrey

The Inn

Like the phoenix of old, the Swan has risen out of the ashes of a disastrous fire that destroyed much of the first floor of this 14th-century, tile-hung coaching inn in 2004. The impressive reincarnation has seen the once traditional interior transformed to create a cool, modern bar with wooden floor, chunky scrubbed tables and chairs, subtle spotlighting and a long, sleek bar lined with gleaming beer pumps and huge vases of lilies.

A trendy, minimalist space it may be, with the adjoining dining room quite formal and upmarket, but this has not obscured the Swan's original function as a cracking village pub: the atmosphere is relaxed and you can still call in for a pint of Hogs Back TEA, sit back and peruse the papers.

It was an upstairs function room that bore the brunt of the fire and from this space 11 contemporary bedrooms have been created, all with 21st-century mod cons. Expect to find decor in muted, earthy colours, plasma TV screens, individual stylish furnishings and lavish bathrooms kitted out with posh basins, power showers and top toiletries.

The Swan Inn, Petworth Road, Chiddingfold, Godalming, Surrey GU8 4TY

The Food

The Swan's chef Darren Tidd's bar menu successfully balances the traditional and modern, with decent sandwiches, ham, egg and chips, and calves' liver and bacon featuring alongside fishcakes with smoked salmon and chive sauce, pork medallions with bubble-and-squeak and mustard cream sauce, and duck leg confit.

The kitchen turns out dishes with ease and confidence in the well laid-out dining room: anything from starters like seared foie gras with warm Sauternes butter sauce, or leek and gruyère tart with dressed leaves and balsamic dressing, to interesting main dishes of asparagus and roasted pepper risotto with pesto and parmesan, and braised lamb shank on celeriac puree with sun-dried tomato and mint sauce.

If you have room for a pudding, why not try the roasted figs with nougat ice cream or the warm chocolate and hazelnut brownie. Alternatively, opt for a plate of French cheeses with a glass of Warres 1988 vintage port. The prettily landscaped terraced garden, decked out with flower-filled urns, teak tubs, terracotta pots and upmarket benches and brollies, makes a perfect alfresco dining option for balmy days.

The Essentials

Time at the Bar!
11am-11pm (Sun 10.30pm)
Food: 12-2.30pm (3pm Sat-Sun),
6.30-10pm

What's the Damage?
Main courses from £9.45

Bitter Experience:
Fuller's London Pride,
Hogs Back TEA

Sticky Fingers:
Children welcome, small portions available

Muddy Paws:
Dogs welcome in the bar if on leads

Zzzzz:
11 rooms, £75-£145

Anything Else?
Terrace, garden, car park

What To Do

Shop

GUILDFORD HIGH STREET

The cobbled High Street has a wide range of shops behind traditional frontages, criss-crossed with lanes and alleyways lined with the nation's favourites and an eclectic mix of individual shops. Heal's on Tunsgate is the place for quality contemporary furniture and stylish accessories. On the fashion front, you'll find a trendy Fat Face store, Karen Millen for womenswear and footware, Amanda Graham in the Tunsgate Centre for designer ladies fashion specialising in Basler and Hauber, and Barbour for quality country clothing and accessories.

Amanda Graham

12 Tunsgate, Guildford, Surrey GU1 3QZ

01483 306543

Barbour

Tunsgate, Guildford, Surrey GU1 3QZ

01483 538365 www.barbour.com

Fat Face

9-13 Market Street, Guildford, Surrey

01483 449695 www.fatface.com

Heal's

Tunsgate, Guildford, Surrey GU1 3QU

01483 796500 www.heals.co.uk

Karen Millen

120 High Street, Guildford, Surrey GU1 3HQ

01483 451621 www.karenmillen.com

SECRETTS FARM SHOP

A delightful farm shop crammed with fruit and veg picked in the market garden each day. An extensive delicatessen offers 300 cheeses, cooked meats, salads and delicious individual dishes prepared in the kitchens. Garden furniture and barbecues are on sale.

Hurst Farm, Chapel Lane, Nilford, Godalming, Surrey GU8 5HU

01483 520500

www.secretts.co.uk

Visit

HATCHLANDS PARK

The National Trust runs this elegant 18th-century mansion set in stunning landscaped parkland. Robert Adams designed much of the interior, which also houses the world's largest collection of keyboard instruments, many of which are associated with Purcell, JC Bach, Chopin and Elgar. Music recitals and concerts are run regularly both at lunchtime and in the evening. There's also a very pretty formal garden designed by Gertrude Jekyll.

East Clandon, Guildford, Surrey GU4 7RT

01483 222482

www.nationaltrust.org.uk

JANE AUSTEN'S HOUSE

Jane Austen lived in this handsome 17th-century house for the last eight years of her life, and penned *Mansfield Park* and *Persuasion* here. The rooms she lived and wrote in are perfectly preserved, and if you walk round the pretty garden, you'll see beautiful plants of the period. Her mother and sister are buried in nearby Chawton churchyard.

Chawton, Alton, Hampshire GU34 1SD

01420 83262

www.janeaustenmuseum.org.uk

PETWORTH HOUSE

This vast late 17th-century mansion is set in a beautiful park, landscaped by Capability Brown and immortalised in Turner's paintings. Works by Turner and Van Dyck, sculpture, furniture and carvings can be seen in the gallery, one of the finest collections in the country.

Petworth, West Sussex GU28 0AE

01798 342207

www.nationaltrust.org.uk

Activity

HOT-AIR BALLOONING

Float over three counties with your loved one and nothing but a bottle of champagne to keep you company (apart from the pilot, of course). The wind takes you wherever it will, but you're guaranteed to see some of the most beautiful countryside in rural southern England.

Horizon Balloons

Blacknest Industrial Park, Blacknest, Alton, Hampshire GU34 4PX

01420 520505

www.horizonballooning.co.uk

WINKWORTH ARBORETUM

Lose yourself in the tranquil hillside woodland, wander among the award-winning collection of thousands of rare shrubs and trees, and imagine yourself in New England in the fall – Winkworth is most famous for autumn hues, but magnolias, cherries, azaleas and bluebells ensure year-round colour.

Hascombe Road, Godalming, Surrey GU8 4AD

01483 208477

www.nationaltrust.org.uk

The Walk - The Lost Canal at Alfold

Take a walk through the wild woods along a derelict canal tow path.

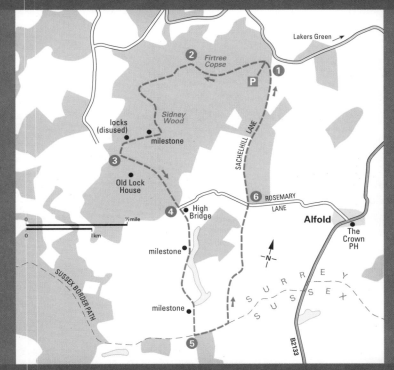

Walk Details

LENGTH: 4.75 miles (7.7km)

TIME: 2hrs

ASCENT: 164ft (50m)

PATHS: Old canal tow path, field and forest paths, muddy after rain

SUGGESTED MAP: aqua3 OS Explorer 134 Crawley & Horsham

GRID REFERENCE: TQ 026350

PARKING: Forestry Commission car park between Alfold and Dunsfold

1 From the car park, walk back towards the road for 35yds (32m) until you see the track on the left, marked by a concrete post with a small Wey South Path waymark near the top. Turn left; then keep right at the fork 300yds (274m) further on. Cross the tarmac drive at the public bridleway signpost and follow the waymarked path around the edge of Firtree Copse.

2 Wey South Path meets the canal at the gate. Turn left, and follow the tow path for 1 mile (1.6km). Notice the gentle slope as you pass the Arun 13/Wey 10 milestone; it's the only clue that this was once the site of a 6-lock flight.

3 A gravelled track now crosses the canal at Sydney Court. Leave the tow path here and turn left, following the waymarked route across the bridleway crossroads to reach High Bridge.

4 Zig-zag right and left across Rosemary Lane; rejoin the old tow path. After 0.5 mile (800m) look out for the Arun 11.5/Wey 11.5 milestone, and continue for 150yds (137m) until the Sussex Border Path crosses the canal.

5 Turn left, and follow the Sussex Border Path for 350yds (320m) until the track bends sharply right. Turn left through a metal field gate, and follow the hedge on the right. A 2nd gate leads past a cottage; now, follow the public bridleway signpost that points your way through 2 fields, and through another gate on

to a path leading out to Rosemary Lane. You can turn right here, to make a 0.5 mile (800m) diversion to The Crown at Alfold.

6 Otherwise, cross over the lane and follow waymarked bridleway for 0.5 mile (800m). Now turn left at public footpath signpost then, just past prominent sign ('Riding by permit only'), turn right to walk along waymarked footpath through woods. Fork right a short way further on and then continue over 2 stiles and follow path just inside woodland edge until it bears left and then meets Wey South Path at waymark post. Turn left, and follow path to Sidney Wood car park road, before turning left again for a short distance to return to your car.

The Albert Arms

Surrey

The Inn

Money has been lavished on this impressive, white-painted pub on the corner of Park Street and Esher's busy high street; it's one of a handful of thriving eateries developed by Jonathan Dunne that includes a cafe around the corner and a fine dining restaurant a few doors away. Swing open the doors to the pub and you are immediately hit by style, be it the sleek mahogany bar, the polished oak flooring in the elegant dining room, or the large plasma TV screen in the lively bar area, which draws punters in for the racing and rugby at weekends. Live weekend jazz, private dining rooms and regular wine courses add to the appeal of this classy town-centre inn.

Simple rooms are just a short stroll away in a peaceful mews building, well removed from the hustle and bustle of both pub and high street. Although quite small, all six rooms have been carefully designed and equipped with style and taste. Expect superior beds with quality linen, 30-channel TV, mini hi-fi system, internet access, and über-trendy wet rooms.

The Food

Vast menus offer an eclectic choice, from traditional favourites such as calves' liver and bacon, grilled Dover sole, rack of lamb with garlic sauce, or the pub's speciality 28-day matured Angus steaks – grilled T-bone or sirloin with pepper sauce – to fish stew, roasted quail on tagliatelle with pesto, or sea bass cooked in chilli, lime and wine sauce.

Starters and puddings have a slightly retro feel. You can take in a classic prawn cocktail or crab claws in garlic butter, and if you've room to squeeze in a pudding, then try the home-made profiteroles with chocolate sauce. On Sundays a big crowd pleaser is the Albert's famous roast – sirloin of beef served with Yorkshire pudding and all the trimmings.

The mind-boggling range of drinks includes more than 30 wines available by the glass, eight tip-top ales from local microbreweries (including Hogs Back TEA and Surrey Hills Shere Drop), and a raft of spirits. If you like the wine you quaffed with your meal, then why not buy a case to take home with you along the road at Jonathan's wine store or on line at the Albert Wine Company, where you have 700 to choose from.

The Essentials

Time at the Bar!
10.30am-11pm
(Thu-Sat 10.30am-12 midnight)
Food: 12-2.45pm, 7-10pm,
Sun 12-4pm (no food Sun evening)

What's the Damage?
Main courses from £12

Bitter Experience:
Fuller's London Pride, Surrey Hills
Shere Drop, Brakspear, guest beers

Sticky Fingers:
Children welcome, children's menu
Sunday lunch only

Muddy Paws:
No dogs

Zzzzz:
10 rooms, £110-£150

Anything Else?
Car park (but not directly linked)

What To Do

Shop

KINGSTON ANTIQUES MARKET

Eighty independent dealers are housed in the Antiques Market, a great place to start a day of full-blown retail therapy in Kingston. The world-famous Bentalls department store is just down the road (for that Missoni or Nicole Farhi something) and Kingston Ancient Market is the place for locally grown and produced fruit, vegetables and meat.

29-31 London Road, Kingston upon Thames, Surrey KT2 6ND
020 8549 2004
www.kingstonantiques.co.uk

KEW GARDENS

Kew's Victoria Plaza is home to the Garden Shop selling a huge range of plants, shrubs and bulbs. Pick up cherry oil, preserves, organic ginger and chocolate fudge at The Cook Shop. The Bookshop, on the same site, stocks a fantastic variety of titles for gardeners at every level.

Royal Botanic Gardens, Kew, Richmond, Surrey TW9 3AB
020 8332 5655
www.kew.org

GARSON FARM SHOP

Garson Farm has over 40 different Pick Your Own crops between May and Sep. The shop, housed in renovated old farm buildings, prides itself on its meats and dairy products, fresh fruit, vegetables, cakes and ice creams. And if you're a keen gardener, visit the garden centre, which sells plants, garden tools, BBQs, furniture and clothing. There's also a restaurant on-site.

Winterdown Road, Esher, Surrey KT10 8LS
01372 464389
www.garsons.co.uk

Visit

THE HOMEWOOD

Recently acquired by the National Trust, this modernist masterpiece was designed and built as a 'party house' for his parents by Patrick Gwynne when he was only 24. It's a perfect example of form and function working in harmony – dramatically stark from the outside, but pure luxury inside. The dressing room at the top of the stairs is simply a stroke of genius.

Portsmouth Road, Esher, Surrey KT10 9LJ
01372 476424
www.nationaltrust.org.uk

CLAREMONT HOUSE & LANDSCAPE GARDENS

This stunning Palladian mansion was built in the 1700s by Capability Brown for Clive of India – it's now a private school, but it opens for visitors at the weekends. While you are here, take the chance to wander round the National Trust's landscaped gardens, and don't miss the unique turf amphitheatre rising magnificently above the lake.

Portsmouth Road, Esher, Surrey KT10 9JG
01372 467841
www.nationaltrust.org.uk

HAMPTON COURT PALACE

An amazing place, just as a royal palace should be. Come to see the magnificent state apartments of William III and Henry VIII, the starkly imposing Tudor kitchens, the hammerbeamed great hall, and fine Renaissance works of art in the Picture Gallery, or lose yourself in the famous Maze and the 60 acres of beautiful riverside gardens.

Hampton Court, Surrey KT8 9AU
0870 752 7777
www.hrp.org.uk

Activity

BROOKLANDS MUSEUM

Brooklands has the distinction of being the first purpose-built motor racing circuit in the world. Now it's a museum and venue for any number of events – if you're a Jaguar or Morris and Austin nut, there are regular 'enthusiasts days out'. Their pride and joy is the Napier Railton collection, Grand Prix and Campbell exhibitions – so you can dream about being the next Stirling Moss to your heart's content. There's a shop selling motoring memorabilia and the Sunbeam Tea Room, too.

Brooklands Road, Weybridge, Surrey KT13 0QN
01932 857381
www.brooklandsmuseum.com

SANDOWN PARK RACES

Enjoy a day at the races – Sandown Park run both flat and National Hunt racing fixtures throughout the year. The views from the racecourse are spectacular, and you can spot famous London landmarks such as The London Eye and the Gherkin from a place in the stands.

Portsmouth Road, Esher, Surrey KT10 9AJ
01372 464348
www.sandown.co.uk

THAMES PASSENGER BOAT

View some of the most historic landmarks of London and, in the summer months, alight to explore the various sites along the way by taking a scheduled, fully licensed passenger boat between Richmond, Kingston and Hampton Court.

Turk Launches, Town End Pier, 68 High Street, Kingston, Surrey KT1 1HR
020 8546 2434
www.turks.co.uk

The Walk - *Anyone for Real Tennis?*

Learn about the game of kings on a walk through the regal landscape of Hampton Court.

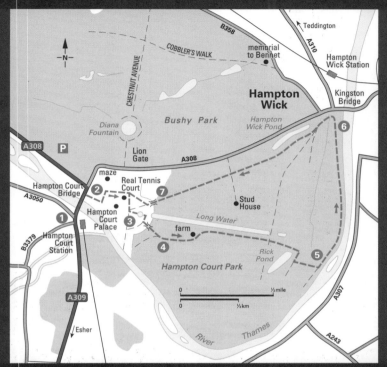

Walk Details

LENGTH: 4.75 miles (7.7km)

TIME: 1hr 45min

ASCENT: Negligible

PATHS: Gravel, tarmac and riverside tracks

SUGGESTED MAP: aqua3 OS Explorer 161 London South

GRID REFERENCE: TQ 174697 Hampton Court rail

PARKING: Car park in Hampton Court Road

1 Cross Hampton Court Bridge, turn right through the main gates to Hampton Court Palace and walk along the wide sweeping drive. Just before reaching the palace turn left through the gatehouse and then walk under the arch.

2 Turn right just before the tea room. Walk through the gateway and along the path through the gardens. At the end, on the right, is the real tennis court building. Pass through another gateway and then turn sharp right to walk alongside the real tennis court and past the entrance to it. King Henry VIII played real tennis here, as did Charles I. Today, the Earl of Wessex and his wife Sophie are members of the 700-strong members-only club.

3 Take the central gravel path in front of the palace and walk past the fountain, then walk towards the railings overlooking Long Water, an artificial lake nearly 0.75 mile (1.2km) in length. Head towards the footbridge on the right and go through the wrought-iron gates.

4 After 220yds (201m) the footpath bears left and joins the tarmac track. Follow this, turning left by some farm buildings, after which the path runs parallel to Long Water. Where the lake ends, continue ahead at the crossing of tracks and bear right to skirt the left side of Rick Pond. Turn left through the metal gate, walk along the enclosed footpath and through the gate to reach the River Thames.

5 Turn left along this riverside path and follow it for 0.75 mile (1.2km) to Kingston Bridge. Here, join the road leading to the roundabout.

6 At the end of the row of houses turn left through the gateway. Immediately after the cattle grid bear right along the grassy path running along the left side of the boomerang-shaped Hampton Wick Pond. Follow the straight path for about 0.75 mile (1.2km) back to Hampton Court Palace.

7 Bear right to cross the footbridge and follow the footpath back to the real tennis court, from where you can retrace your steps to the gatehouse and the start of the walk over Hampton Court Bridge and back into Hampton Court Road.

The Beacon

Kent

The Inn

With open fires to toast your toes in winter and the famous far-reaching view best appreciated over drinks on the terrace, The Beacon seems to have found the ultimate recipe for all-year-round appeal.

The gorgeous late Victorian building impresses with a sense of space and wealth of ornate period details – in particular the magnificent stained glass, oak panelling and decorative ceilings – while the clubby bar scores highly in terms of creature comforts, with attentive service, good beer and an impressive range of wines by the glass.

Bedrooms, reached via a grand wooden staircase, are comfortable. There's antique furniture and a posh bathroom with a roll-top slipper bath in the pretty Georgian Room; the more spacious Colonial Room has bold African prints and a stunning outlook over the surrounding countryside; while the third room, a single, works perfectly with its fresh contemporary styling and light, uncluttered feel. All are equipped with plump cushions, comfortable beds and a relaxed, peaceful air. The Beacon is a perfect weekend bolt hole with the Weald of Kent on its doorstep.

The Beacon, Tea Garden Lane, Rusthall, Tunbridge Wells, Kent TN3 9JH

The Essentials

Time at the Bar!
11am-11pm
Food: 11am-2.30pm

What's the Damage?
Main courses from £8.50

Bitter Experience:
Harvey's Sussex Best, Timothy Taylor
Landlord, Larkin's Traditional

Sticky Fingers:
Children welcome; small portions
available

Muddy Paws:
Dogs welcome in the bar

Zzzzz:
3 rooms, £68.50-£97

Anything Else?
Terrace, garden, 2 car parks

The Food

Light floods through big windows into the spacious, formally laid dining room, which does well with its food, as long as you're not looking for culinary fireworks. Slow cooking is a favoured method, whether lamb shank or belly pork, and there are easy British classics like haddock fillet battered in Harvey's ale with hand-cut chips and mushy peas.

Alternatives include cheese fondue with crusty bread, crudités and tiger prawns, or dishes that come with the occasional Mediterranean or Asian twist – roasted red onion and butternut squash in a puff pastry parcel with lemon and mint pesto, say, or scallops and tiger prawns with chilli noodles.

If you prefer to have a meal in the bar, you can order the likes of rib-eye steak with chips, and lambs' liver and bacon served with rich onion gravy. And if you can't resist ordering the apple sticky toffee pudding for afters, and manage to polish off all the accompanying butterscotch ice cream, you can always make amends with a stroll in The Beacon's delightful wooded grounds to the chalybeate spring, which is similar to the one that made nearby Royal Tunbridge Wells famous.

What To Do

Shop

ANTIQUE SHOPPING IN ROYAL TUNBRIDGE WELLS

Pop along to the Pantiles, famed for its colonnaded streets, for some of Kent's best-known antique shops. Antique and modern jewellery is at Chapel Place Antiques, for a quality range of Georgian, Victorian and Edwardian furniture call into Pantiles Antiques, and if you're interested in Chinese antiques, try Yiju. Elsewhere, Up Country has a good selection of country furniture and rural artefacts, while the Architectural Stores on St John's Road has antique fireplaces, stained glass and salvage pieces.

Chapel Place Antiques

9 Chapel Place, Tunbridge Wells TN1 1YQ

01892 546561

Pantiles Antiques

31 The Pantiles, Tunbridge Wells TN2 5TD

01892 531291

Yiju

27 The Pantiles, Tunbridge Wells TN2 5TN

01892 517000 www.yiju.co.uk

Up Country

The Old Corn Stores, 68 St John's Road, Tunbridge Wells TN4 9PE

01892 523341

www.upcountryantiques.co.uk

Architectural Stores

55 St John's Road, Tunbridge Wells TN4 9TP

01892 540368

www.architecturalstores.com

YALDING ORGANIC GARDENS

Tour the gardens then browse around the shop where you can buy books on organic gardening, unusual ornamentals and herb and vegetable plants in season.

Benover Road, Yalding, Maidstone, Kent ME18 6EX

01622 814650

www.gardenorganic.org.uk

Visit

HEVER CASTLE

Situated deep in the countryside outside the small town of Edenbridge and probably best known as Anne Boleyn's childhood home, 13th-century Hever Castle is arranged around a courtyard complete with a romantic-looking drawbridge. With its award-winning gardens, lake, topiary, rose garden, yew and water mazes, the setting is completely irresistible.

Hever, Edenbridge, Kent TN8 7NG

01732 865224

www.hevercastle.co.uk

PENSHURST PLACE

Sir Philip Sidney, one of the great heroes of the Elizabethan era, was born here in 1554 and his descendants are still in residence. Visit the staterooms en route to the baron's hall and then enjoy the Tudor walled gardens, the toy museum and the woodland trail before relaxing with a well-earned cup of tea in the garden tea room.

Penshurst, Tonbridge, Kent TN11 8DG

01892 870307

www.penshurstplace.com

CHARTWELL

The former home of great British statesman Sir Winston Churchill is filled with reminders of the renowned prime minister, from his hat and uniforms to gifts presented by Stalin and Roosevelt. An exhibition gives you an insight into his life at Chartwell and you can view his studio and stroll through the gardens, which have glorious views across the Weald.

Mapleton Road, Westerham, Kent TN16 1PS

01732 866368

www.nationaltrust.org.uk

Activity

CYCLING

Head off to Bedgebury Forest near Goudhurst for easy cycling along 6 miles (10km) of surfaced track or, for the more adventurous, 7 miles (12km) of challenging single track for mountain bikes. You can hire bikes at the visitor centre bike shop (01580 879694).

Park Lane, Goudhurst, Kent TN17 2SL

01580 879920

www.forestry.gov.uk

HERITAGE WALKING TRAIL

Pick up a leaflet on the Royal Tunbridge Wells Heritage Walking Trail and amble through 400 years of history. The trail commemorates notable figures from Britain's past connected with the town.

Tourist Information Centre, Old Fish Market, The Pantiles, Tunbridge Wells, Kent TN2 5TN

01892 515675

www.visittunbridgewells.com

BEWL WATER

At the largest lake in the Southeast you can pedal or walk the 12.5 mile (20km) cycle route around the reservoir (map and bike hire is available at the visitor centre), buy a permit and fish for trout, or join day courses and learn to sail and windsurf on the lake.

Lamberhurst, Kent TN3 8JH

01892 890661

Outdoor Centre 01892 890716

www.bewlwater.org

www.bewlwindsurfing.co.uk

www.cuckmere-cycle.co.uk

The Walk - Royal Passion at Hever

Memories of King Henry VIII and Anne Boleyn on this circular walk.

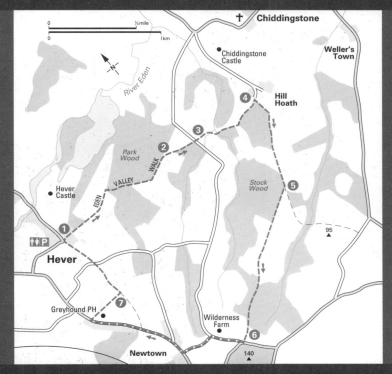

Walk Details

LENGTH: 3.5 miles (5.7km)

TIME: 2hrs

ASCENT: 279ft (85m)

PATHS: Paths, grassy tracks and field edges, some roads, 6 stiles

SUGGESTED MAP: aqua3 OS Explorer 147 Sevenoaks & Tonbridge

GRID REFERENCE: TQ 476448

PARKING: Car park by Hever Castle

❶ Walk under the lychgate and go through the churchyard following the Eden Valley Walk. The path goes downhill, across the bridge and soon becomes a narrow lane parallel to the road, offering occasional glimpses of the lake at Hever Castle. The lake looks natural but it was actually created by William Waldorf Astor when he bought the castle in 1903. The path now bends round, goes through woodland, across another bridge and finally opens out.

❷ When you come to the house, climb the gate following the Eden Valley Walk (follow it all the way to Point 4). Pass another house, then take the track on the righthand side, which winds round the edge of the meadow to woodland. When you come to the tarmac road, cross it and pop over the stile.

❸ Continue along enclosed track, which can get very muddy, crossing 2 more stiles and gradually heading uphill. Another stile leads you past deer fencing and through the gate on to the tarmac road at Hill Hoath.

❹ Now turn back to right and go through the large gate, so that you seem to be doubling back on yourself. This leads to a broad, grassy track. Walk ahead (don't be tempted into crossing stile on the left) and walk between trees, passing the lake on your lefthand side. Soon enter much thicker woodland and the track becomes narrower, but is still clear to follow.

❺ At the branching of footpaths, bear right. Be warned, this can be very muddy. Continue down the track, passing another 2 areas of woodland until you reach the road.

❻ Turn right here and walk to Wilderness Farm, then take the road that leads to the left opposite the farm. At another road turn right and walk up, past the road that leads to the right. Continue ahead to take the footpath on the right that runs alongside the Greyhound pub.

❼ When you come to a fork by 2 stiles turn left, then walk around the edge of the field and past the pond. Continue ahead to the lane, where you turn left, then take the footpath on the right. Follow this back into Hever and return to the car park.

The George Hotel

Kent

The Inn

Old-world charm with modern trimmings is a good way to describe this inn, one of Cranbrook's most historic landmark buildings. An open-plan bar/brasserie kitted out with pale wood (floor and tables) and leather sofas (ideal for sinking into with a pint of Harvey's Best) creates a welcoming first impression. It contrasts nicely with the full suit of armour standing guard at the bottom of a magnificent 14th-century staircase with the impressive half-timbered, chandeliered restaurant beyond. There's a relaxed and informal atmosphere that comes through in a pleasant mix of local drinkers and long-distance diners.

Climb that ancient staircase and you will find that no two bedrooms are the same, although some have exposed brick and timber, bulging walls and the odd wonky floor in common. All have been refurbished to an exacting standard and decorated with an eye for detail. While the best room in the house has a striking antique four-poster bed, others blend ancient features with a more modern feel, and the bathrooms, in particular, are very up to date and equipped with all the comforts such as fluffy white towels, bathrobes and complimentary bath products by Gilchrist & Soames.

The Food

The restaurant may date from the 16th century and come with a big inglenook, mullioned windows and lots of exposed timber, but the look and style is very contemporary, with undressed oak tables, bare floorboards and high-backed leather chairs. This is a place where food takes centre stage. The menu (served in both the restaurant and the brasserie) is an ambitious collection of upmarket pub dishes with brasserie leanings: think twice-baked goats' cheese soufflé served with a crisp salad and shallot and balsamic dressing; chunky shepherd's pie made with locally reared lamb and accompanied by honey and mustard roasted carrots; and Harvey's beer-battered cod with hand-cut chips and creamed peas.

A range of influences combine with local sourcing, and the food is pitched exactly right for the surroundings: what the kitchen delivers is fresh, honestly prepared dishes with bags of flavour. Desserts are a mixture of old favourites like zesty lemon meringue pie served with vanilla ice cream or more of-the-moment interpretations like hot chocolate fondant with white chocolate ice cream and a raspberry shake.

The Essentials

Time at the Bar!
11am-11pm
Food: 12-3pm, 6-9.30pm

What's the Damage?
Main courses from £9.50

Bitter Experience:
Harvey's Sussex Ale, Adnams

Sticky Fingers:
Children welcome, children's menu

Muddy Paws:
Dogs welcome in the bar

Zzzzz:
12 rooms, £70-£135

Anything Else?
Small terrace, car park

What To Do

Shop

RYE ART GALLERY

Comprising two historic buildings, the permanent collection of fine art on display in this town-centre gallery includes works by Lowry, Epstein and Eric Gill. The Gallery Trust was founded in 1957 by flower, landscape and interiors artist Mary Stormont who eloped to Rye in 1957 with landscape and portrait artist Howard Stormont. The ever-changing themed and general exhibitions cover many fields of the creative arts including painting, glasswork, sculpture, metalwork and prints – many for sale.

107 High Street, Rye, East Sussex TN31 7JE
01797 222433
www.ryeartgallery.co.uk

THE WEALD SMOKERY

An ultra-traditional smokery, using oak shavings and sawdust to hot or cold smoke the raw material in kilns or over open fires. The farm shop sells a comprehensive choice of products over the entire meat, fish and fowl range, including smoked venison, trout and cuts of pork, much of it sourced locally.

Mount Farm, Flimwell,
East Sussex TN5 7QL
01580 879601
www.wealdsmokery.co.uk

Visit

BIDDENDEN VINEYARDS

Around 22 acres of vines bask in the sunshine in the Kentish Weald. Nine different types of grape are planted, with more than a nod towards German varietals. Indulge in a self-guided tour before sampling a range of red, white, rosé and sparkling wines. The vineyard shop also sells a range of ciders produced from Kent apples.

Gribble Bridge Lane, Biddenden,
Kent TN27 8DF
01580 291726
www.biddendenvineyards.com

KENT & EAST SUSSEX RAILWAY

An atmospheric evocation of rural branch lines in Edwardian times. The railway line runs through some pretty villages in the Rother Valley, linking Tenterden and Bodiam in over 10 miles (16km) of (largely) steam-hauled nostalgia. Hands-on driving experiences are available.

Station Road, Tenterden, Kent TN30 6HE
0870 600 6074
www.kesr.org.uk

LEEDS CASTLE

The classic English castle, in the midst of a huge lake-cum-moat is familiar from many films that have featured its medieval splendour. It is used today as a venue for major political conferences and all the trappings are thus *in situ*, from magnificent tapestries and fine furnishings to paintings and centuries' worth of ephemera, including a collection of (canine!) dog-collars. There's also themed gardens, a maze and a vineyard.

Maidstone, Kent ME17 1PL
01622 765400
www.leeds-castle.com

Activity

CLAY PIGEON SHOOTING

Instruction for novices is available at the school and all the equipment is on hand for the use of more experienced shooters.

West Kent Shooting School,
Paddock Wood, Kent TN12 7DG
01892 834306
www.wkss.demon.co.uk

HEADCORN AIRFIELD

Book a pleasure flight across the Weald, the South Downs and the south coast from here, or take a trial lesson with an experienced instructor. You can try flying a light aircraft or even a small helicopter. The Lashenden Air Warfare Museum is also based here, with World War II ephemera and a V1 flying bomb.

Headcorn, Ashford,
Kent TN27 9HX
01622 891539
www.headcornaerodrome.co.uk

HONNINGTON EQUESTRIAN CENTRE

Beginners and improvers can book riding lessons or take part in short pony treks on this large country estate near Tunbridge Wells.

Vauxhall Lane, Southborough,
Tunbridge Wells, Kent TN4 0XD
01892 531154
www.honnington.com

The Walk - Sissinghurst, A Gardener's Delight

A lovely, easy walk to the famous garden created by Vita Sackville-West.

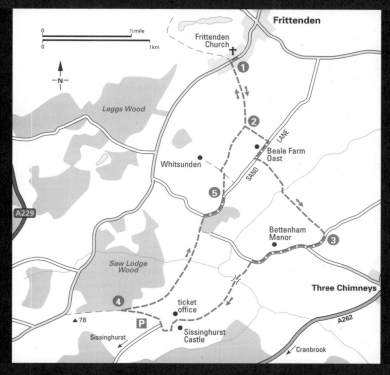

Walk Details

LENGTH: 3 miles (4.8km)

TIME: 2hrs

ASCENT: 33ft (10m)

PATHS: Well-marked field paths and woodland tracks

SUGGESTED MAP: aqua3 OS Explorer 137 Ashford

GRID REFERENCE: TQ 814409

PARKING: On street in Frittenden

❶ With your back to Frittenden church, turn right, then turn left down the pathway by the hall. Cross the stile and walk straight ahead over the field, through the gate and across another field. Go through the kissing gate, then straight ahead again – it's clearly marked. At the gap in the hedge cross the little wooden bridge and head to the telegraph pole. Branch left.

❷ Nip over the stile, go across the next field, over another stile and on to the tarmac lane to turn right past Beale Farm Oast. At the next house, turn left and walk up the track until you pass the old barn. Turn right just after the barn, continue ahead over 2 more stiles and eventually cross footbridge to the right of a clump of trees. Walk a few paces left, continue in the same direction up the edge of the field then turn left again to cross another bridge. Scramble through some scrub and follow the path ahead to another stile and on to the road.

❸ Turn right, then turn right again at the road junction. You pass Bettenham Manor, turn left up the bridleway, over the bridge, then pass Sissinghurst Castle, keeping the building on your left. Walk up to the oast houses, then bear left around them, past the ticket office and up the driveway. Turn left, then right, and walk by the side of the car parks to the stile. Cross into field, then bear right in a few paces to cross a stile by some cottages.

❹ Turn right and walk back past the cottages, then bear left along the path through the trees. Continue ahead along the tree-lined track. Now cross the stream and keep following the bridleway. When you come to the road, cross over and walk up Sand Lane.

❺ Eventually reach the stile on the lefthand side, cross and then head diagonally across the field to another stile in the fence ahead of you. Continue diagonally, passing a dip in the field. Keep the church spire ahead and proceed to cross another stile. The path is clear ahead, then veers to the telegraph pole where you go left, heading for the church spire. Cross the bridge and walk back into the village.

The Bell Hotel

Kent

The Inn

Flanked on one side by the River Stour and by ancient timber-framed houses on the other, the solid 19th-century exterior of the Bell makes a convincing, traditional-looking inn. Yet the interior comes as quite a surprise: modern, light and airy, with restored parquet and modern light wood floors, big, slouchy armchairs and sofas, and contemporary artwork by local artists. The bar may serve up pints of Shepherd Neame Spitfire, but it, too, has a clean contemporary appeal, with low-slung coffee tables and expansive leather seating, while the brasserie follows suit with an equally up-to-date look.

All the bedrooms are chic, especially the ones in bolder colours (room 18, for example, is in deepest red). Top choice, however, is a light-coloured suite with a modern four-poster bed and a balcony looking onto the river. Rooms may come in all shapes and sizes, but comfortable beds, crisp linen, soft duvets, digital radios and flat-screen TVs with Freeview, alongside well-equipped bathrooms with sunflower-head power showers, are standard

The Essentials

Time at the Bar!
10am-11pm
Food: 12-2.30pm, 7-9.30pm

What's the Damage?
Main courses from £10.25

Bitter Experience:
Shepherd Neame Spitfire

Sticky Fingers:
Children welcome; children's menu

Muddy Paws:
Dogs welcome

Zzzzz:
34 rooms, £95-£165

Anything Else?
Terrace, car park, conservatory

The Food

The brasserie extends into a light and airy conservatory and is noted for impeccable service and cooking that puts clever spins on conventional ideas. Proximity to the sea means that the kitchen is noted for the quality of its fresh local fish – and only non-threatened species at that – but look out for Romney Marsh lamb, free-range pork and locally reared beef, which provides burgers or rib-eye steaks. While the cooking may not be cutting edge, it draws plenty of admirers for its reliability and generous portion sizes.

Try a stack of aromatic spiced fishcakes with a pickled cucumber and carrot salad, or rustic Sandwich Bay chowder with roasted vine tomatoes and garlic bruschetta for starters, then move on to honey-glazed duck breast with a Victoria plum compote, crushed organic Kent mids and summertime vegetables, or grilled mackerel fillets on Kentish wholegrain mustard mash with tomato and red onion salad and rustic salsa verde. Finish with one of the home-made puds, such as blackberry crème brûlée with shortbread.

What To Do

Shop

CASTLE ART GALLERY
Browse and/or buy from an extraordinary collection of original and eclectic paintings, jewellery and sculpture in this cutting-edge gallery and cafe.

76 Castle Street, Canterbury, Kent CT1 2QD
01227 766616
www.castlearts.co.uk

CHANDLER & DUNN
This farm shop sells delicious well-marbled, home-reared meat from rare Sussex cattle that has been hung for three weeks, as well as home-reared lamb and locally produced pork.

The Laurels, Lower Goldstone, Ash,
Canterbury, Kent CT3 2DY
01304 814 245
www.chandleranddunn.co.uk

ELHAM VALLEY VINEYARDS
Set among rolling fields in the Kent Downs, this long-established winery grows three white grape varieties in a sheltered tranquil valley. You are invited to thoroughly sample the wares before making your choice from the shop.

Breach, Barham, Canterbury, Kent CT4 6LN
01227 832022

MORELLI'S
This original, kitsch ice cream parlour is a fantastic 1950s Formica fantasy. Relive an episode of *Happy Days* and relax on the candy floss-pink leatherette banquettes, listen to the rock and roll hits on the juke box and glory in the stupendous ice cream sundaes.

14 Victoria Parade, Broadstairs,
Kent CT10 1QS
01843 863500
www.morellis.com

Visit

CANTERBURY CATHEDRAL
At the heart of the historic city of Canterbury, this magnificent cathedral has countless interesting links to many people in history, notably Thomas à Becket. Spend time in the peaceful gardens, perfect for contemplation.

11 The Precincts, Canterbury, Kent CT1 2EH
01227 762862
www.canterbury-cathedral.org

HIGHAM PARK HOUSE & GARDENS
This extraordinary Palladian mansion has been brought to life by three intrepid renovators when it became neglected after being used as a hospital during World War II. The interior now has an elegant Italian marble staircase, and a wonderful Portland stone floor in the grand hall has been revealed. Outside, there's a stunning sunken Italian water garden and 25 acres to stroll round.

Bridge, Canterbury, Kent CT4 5BE
01227 830830
www.higham-park.co.uk

QUEX MUSEUM, HOUSE & GARDENS
Built as a Regency gentleman's country residence, this was later home to the great Victorian explorer Major Powell-Cotton, and his family still live here. Much of his expedition collection is on show, with splendid pieces of oriental furniture, clocks, silver and paintings. There's also a very English country garden, complete with the heady scent of old roses and meandering paths.

Quex Park, Birchington, Kent CT7 0BH
01843 842168
www.quexmuseum.org

Activity

BIKE RIDE
You can hire all sorts of bikes here, and the helpful team will suggest several routes for all abilities, in and around Canterbury. The routes include an enjoyable flat ride through some lovely countryside to Herne Bay. This old railway line cycle track is called the Crab & Winkle Way.

Downland Cycles
The Malthouse, St Stephens Road,
Canterbury, Kent CT2 7JA
01227 479643
www.downlandcycles.co.uk

GOLF AT ROYAL ST GEORGE'S
Take the opportunity to play 18 holes on this stunning links course, following the footsteps of the likes of Pros such as Palmer, Lyle and Norman. Home to many major tournaments, including the Open Championship and the Walker Cup, Royal St George's is a cracking course – and your handicap might even improve.

Royal St George's Golf Club, Sandwich,
Kent CT13 9PB
01304 613090
www.royalstgeorges.com

HERITAGE TRAIN TRIP
The East Kent Railway was built in the early 1900s to serve the local coal mines; the station here hasn't changed since then, so you get an accurate snapshot of the past. Take a trip on one of the genuine electric trains, which will transport you back to a time when air conditioning was an open window.

East Kent Railway, Station Road,
Sherperdswell, Kent CT15 7PD
01304 832042
www.eastkentrailway.com

The Walk - A Picturesque Trail in Sandwich

Enjoy the quiet English charm of Sandwich on this gentle town trail.

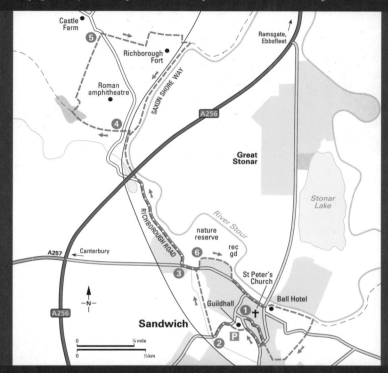

Walk Details

LENGTH: 3 miles (4.8km)

TIME: 1hr 30min

ASCENT: 98ft (30m)

PATHS: Easy town streets and field tracks, 9 stiles

SUGGESTED MAP: aqua3 OS Explorer 150 Canterbury & the Isle of Thanet

GRID REFERENCE: TR 351582

PARKING: Behind the Guildhall in Sandwich

1 From St Peter's Church in the town centre, walk down St Peter's Street to The Chain. Turn right into Galliard Street; walk to New Street. Continue to the Guildhall. Go left, through the car park and up to Rope Walk, a long, straight area used by rope makers to lay out their ropes.
2 Turn right and, when you reach the road, cross over and turn right down The Butts. At the main road turn left, cross over and turn right up Richborough Road.
3 Walk ahead, past the scrapyard, and go through the gate to join the footpath on the right. Follow the track round, under the main road and up to the railway line. Cross the stile and the rail line with care, then go over 2 more stiles and on to road.

4 Cross over the road, go over another stile, then walk across the field to the trees, heading for the 3rd telegraph pole. The path now plunges into the wood and continues up the wide track. Where it splits, fork right and go through the trees to the stile. Now follow the fence line and cross 2 more stiles over 2 fields to join the road.
5 Cross over the road and walk up the track ahead. Richborough Fort is ahead. The path runs around the fort with expansive views. At the bottom of the track turn right along the end of the garden. Nip over the stile and back over the railway, leaving it by another stile. The path now leads to the right, over the neglected-looking lock and back

beside the river. You will eventually rejoin the road, and retrace your steps to the end of Richborough Road where you turn left.
6 Go left through the kissing gate, pass the nature reserve and go round the edge of the recreation ground. Turn right through the gate, and on to Strand Street. Turn left. Then turn left again in front of the Bell Hotel and right past the Barbican. Walk along the river bank, following the line of the old town wall. At the bend in the river, turn right to the road. Cross over, continue along the footpath, pass the bowling green, then turn right down the steps into Mill Wall Place. Cross over and go back along King Street to the start.

The Kings Head Inn

Oxfordshire

The Inn

A more delightful or typically English spot must surely
be hard to find, and facing the well-kept village green
with its meandering brook and border-patrolling ducks,
the Kings Head looks like the quintessential Cotswold
pub. It dates back to the 15th century and stands smack
on the Gloucestershire border in the picture-perfect
village of Bledington.

Step through the old-fashioned latch door into the
original low-beamed and stone-walled bar, find an
ancient settle by the crackling log fire in the huge stone
inglenook and cosy up with a foaming pint of Hooky,
brewed in nearby Hook Norton. You can eat a meal
here seated at a rustic oak table or head next door to
the informal dining room, decked out with solid oak
furniture on flagstones.

Archie and Nicola Orr-Ewing have worked their magic
on this former cider house, creating a classy rural
atmosphere. Comfort, charm and style also sum up the
12 elegant bedrooms, which are split between the pub
and a converted barn, and they have all been tastefully
kitted out by Nicola with plump cushions on big beds,
fresh flowers, CD and video players, and posh toiletries
in the fully tiled bathrooms.

The Kings Head Inn, The Green, Bledington, Chipping Norton, Oxfordshire OX7 6XQ

The Essentials

Time at the Bar!
11.30am-3pm, 6-11pm (all day Fri-Sat)

What's the Damage?
Main courses from £9.95

Bitter Experience:
Hook Norton Hooky, guest beers

Sticky Fingers:
Children welcome, children's menu

Muddy Paws:
Dogs welcome in the bar

Zzzzz:
12 rooms, £70-£125

Anything Else?
Courtyard, garden, car park

The Food

Fresh local produce, notably free-range and organic ingredients and game from local estates, features on the ever-changing menus. The Aberdeen Angus beef is sourced from the Orr-Ewing family farm in Fifield and is hung for 21 days to enhance its unique flavour, so why not try the chargrilled fillet, served with green salad and pommes frites?

Modern influences on traditional English dishes can be seen in lamb cutlets with garlic roasted potatoes and redcurrant and mint salsa, chargrilled chicken with herb and shallot butter, or venison with bubble and squeak and sage and mustard butter.

Starters take in potted shrimps with lemon butter and devilled lambs' kidneys, while home-made puddings run to chocolate caramel brownie with vanilla ice cream or apple and plum crumble – or there could be some unusual English cheeses, perhaps Cotswold organic brie made at Kirkham Farm in Stow-on-the-Wold. Lighter lunchtime bar meals are listed on the chalkboard. In addition to a choice of four real ales, you can sample some first-rate wines from local independent merchants (ten are available by the glass), and a good range of bottled ciders.

What To Do

Shop

BURFORD GARDEN COMPANY

A huge range of interior furnishings, garden plants and products, on a 15-acre site just outside the town. Follow the signs on the A40. There's also an organic food shop and restaurant. Burford itself is renowned for its picturesque main street lined with gift shops, antique shops, old inns and tea rooms.

Shilton Road, Burford,
Oxfordshire OX18 4PA
01993 823117
www.burford.co.uk

OLD FARM FARM SHOP

Established in 2004, this growing farm shop sells home-reared lamb, beef and Old Spot pork, as well as a host of locally produced goodies, from jams, honey, cheese (brie made in Lower Slaughter), ice cream, yoghurts and apple juice.

Dorn, Moreton-in-Marsh,
Gloucestershire GL56 9NS
01608 650394
www.oldfarmdorn.co.uk

RED RAG GALLERY

Art lovers will enjoy Stow's Red Rag Gallery, a cluster of rooms lined with contemporary art and paintings. Then there's Foundation, selling stylish clothes and shoes. With its winding streets lined with shops, Stow-on-the-Wold has something for everyone.

5-7 Church Street, Stow-on-the-Wold,
Gloucestershire GL54 1BB
01451 832563
www.redraggallery.co.uk

Foundation
The Square, Stow-on-the-Wold,
Gloucestershire GL54 1AB
01451 832453
www.shopfoundation.com

Visit

CHASTLETON HOUSE

Chastleton House is both a national monument and a family home. Filled with a mixture of unusual and everyday objects, furniture and textiles collected since its completion in 1612, the house has been continuously occupied by one family for 400 years. The gardens recall typical Elizabethan and Jacobean designs, and it was here in 1865 that the rules of modern croquet were codified.

Chastleton, Moreton-in-Marsh,
Oxfordshire GL56 0SU
01608 674355
www.nationaltrust.org.uk

HIDCOTE MANOR GARDEN

Designed and created by the horticulturalist Major Lawrence Johnston, Hidcote is the perfect embodiment of the Arts and Crafts style of garden landscaping. The garden is arranged as a series of outdoor rooms, each with a different character and separated by hedges and walks of many different species. Also of note are Hidcote's rare shrubs and trees and magnificent herbaceous borders.

Hidcote Bartrim, Chipping Campden,
Gloucestershire GL55 6LR
01386 438333
www.nationaltrust.org.uk

ROLLRIGHT STONES

On the sides of the road between Great and Little Rollright village. The Rollright Stones are two curious Bronze Age clusters of stones that assumed their identity in medieval myth – some say they are a conquering king and his men turned to stone.

www.rollrightstones.co.uk

Activity

COTSWOLD FALCONRY CENTRE

Experience the Eagle Day (for two people) at Batsford Park and learn the correct way to handle an eagle, before taking a 4x4 trip into the Cotswolds to fly one for yourself.

Batsford Park, Moreton-in-Marsh,
Gloucestershire GL56 9QB
01386 701043
www.cotswold-falconry.co.uk

GLOUCESTERSHIRE WARWICKSHIRE RAILWAY

Dubbed as 'the friendly line in the Cotswolds', this diesel and steam railway is run wholly by volunteers. Since 1981 these dedicated enthusiasts have restored more than 10 miles (16km) of railway line, together with platforms, buildings, steam and diesel locomotives and rolling stock. In addition to a scheduled service, the GWR hosts various galas and enthusiasts' events throughout the year, and there's also the chance to learn to drive a diesel locomotive.

The Railway Station, Toddington,
Gloucestershire GL54 5DT
www.gwsr.com

WALKING

The Cotswold Way runs for just over 100 miles (161km), starting in the city of Bath and finishing in the lovely old Cotswold market town of Chipping Campden. En route it follows the Cotswolds' western escarpment, with its breathtaking views and picturesque honey-stoned villages. Follow linear stretches of the route or devise your own manageable half-day circular walk along the way.

www.nationaltrail.co.uk/cotswold
www.cotswold-way.co.uk

The Walk - *The Rollright Stones*

An ancient and mythical site near Chipping Norton.

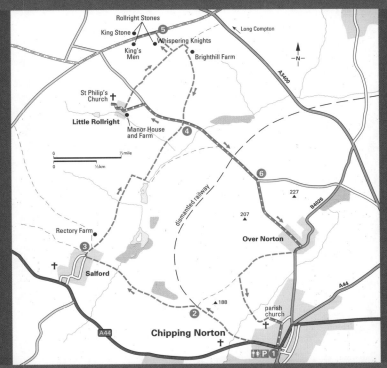

Walk Details

LENGTH: 8 miles (12.9km)

TIME: 4hrs

ASCENT: 295ft (90m)

PATHS: Field paths and tracks, country roads, 9 stiles

SUGGESTED MAP: aqua3 OS Explorer 191 Banbury, Bicester & Chipping Norton

GRID REFERENCE: SP 312270

PARKING: Free car park off A44, in centre of Chipping Norton

❶ Follow the A44 downhill. Pass Penhurst School, then veer right, through the kissing gate. Skirt the lefthand edge of the recreation ground and aim for the gate. Descend to the bridge and, when the path forks, keep right. Go up slope to 3 stiles and keep ahead along right edge of field. Make for gate and drop down to double gates in corner.
❷ Cross the track just beyond the gates. Walk towards Salford, keeping the hedge left. Continue into village. Turn right by patch of grass ('Trout Lakes – Rectory Farm').
❸ Follow track to righthand bend. Go ahead here, following field edge. Make for gate ahead. Turn right in next field. About 100yds (91m) before field corner, turn left. Follow

path across to opening in boundary. Veer left, then right to skirt field. Cross the stream. Maintain direction in the next field to reach the road.
❹ Turn left, then left again for Little Rollright. Visit the church, then retrace route to D'Arcy Dalton Way on left. Follow path up field slope to road. Cross over. Continue between fields. Head for trees and approach the stile. Don't cross it; instead, turn left and skirt the field, passing close to Whispering Knights.
❺ At the road, turn left to visit the Rollright Stones. Return to Whispering Knights, head down the field to the stile and cross it to reach another. Continue along the grassy path. Turn right at the stile towards Brighthill Farm. Pass

beside the buildings to the stile. Head diagonally right down the field to a further stile. Keep the boundary on your right and head for the stile in bottom right corner of the field. Make for the bottom right corner of the next field. Go through the gate and skirt the field; turn left at road.
❻ Keep right at the fork and head towards Over Norton. Walk through the village to T-junction. Turn right. When road swings to left by Cleeves Corner, join track ('Salford'). When the hedge gives way, look for a waymark on the left. Follow the path down the slope, make for 2 kissing gates; follow path alongside the wall to reach church. Join Church Lane. Follow it as far as T-junction. Turn right and return to the town centre.

The Falkland Arms

Oxfordshire

The Inn

The unspoilt and historic village of Great Tew, one of the prettiest Cotswold villages, provides the tranquil setting for this 500-year-old, creeper-clad stone inn. Hidden away at the end of a row of charming thatched cottages opposite the church – the quintessential English village scene – The Falkland Arms is a real classic gem. It must be close to everybody's ideal country pub, with worn flagstones, rough stone walls, rustic settles, a log fire glowing in the inglenook, and a prized collection of hundreds of jugs and mugs hanging from sagging old beams in the time-honoured main bar. Down a couple of steps is the cosy beamed dining room where evening meals are served – booking is always advisable.

Tucked beneath the heavy thatch are five cottagey bedrooms, two with impressive four-poster beds and three with old iron bedsteads, all furnished with antiques and decorated in warm mellow colours. The largest, up a second flight of steep steps under the eaves, has a pitched ceiling, exposed timbers and wonderfully serene views through leaded windows across the Tew Valley.

The Falkland Arms, Great Tew, Chipping Norton, Oxfordshire OX7 4DB

The Essentials

Time at the Bar!
11.30am-2.30pm (3pm weekends),
6-11pm (7-10.30pm Sun).
Open all day summer weekends.
Food: 12-2pm, 7-8pm.
No food Sun evening

What's the Damage?
Main courses from £8 bar lunch,
£11.50 eves in the restaurant

Bitter Experience:
Wadworth IPA, 6X & seasonal ales,
3 guest beers

Sticky Fingers:
Children welcome in the restaurant at
lunchtimes only. No children overnight

Muddy Paws:
Dogs allowed in the bar

Zzzzz:
5 rooms, £85-£110

Anything Else?
Garden, car park, live folk music
Sun evening

The Food

As well as buckets of character and historic charm, you'll find a spectacular range of real ales, heady farm ciders, over 40 malt whiskies and a raft of country wines to choose from behind the bar counter. Food is freshly prepared from locally produced ingredients by Paul Barlow-Heal, his short blackboard menus offering good value for money. Lunchtime dishes, served in the bar and garden, may take in chicken and thyme casserole with baby vegetables, beef and ale pie, local pork and ale sausages with mash and cider gravy, and a range of filled baguettes and ploughman's lunches.

More adventurous evening meals may offer slow-cooked lamb shank with rosemary and garlic, and chicken pan-fried with bacon and mushrooms and an Oxford blue cheese sauce, followed by warm sticky toffee pudding with vanilla ice cream. Evening bar snacks are limited to plates of English cheese with bread and chutney or hand-raised pork pies, great with a pint of Wadworth 6X. A pretty garden shaded by a large hornbeam tree, complete

What To Do

Shop

DAYLESFORD ORGANIC FARMSHOP
Quite the most luxurious farm shop you are ever likely to come across: award-winning cheeses from the creamery, breads, pastries, cakes and biscuits from the bakery and fresh meat from their Staffordshire estate. A foodie's heaven.

Daylesford, Kingham,
Gloucestershire GL56 0YG
01608 731700
www.daylesfordorganic.com

INSPIRES ART GALLERY
In the heart of historic Oxford is this refreshing contemporary art gallery, inspired by friends Danielle Walker and Emily Ashley. The gallery specialises in the best of contemporary art.

27 Little Clarendon Street, Oxford,
Oxfordshire OX1 2HU
01865 556555
www.inspires.co.uk

LIZZIE JAMES
For women who need spoiling – a fun environment, offering Armani Jeans, Nicole Farhi, Kenzo, Missoni, Moschino and more.

36 Little Clarendon Street, Oxford,
Oxfordshire OX1 2HU
01865 512936
www.lizziejames.com

LONDON HOUSE ANTIQUES
A well-established antiques centre, with 14 dealers who are knowledgeable and friendly. You will find furniture, clocks, pottery and porcelain, silver, jewellery, antique lighting and decorative items.

High Street, Moreton in Marsh,
Gloucestershire GL56 0AH
01608 651084
www.london-house-antiques.co.uk

Visit

BLENHEIM PALACE
Set in 2,100 acres of beautiful parkland, this exquisite baroque palace, home to the 11th Duke of Marlborough, is surrounded by sweeping lawns, formal gardens and a magnificent lake. Inside, intricate carvings, hand-painted ceilings and amazing porcelain collections, tapestries and paintings displayed in each room delight at every turn.

Woodstock, Oxfordshire OX20 1PX
0870 060 2080
www.blenheimpalace.com

CHASTLETON HOUSE
This fine Jacobean house is a unique 400-year-old time capsule containing rare tapestries, portraits and personal belongings. On the lawns beside the classic Elizabethan topiary garden, the rules of modern croquet were first laid down. An idyllic setting – advance booking advised.

Chastleton, Moreton in Marsh,
Oxfordshire GL56 0SU
01608 674355
www.nationaltrust.org.uk

ROYAL SHAKESPEARE THEATRE
This is one of the world's most iconic theatrical sites and represents a vision of Shakespearean acting, history and biography that is unrivalled. Set in the beautiful Warwickshire countryside on the banks of the River Avon, Stratford upon Avon, the birthplace of William Shakespeare, is steeped in culture and history.

Waterside, Stratford upon Avon,
Warwickshire CV37 6BB
01789 403444
www.rsc.org.uk

Activity

BALLOONING
Drift slowly with the wind and a glass of champagne over the beautiful Cotswold landscape. There are launch sites at Cirencester, Stroud, Bourton on the Water and Cotswold Water Park.

Ballooning in the Cotswolds
Fallowfield, Itlay, Daglingworth,
Cirencester, Gloucestershire GL7 7HZ
01285 885848
www.ballooninginthecotswolds.co.uk

CYCLING
Cycles – and even tandems – are available for daily hire, with detailed cycling routes and maps provided so that you can enjoy the quieter back roads of the Cotswolds.

Cotswold Country Cycles
Longlands Farm Cottage, Chipping
Campden, Gloucestershire GL55 6LJ
01386 438706
www.cotswoldcountrycycles.com

FISHING
Lemington Lakes is set in 75 acres near the River Stour and offers coarse fishing and the promise of big carp.

Lemington Lakes
Todenham Road, Moreton in Marsh,
Gloucestershire GL56 9NP
01608 650872
www.lemingtonlakes.co.uk

SAILING
The busy and lively Oxford Sailing Club is an RYA-certified training centre, running sailing, windsurfing and power boating courses.

Oxford Sailing Club
Farmoor Reservoir, Oxford,
Oxfordshire OX2 9NS
01865 863201
www.oxfordsailingclub.com

The Walk - *A Rare Plot at Great Tew*

A walk through a lovely village and some undulating countryside.

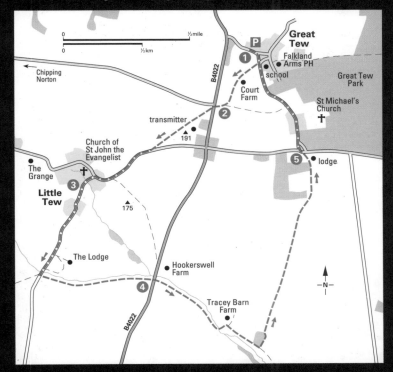

Walk Details

LENGTH: 4 miles (6.4km)

TIME: 1hr 45min

ASCENT: 150ft (46m)

PATHS: Field paths and tracks, stretches of quiet road, 3 stiles

SUGGESTED MAP: aqua3 OS Explorer 191 Banbury, Bicester & Chipping Norton

GRID REFERENCE: SP 395293

PARKING: Free car park in Great Tew

❶ From the car park turn left, pass the turning to Great Tew, follow the road as it bends to the right and as it straightens out turn right at the footpath sign ('Little Tew'). Go diagonally across the field, heading for the farm outbuildings on the brow of the hill. Cross the stile in front of them to the gate and stile and keep the field boundary on your right. Follow it along to pair of galvanised gates and a stile leading out to the road at the junction.

❷ Cross over and take the path ('Little Tew'). Head diagonally across the field, passing to the right of the transmitter. On reaching the road, turn right and walk down the hill into Little Tew. Pass through the village and turn left at the turning

for Enstone. On the corner is the Church of St John the Evangelist.

❸ Follow the road out of Little Tew and look for the entrance to The Lodge on the left. Continue for a few paces to some white railings, then turn immediately left at the opening in the hedge leading into the field. Keep along the left boundary and make for the galvanised gate in the field corner. Continue ahead on the grassy path, passing the house over on the left. Keep ahead on the clear track to the kissing gate leading out to the road.

❹ Cross over and follow the track ('Sandford'). Keep alongside the trees and then round to left towards the house. As you approach it, turn right and join another track heading

southeast. Keep the fence on the right and make for the gate by the trees. Continue for few paces to the gate and the waymark on the left. Take the path, keeping the belt of woodland and the field edge on your left. Beyond some trees, continue ahead into the next field, again beside the tongue of woodland. Pass into the next field and continue alongside the trees. Approach the lodge and keep to the left of it.

❺ Follow the drive to meet the road, cross over to the junction and take the turning ('Great Tew'). Pass the entrance to St Michael's Church (a fine medieval church) on the right. Look for the village school, also on right, and then, just beyond turning to Great Tew, return to the car park.

The Trout Inn
Oxfordshire

The Inn

The setting – smack on the banks of the infant River Thames – is straight out of *Wind in the Willows*, and you can imagine Ratty and Toad enjoying a pint of Ramsbury Gold on the riverside. Narrow boaters, fishing folk and Thames Path walkers rarely pass it by: the lure of a refreshing drink in the garden or in the stone-flagged bar, with its roaring winter fire, old settles and fishing paraphernalia proves too tempting, whatever the weather.

Since the arrival of practised hoteliers Gareth and Helen Pugh in 2006, and with the subsequent refurbishment of the restaurant and six bedrooms, this 17th-century inn now offers first-class food and accommodation.

Rooms really have been given the boutique hotel treatment – all are individually designed with quality fabrics, soft Farrow & Ball colours, antique furnishings, big lamps and mod cons like flat-screen TVs, DVD and CD players and clock radios. Room Five has a brass bed, Room Four a claw-foot bath, Room Six a big sleigh bed and private terrace, while all have fresh coffee and posh bathrooms with Molton Brown smellies.

The Essentials

Time at the Bar!
11.30-3.30pm, 6-11pm
(closed Sun evening in winter)
Food: 12-2pm, 7-9pm

What's the Damage?
Main courses from £10.95

Bitter Experience:
Youngs Bitter, Ramsbury Ales

Sticky Fingers:
Children welcome, children's
menu

Muddy Paws:
Dogs welcome

Zzzzz:
6 rooms, £100-£130

Anything Else?
Garden, car park

The Food

Chef Robbie Ellis is passionate about sourcing the best produce from top local suppliers, and his innovative daily menus reflect the seasonal larder. Nearby shoots provide pheasant, wild duck and partridge – the latter roasted and served with dauphinois potatoes, braised red cabbage and a redcurrant jus. Faringdon and Abingdon butchers supply Cotswold lamb, perhaps a roast rump served with herb lentils, gratin potatoes and red wine jus, and Angus sirloin steak, which comes traditionally with chips, salad and béarnaise sauce. Soft fruits and vegetables are from Buscot Park down the road, and the day's fish delivery from Cornwall may yield baked whole black bream with sauté potatoes and a warm green bean and rocket salad.

To start, there may be scallops with pan-fried chorizo, pureed shallots and rosemary jus, or carpaccio of seared beef with horseradish crème fraîche. Round off with rich chocolate tart with mango sorbet or a plate of local cheeses, say Cerney goats', Stinking Bishop and Cotswold Blue. The wine list has some classic vintages from small vineyards and offers excellent tasting notes.

What To Do

Shop

BURFORD

The long main street of this lovely Cotswold town descends steeply down the hill and is lined with pretty grey-gabled houses, tea shops and a wide variety of craft and antique shops, clothes boutiques and art galleries, and much more, including a traditional English butchers (WJ Castle & Jesse Smith), who has prize-winning sausages.

Gateway Antiques
Cheltenham Road, Burford,
Oxfordshire OX18 4JA
01993 823678
www.gatewayantiques.co.uk

Boxroom Antiques
59 High Street, Burford,
Oxfordshire OX18 4QA
01993 824268

WJ Castle & Jesse Smith Butchers
High Street, Burford,
Oxfordshire OX18 4RG
01993 822113
www.jessesmithbutchers.co.uk

TRADITIONAL CHRISTMAS SHOP

This specialist shop is about much more than tinsel and glitter with a Christmas theme. Here you will find dozens of real collectors' items that are stocked throughout the year. A variety of Good Luck incense-burning character vessels rub shoulders with figures from Tchaikovsky's *Nutcracker*, there are carved wooden Nativity sets and a small collection of Russian nesting dolls. A large selection of the Christmas Tree decorations is German, mainly hand-crafted in wood, porcelain and brass.

High Street, Lechlade,
Gloucestershire GL7 3AD
01367 253184
www.thechristmasshop.org

FOXBURY FARM SHOP

Former National Producer of the Year winner, Foxbury Farm Shop stocks the full range of farm meats – beef, lamb, Gloucester Old Spot pork, chicken and duck – as well milk, bread and locally grown veg, plus cheeses, delicious chutneys and local wines and bottled beers.

Burford Road, Brize Norton,
Oxfordshire OX18 3NX
01993 867385
www.foxburyfarm.co.uk

Visit

BUSCOT PARK

This late 18th-century neo-classical mansion contains the fine paintings and furniture of the Faringdon Collection Trust. Within the grounds are an Italianate water garden and a large walled garden. The church at Buscot has some fine examples of stained glass from the firm of Morris and Co, founded by Arts and Crafts man William Morris in 1861.

Faringdon, Oxfordshire SN7 8BU
01367 240786
www.buscotpark.com

THE PENDON MUSEUM

The museum at Long Wittenham reproduces in miniature scenes of the English countryside around 1930 – an evocative depiction of a bygone era. Exquisitely modelled cottages, farms, fields and chalky lanes recall the quiet charm of the Vale of White Horse. The museum has railway relics and a reconstructed GWR signal box.

Long Wittenham, Abingdon,
Oxfordshire OX14 4QD
01865 407365
www.pendonmuseum.com

MINSTER LOVELL HALL & DOVECOTE

One of the prettiest and most unspoilt old villages in the area; there's an attractive 15th-century church, a stone bridge over the River Windrush, and the imposing and extensive ruins of Minster Lovell Hall, steeped in history and legend. The medieval dovecote nearby survives intact.

www.english-heritage.org.uk

Activity

OXFORD WALKING TOUR

Thomas Hardy's Jude likened Oxford to 'the heavenly Jerusalem'. Its history, beauty and tradition are admired throughout the globe, and the city ranks in importance alongside Rome, Athens and Paris. The best way to appreciate the ancient colleges and historic buildings of this world-class city is on a walking tour. Numerous facts about Oxford and its university life are provided by experienced guides.

01865 250551
www.visitoxford.org

CYCLING

Leave the car behind and explore Oxfordshire's back lanes and byways the healthy way. The Hanson Way, part of the National Cycle Network, heads north from Abingdon to Radley, Kennington and Oxford. Alternatively, cycle south to the picturesque village of Sutton Courtenay; in the churchyard you'll find the grave of controversial writer George Orwell.

Pedal Power, 92 The Vineyard, Oxford Road,
Abingdon, Oxfordshire OX14 3PB
01235 525123

The Walk - From Buscot To Kelmscott

A chance to see the home of 19th-century craftsman and designer William Morris.

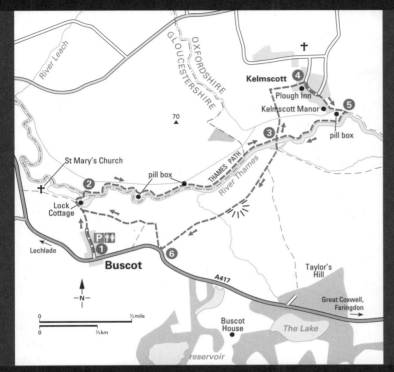

Walk Details

LENGTH: 4.75 miles (7.7km)

TIME: 2hrs

ASCENT: 82ft (25m)

PATHS: Riverside paths, fields, village lanes, 7 stiles

SUGGESTED MAP: aqua3 OS Explorer 1 70 Abingdon, Wantage & Vale of White Horse

GRID REFERENCE: SU 231976

PARKING: National Trust car park (free) in Buscot, signed 'Buscot Weir'

❶ Turn left. Walk back into Buscot to admire the arcaded pump. Retrace your steps and continue along the road, signed to the weir. The road becomes a track. Follow it round the edge of Village Field and cross the bridge. Keep right, to pass Lock Cottage. Follow the footpath over the weir. Bear left and continue, crossing the lock gate.

❷ Turn right, cross the stile and follow the path beside the river. Soon bear left and cross the bridge, with a view left to the main weir. Turn right; follow the Thames Path beside the meandering river. Cross the stile and continue past 2 wartime pill boxes and a gate. Go through a pair of gates. The roofs of Kelmscott appear ahead. Go through gateway and on towards the bridge, passing through the trees.

❸ Pass bridge, go through gate. Turn left up the field. At the far side, cross stile and 2 footbridges. Bear left and ahead up hedge (yellow waymarker). At the end turn right along path (possibly overgrown). Follow this into Kelmscott village.

❹ Turn right to pass Plough Inn. Bear left along the road, passing Memorial Cottages and Manor Cottages. Keep right to reach Kelmscott Manor. Keep ahead on the track, pass World War II pill box. Turn right just before the river.

❺ Cross the bridge. Go through the gate to join the Thames Path National Trail. Cross the stile and continue, passing pill box. Go through gate by footbridge; turn left over bridge. Bear left then right over 2nd bridge. Cross stile and walk up track. Soon cross ditch; now head diagonally right across the field. At corner cross the stile and footbridge by the fingerpost. Turn right. Keep ahead up edge of field, with views of Buscot House, left. Follow track downhill, and bend right. Turn left over footbridge. Continue on path diagonally right across next 2 fields.

❻ Go through gate by road. Turn right up drive. Look out for yellow waymarker and take footpath off left. Soon cross stile and veer left along edge of field. Cross stile and footbridge at other end, walk across Village Field. Turn left to retrace your route back to start in Buscot.

The Fleece Inn

Oxfordshire

The Inn

The Witney outpost of the small, independent and hugely successful Peach Pub Company is a ten-bedroomed inn overlooking the beautiful church green in this classic market town. Flanked by gorgeous Georgian houses and making the most of its swanky location, with tables on the green for summer alfresco drinking, The Fleece is proving a hit among Witney residents for its chic decor, laid-back atmosphere and continental-style opening time of 8am for coffee and breakfast sandwiches. The company's unique and stylish formula – leather sofas around low tables, fresh flowers, fat candles and mirrors and modern artwork on warm, earth-coloured walls – has been replicated here, and you can expect a lively, buzzy feel.

The easy-on-the-eye aubergine decor extends upstairs to refurbished rooms, where you'll find deep armchairs, classy throws on big, comfortable beds, quirky motif wall coverings, and contemporary lamps and mirrors. There's free wi-fi throughout, and bathrooms boast power showers and posh White Company toiletries.

The Food

Good modern food is served throughout the day, so you can pop in to peruse the papers, order a pint of Abbot Ale or one of ten decent wines by the glass, and tuck into a delicious deli-board, perhaps a selection of charcuterie or a range of antipasti, both served with bread and chutney. Alternatively, go for a stone-baked pizza, a chargrilled steak, tomato and mozzarella ciabatta sandwich, or a classic Caesar salad.

Lunch and dinner menus extend the choice to include starter- or main-course-size dishes, say, salt and pepper squid with sweet chilli rice noodles or a salad of scallops, black pudding, pancetta and watercress. Alternatively, kick off with potted shrimps, follow with rack of lamb with pea and mint purée, coconut baked bream with sticky rice, fennel and red pepper and coriander broth, or 35-day dry-aged Angus rump steak with chunky chips and peppercorn sauce. Expect fresh, seasonal produce, including free-range and fully traceable meats. To finish, try the milk chocolate tart or the Eton Mess parfait, or opt for a selection of artisan cheeses, served with celery, apples, grapes and home-made chutney.

The Essentials

Time at the Bar!
8am-11pm
Food: 8-11.30am, 12-10pm
(9.30pm Sun)

What's the Damage?
Main courses from £8.95

Bitter Experience:
Greene King IPA
Abbot Ale

Sticky Fingers:
Children welcome; smaller portions

Muddy Paws:
Dogs allowed in the bar

Zzzzz:
10 rooms,£90-£100, single £80

Anything Else?
Garden, car park, private dining room

What To Do

Shop

ANTIQUES IN BURFORD

Burford is a stunning Cotswold village, and it's worth spending time wandering up and down the historic streets, among the dignified old houses and ancient cottages by the River Windrush. Burford is also well known for the quality and range of its antique shops.

Manfred Schotten Antiques

(sporting antiques & memorabilia), 109 High Street, Burford, Oxfordshire OX18 4RG

01993 822302

www.schotten.com

Jonathan Fyson Antiques

50-52 High Street, Burford, Oxfordshire OX18 4QF

01993 823204

Antiques at the George

104 High Street, Burford, Oxfordshire OX18 4QF

01993 823319

THE COTSWOLD POTTERY

Husband and wife artists John and Jude Jelfs have been working here since 1973, and on display in the charming gallery is John's studio work and Jude's sculptural pottery. You can watch the couple while they work.

Clapton Row, Bourton on the Water, Gloucestershire GL54 2DN

01451 820173

www.cotswoldpottery.co.uk

OXFORD CHEESE COMPANY

Oxford Isis and Stinking Bishop are just two of the many cheeses to be found in this extraordinary shop, which sells solely farmhouse cheeses, mostly unpasteurised and sourced direct from the producer.

17 The Covered Market, Oxford OX1 3DY

01865 721420

www.oxfordcheese.co.uk

Visit

BOURTON HOUSE GARDENS

A magnificent ornamental garden, a late 17th-century raised walk, an original kitchen garden, and a gallery of contemporary art housed in the beautiful 16th-century barn.

Bourton on the Hill, Moreton in Marsh, Gloucestershire GL56 9AE

01386 700754

www.bourtonhouse.com

BUSCOT PARK

This stunning late 18th-century house contains the world-famous Faringdon Collection, with paintings by Rembrandt, Reynolds and Murillo, some fine furniture and an Italianate water garden.

Faringdon, Oxfordshire SN7 8BU

01367 240786

www.nationaltrust.org.uk

www.buscotpark.com

CHASTLETON HOUSE

Chastleton is a unique Jacobean house, a 400-year-old time capsule with rare tapestries, portraits and personal belongings. There's a classic Elizabethan topiary garden.

Chastleton, Moreton in Marsh, Oxfordshire GL56 0SU

01608 674355

www.nationaltrust.org.uk

COTSWOLD WILDLIFE PARK

There are 160 acres of parkland and gardens to explore – spot zebras and white rhinos wandering free by the Gothic manor house, and also meerkats, otters, camels, lions, leopards and red pandas. A good way to see the animals is to ride the narrow gauge railway.

Burford, Oxfordshire OX18 4JP

01993 823006

www.cotswoldwildlifepark.co.uk

Activity

BALLOONING

Start from Bourton on the Water, and drift in a hot air balloon over stunning countryside with a glass or two of champagne.

Ballooning in the Cotswolds

Fallowfield, Itlay, Daglingworth, Cirencester, Gloucestershire GL7 7HZ

01285 885848

www.ballooninginthecotswolds.co.uk

BOATING ON THE THAMES

Start at Christchurch College (where Lewis Carroll was Dean) and float down the river in an elegant Edwardian craft with a glass or two of wine, glimpsing an aspect of Oxford rarely seen by visitors.

Oxford River Cruises

34 West Street, Osney Island, Oxford, Oxfordshire OX2 0BQ

08452 269396

www.oxfordrivercruises.com

FISHING

Surrounded by beautiful countryside and woodland views, this 240-acre reservoir is well stocked with rainbow and brown trout, and is great for novices.

Farmoor Reservoir

Oxford, Oxfordshire OX2 9NS

01865 863033

www.farmoor.iofm.net

GOLF

Suitable for experienced golfers or beginners, this delightful 18-hole par 71 course is set in beautiful rolling downs. The club prides itself on its warm welcome to visitors.

Naunton Downs Golf Club

Naunton, Cheltenham, Gloucestershire GL54 3AE

01451 850090

www.nauntondowns.co.uk

The Walk - Town to Country

Head out of town to the environs of a country park.

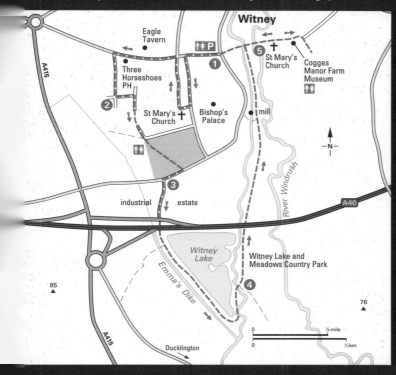

Walk Details

LENGTH: 3.5 miles (5.7km)

TIME: 1hr 30min

ASCENT: Negligible

PATHS: Pavements, meadow and waterside paths, 1 stile

SUGGESTED MAP: aqua3 OS Explorer 180 Oxford

GRID REFERENCE: SP 357096

PARKING: Public car park by Woolgate Shopping Centre, off Witan Way

1 Turn right into Langdale Gate. Walk towards Butter Cross. Turn left immediately before it and walk down the left side of Church Green. (Don't miss the remains of Bishop's Palace and St Mary's Church.) With your back to church, walk along left side of Church Green; turn left at Butter Cross into Corn Street. Keep ahead and, when the street becomes tree-lined, cutting between houses, turn left just beyond Three Horseshoes pub into The Crofts. Follow the road between the terraced houses.

2 Follow The Crofts to the left; turn right at the end. Keep the stone wall left and walk to St Mary's Court. Continue along the alleyway, with the school and spire of St Mary's on the left and, when you reach corner of recreation ground, keep to its right edge, passing a toilet block. Turn right at road then 1st left at pedestrian lights into Station Lane.

3 Follow road through an industrial estate; take path at the end, beneath A40. Avoid footbridge right and proceed through kissing gate. Route now cuts between Witney Lake and surrounding meadows (country park). Walk along lakeside path with Ducklington to right beyond area of scrub. Keep Emma's Dike right and curve to left. Witney church spire is seen at intervals in the distance. On right is River Windrush. Make for the concrete bridge; cross it, branching left to the kissing gate.

4 Keep the field boundary over to the left and look for kissing gate by A40. Pass under it to kissing gate; head north to the stile, keeping your back to the main road. Cross over to the gate and continue with offices left. Pass under the power lines to 2 kissing gates and notice board. Keep ahead, passing to right of the dilapidated mill. Follow path between margins of vegetation and eventually reach spur path to Cogges Manor Farm Museum.

5 To visit the museum, turn right and follow the path to the Priory and St Mary's Church. The museum is next door. Retrace your steps, heading for the town centre. Pass the electricity sub station on the right and continue to the road. Cross over into Langdale Gate and return to the car park.

The Boar's Head

Oxfordshire

The Inn

Bruce and Kay Buchan's handsome half-timbered pub stands in a timeless estate village beneath Ardington Down. Dating back some 400 years and enjoying a lovely spot beside the parish church, it successfully combines being a welcoming village local, a first-class food pub offering top-notch bar and restaurant meals, and a classy inn with three contemporary-styled bedrooms. Log fires blaze in the three light and airy interconnecting rooms – you'll find Ridgeway walkers and local drinkers in the simply furnished bar area, while chunky candles and fresh flowers adorn old pine tables, and tasteful paintings line sunny yellow walls in the two intimate dining rooms.

The idyllic village setting, as well as the pub's proximity to the city of Oxford, the Cotswolds and miles of downland walks, makes it a perfect place to stay. You can relax in one of the three stylishly decorated bedrooms, all with soothing Farrow & Ball colours, thick down duvets, fresh coffee, chocolates and mineral water, and Nutrogena smellies in smart, tiled bathrooms. If you book Room One, you'll be able to luxuriate in the enormous bathroom with its free-standing claw-foot bath.

The Essentials

Time at the Bar!
12-3pm; 6-11pm
Food: 12-2pm; 7-9.30pm

What's the Damage?
Main courses from £12

Bitter Experience:
Hook Norton Hooky; West Berkshire ales; Butts ales

Sticky Fingers:
Children welcome

Muddy Paws:
Dogs allowed in the bar only

Zzzzz:
3 rooms £85-£130

Anything Else?
Garden, patio, car park

The Food

Bruce Buchan offers an accomplished home-grown style of cooking, and his short, innovative menus make good use of seasonal local produce, notably game from the estate, and lamb and pork from surrounding farms, while fish is delivered daily from Cornwall. In addition, bread, ice creams and pasta are made in the kitchen. His restaurant menu goes in for an ambitious and inventive style with some unusual flavour combinations, as seen in a starter of seared foie gras with brioche and rhubarb, and a main course of roast venison with sweet and sour onions. The daily choice may also take in red mullet with ratatouille and chorizo and lamb rump with butter beans and seared kidneys. For pudding, try the irresistible hot pistachio soufflé with iced chocolate cream.

By contrast, the philosophy when it comes to bar food is to keep everything simple. The succinct blackboard choice may list squid tempura with chilli dressing, spaghetti carbonara and sea bass served with rosti and hollandaise. Expect a decent wine list favouring the vineyards of France and some tip-top ale from the West Berkshire brewery.

What To Do

Shop

WANTAGE

The town's focal point is its wonderful and traditional Market Place overlooked by a splendid statue of King Alfred presented to the town in 1877. A bustling market is held here every Wednesday and Saturday, and lining the square are many independent retailers. Just round the corner in Newbury Street is Gus Mills Gallery, stocking original artwork, prints, cards, ceramics, glass and wood carving.

Gus Mills Gallery, Newbury Street, Wantage
Oxfordshire OX12 8BS
01235 770353

ARDINGTON VILLAGE

Ardington is a prime example of a classic estate village. Take a stroll round it and you'll find a butcher's shop, a village stores and a tea room. Many of the old farm outbuildings have been converted into craft shops, workshops, offices, a picture gallery and a pottery, helping to boost the local economy, raise the village's profile and provide much-needed employment for local people.

01235 833200
www.lockinge-estate.co.uk

BROOKLEAS FISH FARM

This small trout farm is fed by the waters of Ginge Brook from neighbouring downland. It's possible to catch a trout to take home here, or simply visit the small farm shop and smokery to buy their delicious fresh or oak-smoked trout, smoked trout paté and locally caught crayfish.

Ludbridge Mill, East Hendred, Wantage,
Oxfordshire OX12 8LN
01235 820500

Visit

KELMSCOTT MANOR

Kelmscott is best known for its connection with William Morris, founder of the Arts and Crafts Movement and remembered for his furnishing designs, rich with flowers, leaves and birds, still popular on fabric and wallpaper. He called the village 'a heaven on earth', and his country home was Kelmscott Manor. Morris is buried in the local churchyard.

Kelmscott, Lechlade,
Gloucestershire GL7 3HJ
01367 252488
www.kelmscottmanor.co.uk

ASHDOWN HOUSE

Now in the care of the National Trust, this fine 17th-century house was built as a hunting lodge by the first Lord Craven. Tall and ornate, Ashdown is reminiscent of a child's dolls' house. Located on the windswept downs between Lambourn and Ashbury and at the heart of spectacular walking country, this extraordinary Dutch-style house is one of the Trust's more unusual acquisitions.

Lambourn, Newbury, Berkshire RG17 8RE
01793 762209
www.nationaltrust.org.uk

GREAT COXWELL BARN

This large monastic stone barn dates from the 13th century and is a remnant of the Cistercian Grange at Coxwell. William Morris said the barn was 'as noble as a cathedral'. It is 152ft (46m) long and 44ft (13m) wide, and has a fine stone-tiled roof and an interesting timber structure.

Great Coxwell, Faringdon, Oxfordshire
01793 762209
www.nationaltrust.org.uk

Activity

RIDGEWAY WALKING

The Ridgeway runs very close to Ardington and is perfect for space, solitude and views to far horizons. Here you can blow away the cobwebs, exploring a dramatic landscape of chalk downland and mysterious ancient long barrows. This is Britain's oldest road and the well-signposted, easy-to-follow trail follows it for 85 miles (137km) between Avebury in Wiltshire and Ivinghoe Beacon in the Chilterns.

01865 810224
www.nationaltrail.co.uk/ridgeway

WILLIAMS F1

Book a tour of the Williams Formula One state-of-the-art conference facility, which has the added bonus of a superb Grand Prix collection – the largest privately owned collection of F1 racing cars. The venue is the prestigious Wantage-based headquarters of one of the world's most successful F1 teams, with facilities to stage a range of activities from pit-stop challenges to corporate race days, from small meetings to product launches.

01235 777900
www.williamsf1conferences.com

FARMOOR RESERVOIR

The largest single area of water in Oxfordshire is the location for excellent trout fishing (day tickets available) and a noted site in the county for birdwatching, especially at Pinkhill Meadow Nature Reserve beside the Thames. You can explore the 4-mile (6km) 'countryside walk' around the reservoir.

Oxford, Oxfordshire OX2 9NS
01865 865551
www.farmoor.iofm.net

The Walk - *Alfred's Greatness Remembered*

Visit the statue of a revered British king before heading for downland country.

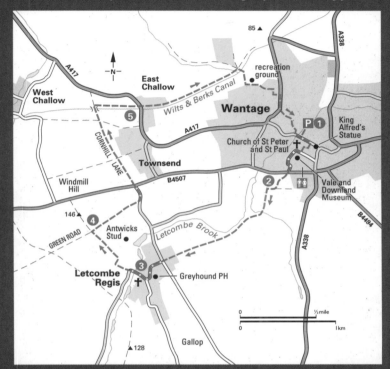

Walk Details

LENGTH: 6 miles (9.7km)

TIME: 2hrs 45min

ASCENT: 150ft (46m)

PATHS: Pavements, tow path, field paths and tracks, 1 stile

SUGGESTED MAP: aqua3 OS Explorer 170 Abingdon, Wantage

GRID REFERENCE: SU 397881

PARKING: Long-stay car park off Mill Street

❶ Keep to the right edge of the car park and look for the pedestrian exit. Turn left into Mill Street and walk up into Market Place. Make for the statue of King Alfred, then follow signs for the museum. Approach the parish Church of St Peter and St Paul; turn left into Church Street. The museum is opposite you at the next junction. Turn right here, avoid Locks Lane and follow Priory Road to the left. Head for Portway and cross to footpath to left of The Croft.

❷ Follow the clear tarmac path as it runs between the fences and playing fields. At length you reach the housing estate; continue ahead into Letcombe Regis and make for the junction with Courthill Road. Keep it on your left and go straight ahead through the village, passing the Greyhound pub and the thatched cottage dated 1698.

❸ Turn right by the church ('Letcombe Bassett and Lambourn') and, when the road bends sharp left, go straight ahead. After a few paces the drive bends right. Keep walking ahead along the path between banks of vegetation, following the path as it curves right, then swings to the left. Pass Antwicks Stud over to the right and then climb gently between the trees and bushes.

❹ Turn right at the next intersection and follow tree-lined track to road. Turn left and make for the junction. Cross, pass alongside the house and follow Cornhill Lane. Begin the gentle descent, cross the track and continue down the slope. Avoid the turning on the right and keep ahead to the footbridge crossing the Wilts and Berks Canal. Turn right and continue, following the tow path.

❺ Cross the A417 and then continue towards Wantage. Follow the drive, then take the parallel path on the right, running alongside a section of restored canal. On reaching tarmac drive, turn right and walk along to the row of houses. Turn left at path junction, pass the recreation ground and follow path as it curves right. Turn left into Wasborough Avenue, then, after lock-up garages, left into St Mary's Way. Turn right and swing left into Belmont. Keep right at the fork, heading for Mill Street. Keep left and the car park is on the left.

157

The Kings Arms
Oxfordshire

The Inn

You can't miss this appealing Georgian building as you approach the centre of Woodstock – it stands on the corner of Market Street, a short stroll from Blenheim Palace. David and Sara Sykes have lovingly restored and refurbished the building, creating a stylish small hotel and a comfortable base from which to explore Oxford and the Cotswolds. Traditional and modern styles blend effortlessly throughout the lively bar, with its worn wooden floor, grand settles, and bold art and stained glass providing a splash of colour. The bistro-style restaurant is in a high-ceilinged old billiard room, replete with rustic mirrors, hanging ferns and chunky candles.

Rooms ramble across several floors and cleverly combine classic Georgian features with a simple, minimalist approach to decor and furnishings. Think low, contemporary beds with colourful throws and scatter cushions, leather chairs, quirky phones, unusual local photographs and fully tiled bathrooms, with trays of fluffy towels and top toiletries from Molton Brown. Breakfast like a king on smoked salmon and scrambled eggs, then browse the boutiques along the historic streets of Woodstock.

The Essentials

Time at the Bar!
11am-11pm
Food: 12-2.30pm, 6.30-9.30pm

What's the Damage?
Main courses from £7.75 (lunch),
£11.50 (dinner)

Bitter Experience:
Marston's Pedigree

Sticky Fingers:
No children under 12 overnight

Muddy Paws:
No dogs

Zzzzz:
14 rooms; double from £140

Anything Else?
Pavement tables

The Food

In the bar, you could do a lot worse than to sup a pint of Hooky and order a selection of nibbles to go with it, from pitted green olives and a slab of creamy Somerset brie to Tyrrell's sea salted crisps with a red pepper and chilli mayonnaise dip. For something more substantial, order a rustic roll filled with hot chicken and bacon, or a plate of home-cooked ham, egg and chips, or head next door into the dining room, which sports a striking black-and-white tiled floor.

Here, you can lunch on tomato and roast shallot soup with chervil cream, salmon and spinach fishcakes on a herb salad with tomato and lime relish, or an organic beefburger served with chips or a classic Caesar salad.

The dinner menu follows a similar modern British style, with starters of scallops with home-made pork scratchings and apple and rocket salad, or duck leg confit with red onion tart and plum tomatoes. Move on to braised lamb shank, pot-roast brisket of beef with red wine sauce, or baked cod with tiger prawn sauce and crispy cured ham. To finish, there may be apple and raspberry cobbler with armagnac ice cream.

What To Do

Shop

CENTRAL

This innovative shop sells high-quality contemporary furnishings and home accessories from leading international designers.
33–35 Little Clarendon Street,
Oxford, Oxfordshire OX1 2HU
01865 311141
www.central-furniture.co.uk

MAISON BLANC

Part of Raymond Blanc's empire, this impressive patisserie – modern, innovative but true to artisan values – sells French bread, made on the premises. Savour an exquisite tarte au citron, millefeuille or croque monsieur in the delightful cafe.
3 Woodstock Road, Oxford,
Oxfordshire OX2 6HA
01865 510974
www.maisonblanc.co.uk

ONE VILLAGE

You'll find all kinds of good-quality, interesting, Fairtrade ethnic goodies under one roof here – durries, hammocks, lighting, bed linen and home accessories.
27–29 Oxford Street, Woodstock,
Oxfordshire OX20 1TH
01993 812866
www.onevillage.org

WELLS STORES AT PEACH CROFT FARM

Long established, this fabulous farm shop sells local and European cheeses, home-made sausages and dry-cured bacon, as well as garden herbs and plants. You can also pick your own soft fruit.
Radley, Abingdon, Oxfordshire OX14 2HP
01235 535978
www.peachcroft.co.uk

Visit

BLENHEIM PALACE

Set in stunning parkland, this majestic palace, designed by Sir John Vanbrugh, with carvings by Grinling Gibbons, is filled with treasures. The Winston Churchill Exhibition is set around the room in which Churchill was born, and extends to his apartments, which are dotted with personal ephemera. In the beautiful grounds, designed by Capability Brown, you can see rare trees and shrubs, and the extraordinary Grand Cascade.
Woodstock, Oxfordshire OX20 1PX
0870 060 2080
www.blenheimpalace.com

BROOK COTTAGE GARDEN

Created in 1964 by an architect and a plantswoman, this delightful 4-acre garden is situated on the west-facing slope of a valley, with colour and interest in abundance. There's a wide range of plants, some rare, with over 50 varieties of clematis scrambling over stone walls.
Well Lane, Alkerton, Banbury,
Oxfordshire OX15 6NL
01295 670303
www.brookcottagegarden.co.uk

CLAYDON HOUSE

This Georgian country house, famous for its rococo and chinoiserie interiors, has been in the Verney family for 380 years. Admire the intricate wood carvings and amazing parquetry staircase. Florence Nightingale was a regular visitor. The house was used as a location for the film *Emma* and the BBC dramatisation of *Vanity Fair*.
Middle Claydon, Buckinghamshire MK18 2EY
01296 730349
www.nationaltrust.org.uk

Activity

GOLF

Built in 1907 and set in 80 acres of mature verdant parkland, this is one of the oldest clubs in the county. The tree-lined fairways and undulating 18-hole course provide an enjoyable challenge for pros and beginners alike.
North Oxford Golf Club
Banbury Road, Oxford, Oxfordshire OX2 8EZ
01865 554924
www.nogc.co.uk

GREYHOUND RACING

For a fun night out, have a flutter on the dogs – there are races every 15 minutes at this modern stadium. Make it a very special evening by hiring a box and dining in style.
GRA Oxford Stadium
Sandy Lane, Oxford, Oxfordshire OX4 6LJ
0870 840 8903
www.lovethedogs.co.uk

OUTDOOR THEATRE

Oxford-based Creation Theatre Company specialises in site-specific productions in unusual locations, such as a ruined abbey and Oxford Castle. The performances are fast-paced, visual and accessible, with the work ranging from Shakespeare to *The Snow Queen*.
01865 766266
www.creationtheatre.co.uk

PUNTING

Enjoy the quintessential Oxford experience! Spend an afternoon lazing about on the river, but before you set off, why not try the restaurant at the boathouse?
Cherwell Boathouse
Bardwell Road, Oxford, Oxfordshire OX2 6ST
01865 515978 (punts); 552746 (restaurant)
www.cherwellboathouse.co.uk

The Walk - A Sweet House at Blenheim Palace

A lengthy walk to one of Britain's top country houses.

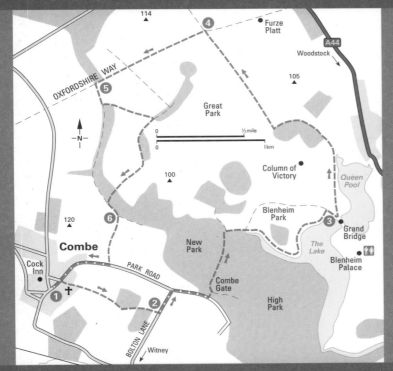

Walk Details

LENGTH: 7 miles (11.3km)

TIME: 3hrs

ASCENT: 150ft (46m)

PATHS: Field paths and tracks, parkland paths and estate drives. Some quiet road walking, 3 stiles

SUGGESTED MAP: aqua3 OS Explorer 180 Oxford

GRID REFERENCE: SP 411158

PARKING: Spaces in centre of Combe

❶ From village green, take road ('East End'). Swing right by village pump into churchyard and keep to left of church. Exit through gap in boundary wall, flanked by 2 gravestones, and begin skirting righthand edge of sports field. After 50yds (46m), branch off into trees, then head diagonally across the field. Cross into next field and keep to right edge of wood. In next field, turn left, still with trees left, and go up slope to woodland corner. Pass through gap in hedge; cross field.

❷ Exit to the road, turn left and keep right at the next junction. Walk to Combe Gate. Go through a kissing gate into Blenheim Palace grounds, keep left at the junction; follow the drive through parkland. As it sweeps left to a cattle grid, veer off to the right by a sign ('visitors are welcome to walk in the park'). Follow the path to a stile. Keep right when the path divides and walk beside the western arm of The Lake.

❸ Eventually reach a tarmac drive. Turn right and walk towards Grand Bridge. As you approach it, turn sharp left, passing between mature trees with Queen Pool on the right. Cross over the cattle grid and keep ahead through the park. With the Column of Victory on your left, follow the drive as it sweeps to right.

❹ Turn left at the cattle grid, in line with the buildings of Furze Platt on the right. Join the Oxfordshire Way, cross the stile and follow the grassy track alongside the trees, then

between the fields. At length, cross the track and continue towards the woodland. Enter the trees and turn left after a few paces to join a clear track running through the wood.

❺ After 150yds (137m) take the 1st left turning, crossing the footbridge to reach the edge of the field. Keep right here, following the obvious path across fields. When you reach the track, turn right. Keep alongside trees to the junction. Turn right and follow the track down through the wood and diagonally left across strip of pasture to opening in trees. Go up to track; cross it to a ladder stile.

❻ Turn left to the hedge then turn right, keeping it and the ditch on the right. Skirt the field to the road then turn right and walk into Combe.

The Miller of Mansfield
Oxfordshire

The Inn

When Paul Suter bought the Miller back in 2005 it was in a sorry state. He lavished money on the historic ivy-clad coaching inn and the finished result is very impressive. What's more, it's in a pretty riverside village, an amble from the Thames Path and smack between the Chilterns and the Berkshire Downs, both classic walking areas. Be prepared for a quirky interior, from the chic bar with its black-lacquered wood floor, leather club chairs and suede bar stools and sand-blasted beams to the smart and airy rear restaurant and the 11 decidedly funky bedrooms.

The bedrooms ramble across the first floor of the 18th-century building and all combine the old (antique fireplaces, rustic wooden floors) with an element of funky 21st-century chic (extravagant marble-tiled bathrooms, Perspex Philippe Starck chairs and bold silk fabrics). Expect vibrant wall coverings, like the metallic Cole & Son floral wallpaper in room seven, and strong colours, notably the lime green-upholstered antique French beds in room two. Added touches include plasma TV screens, fluffy robes and Molton Brown toiletries.

The Essentials

Time at the Bar!
11am-11pm; Sun 12-10.30pm
Food: 12-3pm, 6-9.30pm

What's the Damage?
Main courses from £15

Bitter Experience:
Marlow Rebellion, West Berkshire
Good Old Boy

Sticky Fingers:
Children welcome, small portions

Muddy Paws:
Dogs welcome in bar & bedrooms

Zzzzz:
11 rooms, £110-£175

Anything Else?
Garden terrace, car park

The Food

Chef Gavin Young and his team are passionate about sourcing the best local and British seasonal produce for their daily bar and restaurant menus, and the kitchen prepares everything, from the pastries sold in the bar to the hand-rolled pasta and home-made jams, jellies and chutneys. Locally foraged herbs and garlic and woodland mushrooms make seasonal appearances, as do soft fruit and asparagus from Dorney Court Farm, and top-grade Highland beef from a local Cookham butcher.

In the bar, check out the menu over a pint of Marlow Rebellion and if you are not feeling too peckish, opt for a sandwich such as roast beef, horseradish and rocket; otherwise, tuck into something more hearty and satisfying, say the braised oxtail and kidney pudding or the calves' liver and bacon served with fluffy mash. Also check out the excellent value set lunch menu in the restaurant, or splash out by ordering ballotine of foie gras with toffee apple purée and brioche, followed by monkfish with butternut squash, pak choi and pancetta, and round off with a pudding such as apple tarte tatin.

What To Do

Shop

PANGBOURNE

For many years, particularly during the Edwardian era, Pangbourne was a favourite haunt of writers, artists and anglers. It retains the air of an inland resort today, its reputation helped considerably by the colourful presence of various successful and independent small retailers. Greens is an award-winning butchers specialising in traditional pork sausages and pies, while the organic shop Garlands offers local, seasonal and home-grown fruit and vegetables from certified suppliers, as well as meats, chilled and frozen foods, and honey sourced from the Kennet valley.

www.pangbourne-on-thames.com

Greens Butchers
10 Whitchurch Road, Pangbourne,
Berkshire RG8 7BP
01189 842063

Garlands Organic & Natural
6 Reading Road, Pangbourne,
Berkshire RG8 7LY
01189 844770
www.garlandsorganic.co.uk

THE ORACLE

This is the region's leading fashion destination, with more than 115 retail outlets in addition to three flagship stores: John Lewis, Debenhams and House of Fraser. The Oracle offers a total shopping experience and the bonus of an impressive riverside setting with a wide range of stylish restaurants, cafes and bars, opportunities for alfresco dining when the weather permits and a 10-screen Vue cinema with the latest releases.

Reading, Berkshire RG1 2AG
01189 659000
www.theoracle.com

Visit

BASILDON PARK

This late 18th-century house is one of the Thames Valley's best-loved landmarks. After World War II, Basildon Park was rescued from the brink of destruction by Lord and Lady Iliffe who filled the rooms with magnificent paintings, textiles and furniture. The house played a lead role in the filming of Jane Austen's *Pride & Prejudice* in 2005; the ballroom sequences required 250 extras, and exterior scenes were also filmed here.

Lower Basildon, Reading,
Berkshire RG8 9NR
01494 755558
www.nationaltrust.org.uk

STONOR HOUSE & PARK

Set in magnificent parkland amid the rolling Chiltern Hills, Stonor's 18th-century façade of red brick encloses an E-shaped Elizabethan house with work dating from an earlier era behind it. Within its walls lies a maze of rooms and staircases, with sculptures, tapestries, drawings, paintings and many items of furniture on display. Stonor's delightful grounds regularly play host to craft shows, summer concerts and car rallies.

01491 638587
www.stonor.com

MAPLEDURHAM HOUSE & WATERMILL

The setting for the film *The Eagle Has Landed* is well worth visiting – a fine Elizabethan mansion surrounded by quiet parkland, which runs down to the River Thames. Inside you'll find great oak staircases, moulded ceilings and an impressive collection of paintings and family portraits. Don't miss the watermill, the last working corn and grist mill on the Thames, still using traditional wooden machinery and producing flour for local bakers. You can arrive there by launch from Caversham Promenade.

Mapledurham, Reading,
Berkshire RG4 7TR
01189 723350
www.mapledurham.co.uk

Activity

THE ROYAL BERKSHIRE SHOOTING SCHOOL

This is a rare opportunity to enjoy the challenge and excitement of clay shooting, a satisfying and tremendously popular pastime for many people. The school can simulate almost every form of 'bird' the gun can cope with, from challenging grouse to very high pheasants. Much can be achieved in as little as one hour, even if you've never held a gun before. All equipment is provided.

Tomb Farm, Hook End Lane, Upper Basildon, Reading, Berkshire RG8 8SD
01491 671239
www.rbss.co.uk

THE THAMES PATH

This glorious riverside trail follows Britain's greatest river for 184 miles (294km), starting where it rises in Gloucestershire. Between Wallingford and Reading, the path explores some of the best scenery in the south of England and, in the vicinity of Goring, you can follow part of the trail on a circular walk or complete a section upstream or down and then return by train.

www.thames-path.com

The Walk - *Pangbourne, Fashionable Riverside Resort*

Visit the River Pang and a National Trust meadow on this easy-going walk.

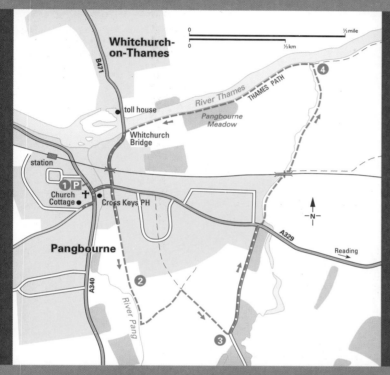

Walk Details

LENGTH: 3 miles (4.8km)

TIME: 1hr 30min

ASCENT: Negligible

PATHS: Field and riverside paths, stretches of road, section of Thames Path, 4 stiles

SUGGESTED MAP: aqua3 OS Explorer 159 Reading, Wokingham & Pangbourne

GRID REFERENCE: SU 633765

PARKING: Car park off A329 in Pangbourne, near railway bridge

INFORMATION: This walk is over the county border in Berkshire

① From the car park turn right to the mini-roundabout; walk along to church and adjoining cottage. Retrace your steps to the main road, keep Cross Keys pub on your right and turn right at the mini-roundabout. Cross the Pang; bear right at the next major junction into The Moors. At the end of the drive continue ahead on the waymarked footpath. Pass alongside various houses and patches of scrub; then go through the tunnel of trees. Further on is a gate with map and information board. Beyond the gate the River Pang can be seen.

② Follow the riverside path. Make for the footbridge. Don't cross it, instead, turn sharp left and walk across open meadow to the stile in the far boundary. Once over, keep alongside the hedge on left and, as you approach a World War II pill box, turn right at path intersection and cross the footbridge. Head for another footbridge on the far side of the field and then look for 3rd bridge with white railings, by the field boundary. Cross the bridge and stile beyond it; then head across the field to the far boundary.

③ Exit to the road and bear left. Follow lane between hedges and oak trees and proceed to A329. Go diagonally right to footpath by sign ('Purley Rise') and follow the path north towards distant trees. Turn right at the next bridge; follow the concrete track as it bends left to run beneath the railway line. Once through it, bear right to stile; then follow track along left edge of field, beside rivulet. Ahead on horizon are hanging woods on north bank of Thames. Pass double gates and bridge on left; continue on footpath as it crosses the gentle lowland landscape. Cross stile; walk across the next field to reach river bank.

④ On reaching River Thames, turn left and head towards Pangbourne. Follow Thames Path to Pangbourne Meadow and up ahead now is Whitchurch Bridge. As you approach it, begin to veer away from the river bank towards the car park. Keep left when you get to road, pass beneath railway line and turn right at next junction. Bear right again at mini-roundabout and return to car park.

The Crazy Bear
Oxfordshire

The Inn

It's a fitting name for a fairly quirky place, but then the Crazy Bear likes to pride itself on being quirky. This 16th-century coaching inn succeeds in weaving its ancient features into a modern look, creating the kind of wonky charm that goes down well with weekenders as well as a crowd as diverse as the proximity to Oxford can conjure up. The place has a genius all of its own, boldly mixing colour and texture in slate floors, exposed stone walls, fake fur carpets, crushed velvet and leather, adding a sprinkling of Asian artefacts and a life-sized stuffed bear for good measure.

But it's in the bedrooms where contemporary interior design and wild imagination have free rein. Arranged higgledy-piggledy throughout the inn and garden, every bedroom is different, but you can choose a theme – art deco, cottage rooms, garden rooms, suites or the opulent infinity suites. Beds are gorgeous, dressed with snowy white linen and frequently, eccentrically, with a bath at the end of them (there may even be a juke box, too), while snazzy bathrooms are state-of-the-art impressive.

The Crazy Bear, Bear Lane, Stadhampton, Oxfordshire OX44 7UR

The Essentials

Time at the Bar!
12pm-12am
Food: 12-9.45pm

What's the Damage?
Main courses from £11.50

Bitter Experience:
Greene King Old Speckled Hen, IPA

Sticky Fingers:
Children welcome, children's menu

Muddy Paws:
No dogs

Zzzzz:
18 rooms, £95-£380

Anything Else?
Terrace, garden, car park

The Food

The Crazy Bear scores highly in terms of creature comforts – diners rave about its pleasant garden and funky bar area. It also does well with its food – you'd be mad not to eat here. There's not only an English restaurant serving all-day breakfasts (with some upmarket choices such as duck eggs benedict or smoked haddock kedgeree if you're not in the mood for a full English), as well as classic prawn cocktail, tournedos Rossini, chargrilled calves' liver and Sunday roasts, but the inn also includes an authentic Thai brasserie.

Here, oriental standards – chicken satay, spring rolls, steamed pork and prawn dumplings, various salads and red and green curries – sit alongside slow pot-roasted ox cheek, steamed baby squid, whole crispy sea bream and braised salmon with Chinese rosé wine, ginger, lime, coriander and soy sauce. If you find it impossible to choose, check out the eight-to-twelve-plate tasting menus. Flexibility is the keyword here, though – for the best of both worlds, head for the bar where both the English and Thai menus are offered.

What To Do

Shop

OXFORD COVERED MARKET

The quality of the fare at this famous market brings foodies from all over the country. Everything is under one roof: fish, cheese, vegetables and flowers. Rick Stein's Food Hero Mr Feller has been working here since 1979, and now it's a family affair – selling organic pork, beef, lamb, home-made sausages and burgers.

M Feller Organic Butchers

54-55 Oxford Covered Market, Oxford, Oxfordshire OX1 3DY

01865 251164

www.mfeller.co.uk

SARAH WISEMAN GALLERY

This is a large, light, airy space exhibiting and selling a wide and contemporary collection of paintings, glass, ceramics, photography and jewellery, made by both established and new artists. Take home a future investment!

40-41 South Parade, Summertown, Oxford, Oxfordshire OX2 7JL

01865 515123

www.wisegal.com

BICESTER SHOPPING VILLAGE

For the ultimate designer shopping experience, head for this stylish complex, one of the best retail outlets in the country. The Shopping Village is home to top designer names such as Christian Dior, Ralph Lauren and Ted Baker. Clothes, shoes, jewellery, household items, lingerie and accessories can all be found here at bargain prices, and there are plenty of places to eat.

50 Pingle Drive, Bicester, Oxfordshire OX26 6WD

01869 323200

www.bicestervillage.com

Visit

BLENHEIM PALACE

Home to 11th Duke of Marlborough and birthplace of Sir Winston Churchill, there's a full day's worth of things to do and see at Blenheim Palace, with its 2,100 acres of parkland designed by Capability Brown, sweeping lawns, formal gardens and a magnificent lake. The Baroque palace has staterooms, carvings, painted ceilings and treasures collected over 300 years. You'll need to break for refreshment at the cafe, restaurant or ice cream parlour, which also sells Blenheim Palace wines and champagne.

Woodstock, Oxfordshire OX20 1PX

01993 811091

www.blenheimpalace.com

WATERPERRY GARDENS

Waterperry is famous for its magnificent herbaceous borders designed by Alan Bloom – but there's also the Mary Rose garden, a tranquil river walk where you might spot darting kingfishers, and a formal and alpine garden. Make sure you have enough space in the car, as the shop produces and sells the largest range of plants in the country. Buy art and crafts here, too, from the gallery housed in a restored 18th-century barn.

Wheatley, Oxfordshire OX33 1JZ

01993 811091

www.waterperrygardens.co.uk

OXFORD

This ancient and picturesque university city dating back to the 8th century sits comfortably on the rivers Cherwell and Thames. With so much to see and do, from taking a tour around the colleges and visiting some fascinating museums to enjoying some first-class shopping, you'll need a day, if not more, to get a real flavour of the city. Highlights include The Oxford Story, the University of Oxford Botanic Garden and the Ashmolean Museum of Art and Archaeology.

www.oxfordcity.co.uk

Activity

PUNT ON THE CHERWELL

What better way to spend a lazy summer day than messing about on the river? At the Cherwell Boat House you can start or end your sojourn with a good lunch on the terrace overlooking the river.

Cherwell Boat House, Bardwell Road, Oxford, Oxfordshire OX2 6SR

01865 515978

www.cherwellboathouse.co.uk

WATCH A CLASSIC FILM

If you're a fan of the classics rather than the blockbusters, The Ultimate Picture Palace is for you – it's Oxford's only remaining independent cinema, showing European and cult movies, and there are regular late-night screenings – a great way to round off the evening.

The Ultimate Picture Palace

Jeune Street, Oxford, Oxfordshire OX4 1BN

01865 245288

HOT-AIR BALLOONING

Take off from South Park or Cutteslowe Park close to Oxford and glide peacefully over the city's dreaming spires, the Thames and surrounding countryside.

Adventure Balloons

01253 844222

www.adventureballoons.co.uk

The Walk - A Very Special Abbey at Dorchester

A stroll around an ancient settlement with some superb views.

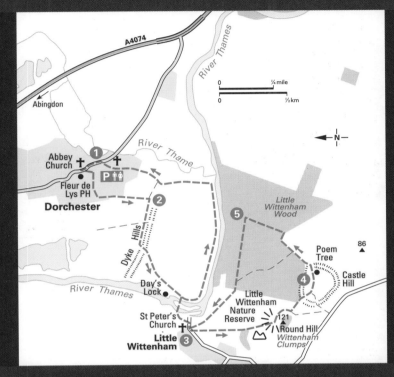

Walk Details

LENGTH: 4.5 miles (7.2km)

TIME: 1hr 45min

ASCENT: 115ft (35m)

PATHS: Field and woodland paths and tracks, stretch of Thames Path and main road with pavement

SUGGESTED MAP: aqua3 OS Explorer 170 Abingdon, Wantage

GRID REFERENCE: SU 578939

PARKING: Parking area in Bridge End at southern end of Dorchester

1 From parking area walk towards centre of Dorchester, keeping the abbey church on right. As you approach Fleur de Lys, turn left into Rotten Row and walk to Mayflower Cottage and Pilgrims. Take the path between the 2 properties and pass beside the allotments. At the row of cottages, veer left to follow the track. Swing right after 60yds (55m) at the sign for Day's Lock. Pass between the fencing and out across the large field. Ahead is the outline of Wittenham Clumps. At the low embankment of Dyke Hills, turn right in front of the fence.
2 Follow the path along field edge, pass over the track and continue. The path, enclosed by hedge and fencing, heads south towards the

Thames river bank. Go through gate and follow path, now unfenced, to footbridge at Day's Lock. Cross river to Lock House Island and head for St Peter's Church, Little Wittenham.
3 Turn left just beyond it, at the entrance to the manor. Keep right at immediate fork, go through the gate and begin steep climb to viewpoint on Round Hill at top. Veer left as you approach the seat, pass 2nd seat and keep left at next fork, heading for Castle Hill. Head towards gates at foot of the hill, avoid stile and go through gate, up flight of steps and into trees. At T-junction, turn left.
4 Emerge from trees and pass the commemorative stone, keeping it on your right. Descend the grassy slope to the gate and pass through trees

to the field. Continue on perimeter, with woodland left. Pass the stile, continue along the field edge and round to the right in corner. Swing left to join the nature trail; follow it through Little Wittenham Wood.
5 At a barrier and T-junction in heart of the wood, turn left and follow the path back to Little Wittenham. Recross the Thames, then turn right to follow the river downstream. On reaching the confluence of Thames and Thame, swing left and head north towards Dorchester. As Thame bends right, keep ahead to the gate. Keep to the right of Dyke Hills to another gate and skirt field to track (Wittenham Lane). Pass the Catholic Church of St Birinus to reach the car park.

The White Hart Inn

Oxfordshire

The Inn

It pays to look historic, and the White Hart certainly has that quality. It is a handsome, ancient inn, with an interior that has been neatly rationalised, yet still remains atmospheric. In the bar, there is an open wood fire, beams, ancient timbers offset by stylish chocolate-coloured sofas and easy chairs, and a lovely atmosphere. The stylish bistro sports simply dressed wooden tables and a menu with a modern British approach.

Smart, contemporary bedrooms are divided between the inn and a converted building at the back, which overlooks a well-dressed and well-maintained terrace, with good-quality wooden furniture and lush plants. Rooms are named after flavours or colours – Spearmint, say, or Olive. Main-house rooms have tremendous character – Blueberry, in particular, has walls and a floor that have moved over the centuries, while the spacious Chocolate has an impressive half-timbered wall. Expect large, comfortable beds, crisp linen, scatter cushions, dressing gowns, cafetières for Columbian coffee, home-made biscuits and smart, modern bathrooms with toy ducks to play with in the bath.

The Essentials

Time at the Bar!
11am-11pm (4pm Sun)
Food: 12.2.30pm, 6.30-9.30pm
(12-4pm Sun)

What's the Damage?
Main courses from £9.95

Bitter Experience:
Brakspear

Sticky Fingers:
Children welcome;
children's menu

Muddy Paws:
No dogs

Zzzzz:
12 rooms, £90-£145

Anything Else?
Terrace, car park

The Food

The open-plan bistro is a pleasant, relaxed environment and it draws crowds for its superior cooking. Seasonal materials are a strength, the appealing, modish menu delivering a roll call that could take in a starter of 100% pure crab cake with fennel and cucumber and tomato salsa, or open ravioli of peas, iceberg velouté, pea shoot salad and sage oil, followed perhaps by roasted seared loin of pork with black pudding and potato dauphinoise, or roast best end of lamb with spinach, confit tomato and thyme butter sauce.

Fish is something of a speciality – the day's catch is detailed on blackboard menus – while desserts can be as homely as apple and cinnamon crumble or as light and stylish as Veuve Clicquot champagne jelly with raspberry mousse and pistachio biscotti. Alternatively, you could just settle in the bar and opt for Welsh rarebit, Brakspear cooked ham and wholegrain mustard sandwich and chips, or wild mushrooms on toast with rocket, poached egg and hollandaise. The wine list is carefully selected, global in choice and extremely reasonably priced.

What To Do

Shop

ABINGDON FARMERS' MARKET
A favourite of Rick Stein and Sophie Grigson, Abingdon Farmers' Market sells locally grown and sourced products, including cheeses, fruit, vegetables and organic meat from rare breed cattle.

Market Place, Abingdon, Oxfordshire
www.tvfm.org.uk

COUNTY DELICACIES
Housed in a splendid old building, County Delicacies is run by a Polish family, specialising in local produce, particularly cheese, ham and bread. But, true to their roots, they stock all sorts of goodies from the continent, including salami and Polish sausage.

35–37 St Mary's Butts, Reading,
Berkshire RG1 2LS
0118 957 4653

O3 GALLERY
This contemporary gallery, Oxford's former prison in the Heritage Quarter, shows and sells work by established and emerging regional artists. The gallery is uniquely round and right next to Carluccio's excellent cafe at Oxford Castle.

Oxford Castle, Oxford, Oxfordshire OX1 1AY
01865 246131
www.o3gallery.co.uk

OXFORD COVERED MARKET
Don't miss this famous market, here since the late 9th century. You'll find a huge and eclectic range of things to buy, including unusual pottery, food, cheese, fish, clothes, furniture, flowers, fruit, and great cookies at Ben's Cookie Shop.

39–41 The Oxford Covered Market, Oxford,
Oxfordshire OX1 3DX
www.oxfordcity.co.uk/shops/market

Visit

MAPLEDURHAM HOUSE & WATERMILL
This grand Elizabethan manor house beside the Thames and sheltered by the Chilterns has portraits, furniture, a great oak staircase and intricate plastered ceilings. The watermill has been on site since Saxon times and is the last one remaining on the River Thames. Cream teas are served in the 14th-century tea rooms.

Mapledurham Estate, Reading,
Berkshire RG4 7TR
0118 972 3350
www.mapledurham.co.uk

RIVER & ROWING MUSEUM
This fascinating modern museum celebrates the River Thames, rowing and Henley. The town held the first university boat race in 1829, established the Royal Regatta in 1839 and has hosted Olympic regattas – the Rowing Gallery traces this history to the present.

Mill Meadows, Henley-on-Thames,
Oxfordshire RG9 1BF
01491 415600
www.rrm.co.uk

STONOR HOUSE & PARK
Home to the Camoys for over 800 years, Stonor is set in the Chilterns with far-reaching views over the deer park. The house is of considerable architectural interest; building started in 1190 and continued over many centuries. It's a family home, containing rare paintings, tapestries and sculptures from America and Europe.

Stonor, Henley-on-Thames,
Oxfordshire RG9 6HF
01491 638587
www.stonor.com

West Wycombe Park

WEST WYCOMBE PARK
The house is one of the most theatrical and Italianate in the country, and is the former home of Sir Francis Dashwood, founder of the Hellfire Club. The façades are formed as classical temples, and the interior has fine painted ceilings, furniture and sculpture. Enjoy the rococo gardens, statues, grottos and ornamental lakes. The house was the location for the film *The Importance of Being Earnest*, starring Judi Dench and Colin Firth.

West Wycombe, Buckinghamshire HP14 3AJ
01494 513569
www.nationaltrust.org.uk

Activity

BALLOONING
Soar over the stunning Chilterns in a hot air balloon, see unique views of Henley and the Thames, and raise a glass or two of champagne on this exhilarating flight of a lifetime.

Henley Ballooning, 7 The Green,
Middle Assendon, Henley-on-Thames,
Oxfordshire RG9 6AT
01491 574101
www.henleyballons.com

BOATING ON THE THAMES
Enjoy a few hours – or a full day – messing about on the river. Originally boat builders in the 16th century, Hoopers now hire out motor and rowing boats. They're located near the Henley Royal Regatta finishing line, by the Hotel du Vin.

J Hooper Boat Hire
54 Ancastle Green, Henley-on-Thames,
Oxfordshire RG9 1TS
01491 576867
www.riverthames.co.uk/boat/hire

The Walk - *A Religious Refuge at Stonor*

A walk that takes you across a beautiful deer park.

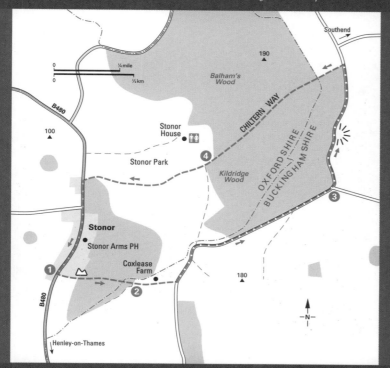

Walk Details

LENGTH: 3.5 miles (5.7km)

TIME: 1hr 15min

ASCENT: 150ft (46m)

PATHS: Wood and parkland paths and tracks, country lanes, 2 stiles

SUGGESTED MAP: aqua3 OS Explorer 171 Chiltern Hills West

GRID REFERENCE: SU 735883

PARKING: Off-road at southern end of Stonor, by barns of Upper Assendon Farm, which straddle road

❶ The chief attraction is Stonor Park and the Elizabethan house. Stonor has a 14th-century Chapel of the Holy Trinity. During the 16th and 17th centuries it was used as a refuge for Catholics. The family endured persecution and imprisonment as a result of their devotion to the faith. Make for the 30mph speed restriction sign at the southern end of Stonor. Turn left at the stile just beyond it to join the footpath. Keep the farm outbuildings on the left and go up the slope towards the trees. Cross the stile into woodland and begin climbing very steeply into the Chilterns. Look for the white arrows on the tree trunks and further up reach the clear track on the bend. Keep ahead, cross the track and pass beside the buildings of Coxlease Farm.

❷ Keep to the right of outbuildings and join the track leading to the farmhouse. Make for the road; turn left. Pass several houses and follow the lane between the hedges. Avoid a path on the right and, further on, the road bends sharp right. Ignore a bridleway on the left for Stonor and keep on the road, which curves left and runs alongside Kildridge Wood. Pass some double wooden gates on the right and keep to the road as it curves round to the right. Turn left after only a few paces, signposted towards Southend.

❸ Keep Kildridge Wood on left still, with views over fields and rolling countryside on the right. Follow lane until you reach turning on left – the Chiltern Way. Follow path beside a pair of brick-and-flint cottages, following the way towards Stonor Park. Cross the junction of tracks and descend between the trees. Some of the trunks carry the CW symbol for the Chiltern Way. Keep left at the fork, passing between laurel bushes and trees. Eventually you reach the deer fence and gate.

❹ Pass alongside tall wire fence. Gradually Stonor House edges into view. Head down towards road and look for the kissing gate in the deer fence. Turn left and head for Stonor. Pass the footpath and turning to Maidensgrove and keep ahead to the Stonor Arms. Walk through the village to return to the parking area.

The Baskerville

Oxfordshire

The Baskerville, 7 Station Road, Lower Shiplake, Henley on Thames, Oxfordshire RG9 3NY

The Inn

On entering, you can see this rambling, brick-built inn is well loved – the smartly maintained, interlinked rooms are filled with plants, flowers and highly polished furniture. It exudes the solidity of places built in the 1930s, and a great period feel is created by half-panelling, a sturdy wood floor in the bar, ceiling beams and lots of knick-knacks, while proximity to the Thames Path is hinted at with full-sized oars – one fastened to a beam in the bar, another forming a banister up to the bedrooms. They certainly know how to serve a decent pint here, too, whether it's Timothy Taylor's Landlord or the more local Hoppit from Loddon Brewery, but food and accommodation are big draws, too. The Baskerville is ideal for some traditional and unpretentious good cheer.

Bedrooms have a classy, comfortable look. Named after local locks, they are light and airy, decorated in beige, creams, browns plus one bold colour, and range from Sonning Lock's cosy twin to Shiplake Lock's large family room. Welcome extra touches include those easily forgotten toothbrushes and razor blades, as well as boiled sweets, biscuits and bottled water.

Room At The Inn, Oxfordshire

The Food

From the start, landlord Graham Cromack set out to attract a clientele seeking much more than a pint and a packet of crisps, and the Baskerville is now well known in the area as a classy dining pub. The menu is straightforward. Dishes don't pretend to be anything more than the written descriptions suggest: grilled sardines with provençale sauce and salsa verde, calves' liver with streaky bacon, sage mash and jus, or rib-eye steak with mustard and brandy sauce – but, because they are well cooked and well presented, the results are more than satisfying.

Substantial lunch dishes such as fish and chips, steak and kidney pie, or smoked haddock and spring onion fish cakes make meals in themselves, while Sunday is kept very traditional, with terrines, soups and organic home-cured salmon to start and roasts of beef, lamb and locally farmed pork. Do save space for excellent puddings like pear and almond crumble with crème anglaise, or individual strawberry and blueberry cheesecakes. Alfresco dining is a major feature, too, with a weekly summer barbecue and a large outdoor eating area.

The Essentials

Time at the Bar!
11.30am-2.30pm, 6-11pm
(7-10.30pm Sun)
Food: 12-2pm (12-3pm Sun),
7-9.30pm (10pm Fri & Sat)

What's the Damage?
Main courses from £12.50

Bitter Experience:
London Pride, Loddon Brewery
Hoppit, Timothy Taylor's Landlord

Sticky Fingers:
Children welcome; children's menu

Muddy Paws:
Dogs welcome

Zzzzz:
4 rooms, £65-£85

Anything Else?
Garden, car park

0118 940 3332, www.thebaskerville.com

What To Do

Shop

BRIGHTWELL VINEYARD

Enjoy award-winning wines from this stunningly located vineyard by the River Thames. Walk through the vines, explore the woodlands and lakeside. You can buy any of their five different wines from the shop, so why not take a bottle down to the river with a picnic?

Rush Court, Shillingford Road, Wallingford, Oxfordshire OX10 8LJ
01491 832354
www.brightwellvineyard.com

COUNTY DELICACIES

This great deli supports small local producers, selling Berkshire ham on the bone, local cheeses, artisan bread and honey. It also has a good reputation for sandwiches.

35-37 St Mary's Butts, Reading, Berkshire RG1 2LS
0118 957 4653

GABRIEL MACHIN

Gabriel Machin sells local Chiltern lamb and free-range Norfolk pork, but he's so much more than just a butcher – there's also a traditional smokehouse on the premises, so take home some smoked Scottish salmon or eel, or cheeses from the vast selection on offer.

7 Market Place, Henley-on-Thames, Oxfordshire RG9 2AA
01491 574377
www.gabrielmachin.co.uk

NOA NOA

You'll be spoiled for choice with the eclectic and elegant collections for women and kids at this fabulous clothing store.

24 Duke Street, Henley-on-Thames, Oxfordshire RG9 1UP
01491 413019

Visit

STRATFIELD SAYE HOUSE

This elegant, intimate house has been home to the Dukes of Wellington since 1817. Inside is a collection of important paintings and fine furniture, as well as an exhibition charting the 1st Duke of Wellington's political and military life. The main parts of the house and stable blocks were built in 1630 by Sir William Pitt. The Pleasure Grounds have many rare trees.

Stratfield Saye, Reading, Berkshire RG7 2BZ
01256 882882
www.stratfield-saye.co.uk

THE VYNE

This stunning 16th-century house dates back to the reign of Henry VIII, who was a regular visitor, as was Elizabeth I. The treasures in the house have been collected over 350 years of ownership. Elegant, wide lawns run from the house to the lake, and the large country park is worth exploring.

Sherborne St John, Basingstoke, Hampshire RG24 9HL
01256 883858
www.nationaltrust.org.uk

WEST GREEN HOUSE GARDENS

Voted one of the top 50 gardens in the country, West Green House Gardens is the work of designer Marylyn Abbott, and a riot of colour, with a delightful walled garden, stunning ornamental kitchen garden and a series of intriguing follies. There's an excellent cafe serving home-grown produce.

Hartley Wintney, Hook, Hampshire RG27 8JB
01252 844611
www.nationaltrust.org.uk
www.westgreenhousegardens.co.uk

Activity

BALLOONING

Virgin have been flying hot air balloons for 20 years, so you're in safe hands. Enjoy a unique perspective of the Oxfordshire landscape hundreds of feet in the air, and take home memories of an unforgettable experience.

Virgin Balloon Flights
0871 663 0035
www.virginballoonflights.co.uk

GOLF

Designed by James Braid in 1907, Henley Golf Club is thought to be one of the best in the county. It's an enjoyable 18 holes.

Henley Golf Club
Harpsden, Henley-on-Thames, Oxfordshire RG9 4HG
01491 575710
www.henleygc.com

MUSIC/THEATRE/COMEDY

There's a wide-ranging programme here – classical concerts, opera, rock music and comedians – something to suit all tastes. There's a good restaurant and bar, too, so make a night of it.

Anvil Arts
The Anvil, Churchill Way, Basingstoke, Hampshire RG21 7QR
01256 844244
www.anvilarts.org.uk

PAINTING

Dabble with oils in the lovely Grade II listed studio in the grounds of Mapledurham Estate. Your teacher is a professional artist.

JoeDaisy Studio
Dons Yard, Mapledurham, Oxfordshire RG4 7TP
0118 948 3155
www.joedaisy.co.uk

The Walk - A House and Home at Greys Court

A walk around a National Trust property in the Chilterns.

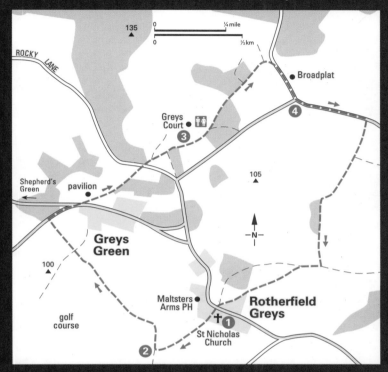

Walk Details

LENGTH: 4 miles (6.4km)

TIME: 1hr 45min

ASCENT: 150ft (45m)

PATHS: Field and parkland paths, drives and tracks, stretches of road (can be busy), 12 stiles

SUGGESTED MAP: aqua3 OS Explorer 171 Chiltern Hills West

GRID REFERENCE: SU 726823

PARKING: Spaces by church at Rotherfield Greys

❶ With the church lychgate on the lefthand side, walk towards Maltsters Arms pub. Turn sharp left before William's Cottage to join the gravel drive. Follow the footpath alongside the churchyard and make for the stile ahead. Head obliquely right, across the field to another stile, pass through gap in hedgerow then veer half-right in the next field. Make for stile, cross and join path. ❷ Turn right; pass between trees, hedges and margins of bracken. The path graduates to a track and passes alongside a golf course before crossing the drive to the gate. Continue ahead to road; turn right. Pass the turning for Shepherd's Green on the left and follow the road along to Greys Green. Veer left

on to green and aim to the right of the pavilion. Join footpath, cross a stile and descend very steeply to next stile. Pass under power lines in pasture and keep the fence on the left. Make for stile, cross lane to footpath and after a few steps reach stile. Continue towards Greys Court. ❸ Walk to the admission kiosk and swing left, following the footpath to next boundary. Continue on the path to the pond and along a section of boardwalk. Pass alongside fence and woodland, avoiding the gate and steps to reach a stile on the left just beyond them, by a corrugated barn. Cross the stile and keep to the righthand side, with the fence and field on your right. Turn right at the drive and make for the road ahead.

Turn right at this junction and continue, passing Broadplat. ❹ Keep left at the next junction and continue along the road to reach the track on right ('Rotherfield Greys'). Continue ahead when track bends to the left, and follow the rough track ahead. Pass a footpath sign and look for a stile on left. Follow path down hillside, keeping belt of woodland on right. Beyond it, continue on the grassy path with the fence on the right. Turn right, across stile in field corner and follow the path alongside fencing. After 60yds (55m), look for stile on left. Cross it and maintain same direction. Make for stile ahead then swing left and follow path up slope and back to the road opposite the church at Rotherfield Greys.

The Cherry Tree Inn
Oxfordshire

The Inn
Perfectly placed for visiting Henley-on-Thames and exploring the Chiltern Hills, this collection of 400-year-old brick-and-flint farm cottages, now enjoying new life as a popular inn, is well worth locating. The Cherry Tree stands in sleepy Stoke Row and is best reached from junction 6 of the M40. Following extensive refurbishment by Paul Gilchrist and chef Richard Coates, who have worked wonders in bringing this old village local bang up to date, there's a confident blend of ancient and modern inside.

A plethora of old beams, worn flagstones and crackling log fires provide a warm, welcoming atmosphere in the bar areas and prove to be the classic backdrop to a wealth of stylish contemporary furnishings – expect to find a palette of soothing earthy colours, soft lighting and squashy sofas. Chunky wooden tables and high-backed chairs lend a sense of occasion to the dining room.

You will not be disappointed with the food or the chic bedrooms in the converted barn. The rooms mirror the contemporary theme of the pub, with stylish furnishings and a host of cosseting extras: plasma screens, fresh Illy coffee, mineral water, bowls of fruit and Molton Brown goodies in the smartly tiled bathrooms. The bedrooms are all named after flowering trees – Cherry, Plum, Pear and Walnut.

The Essentials

Time at the Bar!
12-11pm, Sun 12-10.30pm
Food: 12-3pm (Sun 4pm), 7-10pm;
no food Sun evening

What's the Damage?
Main courses from £10.50

Bitter Experience:
Brakspear Bitter, Hot Goblin

Sticky Fingers:
Children welcome, children's menu

Muddy Paws:
Dogs welcome in the bar

Zzzzz:
4 rooms, £95

Anything Else?
Terrace, garden, car park

The Food

Simplicity, quality, fresh, seasonal and local are the five key words that sum up the philosophy of the food operation at The Cherry Tree, alongside uncomplicated presentation and value for money. Cooking is classic European with a modern twist, as seen in grilled sea bass with roast vegetable couscous and a tomato and chilli dressing, and roast confit duck leg with cassis and green peppercorn sauce.

You could start with the likes of tempura fried squid and courgette with red chilli oil and rocket, or smoked haddock fishcakes with lime hollandaise, then tuck into main courses of roast belly of Old Spot pork with creamed mash, smoked black pudding and cider jus, or braised shank of Chiltern lamb with garlic and herb mash and honey roast vegetables.

The menu recommends a beer with some courses: for a change, try a bottle of Leffe Blond with your skate wing with clam, caper and parsley jus. Pasta, steak sandwiches and wild boar sausages are typical lunch dishes, best enjoyed alfresco in the big garden on warm days. Pudding lovers should try the chocolate and cherry pudding with white chocolate ice cream.

01491 680430, *www.thecherrytreeinn.com*

What To Do

Shop

FARMERS' MARKETS

South Oxfordshire's monthly markets, which are held in Henley, Didcot, Thame and Wallingford, offer everything from fish, meats, sausages and pies to a mouth-watering choice of cheeses, home-made jams, fruits, vegetables, herbs and spices.

Tourist Information Centre, King's Arms Barn, Kings Road, Henley-on-Thames, Oxfordshire RG9 2DG

01491 578034

www.visit-henley.org.uk

HENLEY-ON-THAMES

As well as boating, Henley is known for its quality and variety of shops. Near the town hall is Henley's exhibition centre, which features all manner of artists and collections. The town's four main thoroughfares are lined with shops specialising in antiques, rare books and gifts, in addition to shoe shops, jewellers, and gift and interiors boutiques.

Henley Tourist Information (as above)

Visit

CHILTERN VALLEY WINERY & BREWERY

Situated in an area of outstanding natural beauty, Old Luxters Vineyard is home to Chiltern Valley Wines. The first vines were planted back in 1982 on the slopes of the Chiltern Hills and since the first harvest two years later, the company has produced an increasing range of fine award-winning English wines.

Hambleden, Henley-on-Thames, Oxfordshire RG9 6JW

01491 638330

www.chilternvalley.co.uk

GREYS COURT

The historic National Trust house and the village owe their name to Lord de Grey, who fought at Crecy and became one of the original Knights of the Garter. Greys Court contains a Tudor donkey-wheel well house and the Archbishop's Maze. There are glorious views from the house over the surrounding parkland, and regular events held here include open-air theatre, black-tie picnics and evening walks.

Rotherfield Greys, Henley-on-Thames, Oxfordshire RG9 4PG

01494 755564

www.nationaltrust.org.uk

RIVER & ROWING MUSEUM

The history of rowing, as well as that of the River Thames and Henley, are brought to life through the use of interactive displays and fascinating exhibits housed at this stunning riverside building.

Mill Meadows, Henley-on-Thames, Oxfordshire RG9 1BF

01491 415600

www.rrm.co.uk

THE WARBURG RESERVE

Named after an Oxford botanist and acquired in 1967, the Warburg Reserve is the jewel in the local Wildlife Trust's crown. During daylight hours the air is filled with the song of countless birds and the ground is a richly textured carpet of wild flowers in spring and summer. Orchids and bluebells and more than 900 species of fungi thrive here and a visitor centre puts the site's natural elements into perspective.

Bix, Henley-on-Thames, Oxfordshire

01491 642001

www.bbowt.org.uk

Activity

BALLOONING

Enjoy a birds-eye view of the Thames, Henley and the rolling Chiltern countryside from the basket of a hot-air balloon as it drifts peacefully through the sky from its Henley launch site.

Henley Ballooning

7 The Green, Middle Assendon, Henley-on-Thames, Oxfordshire RG9 6AT

01491 574101

www.henleyballoons.com

BOATING

There is no shortage of opportunities to go boating on the Thames. Hobbs of Henley offer cruises and boats for hire, whether it's row boats, canoes, steamers or motor boats. One of the most popular is a passenger cruise, following the Thames through some of the region's prettiest countryside.

Hobbs of Henley

Station Road, Henley-on-Thames, Oxfordshire RG9 1AZ

01491 572035

www.hobbs-of-henley.com

MIDSOMER MURDERS TRAIL

This world-famous and highly successful TV series now has its own trail. Key locations are part of the route, hidden away in deepest Buckinghamshire and the Vale of Aylesbury. Along the trail, which can be picked up at any point, you discover a world of snug cottages, village greens and quaint old pubs – and maybe the odd corpse or two!

www.visitbuckinghamshire.org

The Walk - *A Maharajah's Gift at Stoke Row*

Discover the link between India and a quiet village in the Chilterns.

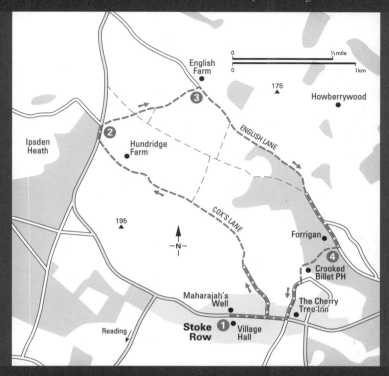

Walk Details

LENGTH: 5 miles (8km)

TIME: 2hrs

ASCENT: 164ft (50m)

PATHS: Field and woodland paths and tracks, road (busy), 8 stiles

SUGGESTED MAP: aqua3 OS Explorer 171 Chiltern Hills West

GRID REFERENCE: SU 678840

PARKING: Roadside parking in Stoke Row; two spaces in village hall car park when hall is not in use

❶ From the car park turn right and walk past the village stores. Enclosed in an exotic cupola you'll see the Maharajah's Well, which was a gift to the village from the Maharajah of Benares in 1863. Turn left into Cox's Lane and follow it as it curves to the left. Soon it dwindles to a track. Continue to the waymark, avoid the footpath on the right and keep ahead on the right of way. The track narrows to a path now, running between trees and hedgerows. Pass the stile and footpath and eventually you reach the outbuildings of Hundridge Farm. Join the track running through woodland and make for the road. ❷ Turn right along the road for several paces, then swing right

at the footpath sign into the wood. Follow the path between the trees and cross the drive. Make for the stile ahead and then go diagonally right in the field, using the waymark posts to guide you. Look for the stile in the corner and cross the lane to the further stile on the opposite side. Head diagonally right inside the field and look for the stile by the hard tennis court. Pass alongside beech hedge to the drive; turn left. As drive sweeps left to house, go forward over cattle grid to field. Continue with the boundary on your left and on reaching the corner, go straight on along the track. ❸ Turn right at English Farm and follow the narrow track known as English Lane. Go past the footpath

and stile on righthand side. Follow the track along edge of woodland. Continue to the junction and keep ahead through trees. Pass timber-framed cottage on lefthand side and house on right called Forrigan. Keep ahead for about 100yds (91m) and swing right at sign ('Stoke Row'). ❹ Cross the stile and cut through the wood to a 2nd stile. Emerge from woodland at a gate and cross pasture to a further patch of woodland. Negotiate next stile within sight of Crooked Billet and go up the gentle slope towards the pub. Turn right at the road, pass the footpath on right, followed by Rose Cottage, and head for the crossroads in centre of Stoke Row. Turn right and return to the start.

The Angel Inn

Buckinghamshire

The Essentials

Time at the Bar!
12-3pm, 7-11pm
Food: 12-2.30pm, 7-9.30pm

What's the Damage?
Main courses from £7.50 (lunch),
£13.50 (dinner)

Bitter Experience:
Greene King Old Speckled Hen

Sticky Fingers:
Children welcome; smaller portions
available

Muddy Paws:
No dogs

Zzzzz:
4 rooms, £85; single £65

Anything Else?
Garden, terrace, car park

The Inn

Trevor Bosch's beautifully restored 16th-century coaching inn turned gastropub-with-rooms has much to recommend it. Come for the stylishly rustic decor – the civilised bar with original wattle and daub walls, exposed beams, warm, yellow-washed walls, and leather sofas fronting the inglenook. Beyond, you'll find small, intimate dining areas, an airy conservatory, and a sun terrace for summer alfresco dining. Add welcome details like big lamps, huge vases of lilies, low lights, glowing fires and attentive service, and you have a very appealing country-style inn.

Old beams, wonky wall timbers and sloping floors in the four upstairs rooms attest to the age of the building. In keeping, rooms are cosy and cottagey, so expect brass beds with colourful bedspreads and cushions, a mix of old and new pine furnishings, added extras like phones, clock-radios and mineral water, and spotless tiled bathrooms with posh Cavendish & Clarke toiletries. Room 4 is spacious and boasts a big bathroom with claw-foot bath and separate walk-in storm shower.

The Food

The extensive British menu has Mediterranean and Pacific Rim influences, and shows great imagination with good use of fresh, locally sourced produce. Fish is the real feature, with daily specials chalked up on the blackboard to take advantage of the latest catch. Try the likes of roast monkfish with samphire and saffron butter sauce, seared sea bass on chargrilled vegetables with sweet chilli dressing, or sea bream with scented pak choi and Thai green curry sauce.

For starters, you might choose roast scallops with chorizo and avocado salsa, spicy salmon fishcakes with lime and ginger mayonnaise, or twice-baked cheese soufflé with garlic and parsley sauce, then move on to beef fillet served with fat-cut chips, baby vegetables and peppercorn sauce, or roast pork fillet wrapped in Parma ham and served on apple mash. Lunchtime extras include sausages on leek mash with red onion gravy, and hot-filled sandwiches (pesto bread with smoked bacon and brie) – and don't miss the good-value set-price lunch menu.

What To Do

Shop

FREDERICK TRANTER

For those who still brave the opprobrium of their peers and indulge in smoking, this is your Mecca, with hand-made cigars from around the world, 25 varieties of blended tobaccos, bespoke pipes and a large range of smoking accessories, including cutters, lighters, humidors, pipe pouches and cigar cases.

37 High Street, Oxford, Oxfordshire OX1 4AN
01865 243543
www.fredericktranter.co.uk

OXFORD COVERED MARKET

Oxford has had a market in some form or other since the late 9th century, and today's modern market is surely every bit as colourful and varied as its medieval precursor. Produce is imported from all over the world, prompting you to look for the unexpected or special gift. If the spice of life is variety, then it will be seen here.

39-41 The Covered Market, Oxford, Oxfordshire OX1 3DX
www.oxfordcity.co.uk/shops/market

THE REAL WOOD FURNITURE COMPANY

Fourteen showrooms display individually crafted pieces of great beauty and originality, from the traditional to the contemporary. As well as bespoke furniture, there are soft furnishings and a wide range of unusual accessories sourced from around the world.

London House, Oxford Street, Woodstock, Oxfordshire OX20 1TS
01993 813887
www.rwfco.co.uk

Visit

THE ASHMOLEAN MUSEUM OF ART & ARCHAEOLOGY

Since opening its doors in 1683, the private collection has emerged into the public domain.

Beaumont Street, Oxford, Oxfordshire OX1 2PH
01865 278000
www.ashmolean.org

KING'S HEAD

In the heart of historic Aylesbury is one of the oldest coaching inns in the country, with links to Cromwell, rare 15th-century stained-glass heraldry, a second-hand bookshop in a medieval courtyard and a bar.

King's Head Passage, Market Square, Aylesbury, Buckinghamshire HP20 2RW
01296 381501
www.nationaltrust.org.uk

STOWE LANDSCAPE GARDENS

Enjoy spectacular views and miles of walks through one of the great English landscape gardens. This is a place full of mystery and hidden meaning, with many monuments and temples, ornamental lakes and wooded valleys to discover.

Buckingham, Buckinghamshire MK18 5EH
01280 822850
www.nationaltrust.org.uk

WADDESDON MANOR

A magnificent house built for the Rothschild family in the style of a 16th-century French chateau. There's also a landscaped park, rococo-style aviary with exotic birds and Rothschild wine to buy.

Waddesdon, Aylesbury, Buckinghamshire HP18 0JH
01296 653226
www.nationaltrust.org.uk
www.waddesdon.org.uk

Activity

BOARSTALL DUCK DECOY

This rare survival of an ingenious 17th-century decoy that uses a lake, a decoy man and a highly trained dog makes for a good tale to drop into a dinner conversation! You'll also find a nature reserve with a wide variety of birds, wildlife, rare trees and a great visitor centre.

Boarstall, Aylesbury, Buckinghamshire HP18 9UX
01844 237488
www.nationaltrust.org.uk

WALK THE RIDGEWAY

Follow the same route used since prehistoric times by travellers, herdsmen and soldiers. The 87-mile (139-km) Ridgeway Trail goes through ancient landscapes, over rolling, open downland to the west of the River Thames, and through secluded valleys and woods in the Chilterns to the east. The Iron Age fort at Pulpit Hill is close by and a visit could be incorporated with a ride on the Chinnor & Princes Risborough Railway.

01865 810224
www.nationaltrail.co.uk/ridgeway

WALKING TOUR OF OXFORD

Discover this magical city on a relaxed and informative tailor-made walking tour, arranged at a time and pick-up point to suit you. When booked in advance, these tours can include visits to places normally closed to the public.

Felicity Tholstrup, 21 Northmoor Road, Oxford, Oxfordshire OX2 6UW
01865 512650
www.hiddenoxford.co.uk

The Walk - A Green Abode at Hartwell

By the River Thame and through the grounds of Hartwell House.

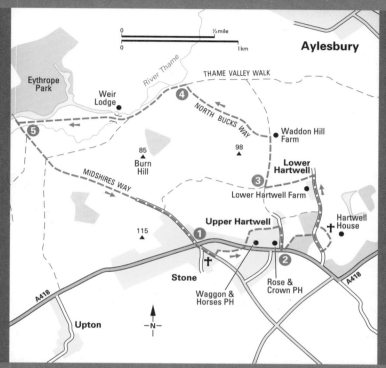

Walk Details

LENGTH: 5 miles (8km)

TIME: 2hrs

ASCENT: 180ft (55m)

PATHS: Field and riverside paths, tracks and lanes, 6 stiles

SUGGESTED MAP: aqua3 OS Explorer 181 Chiltern Hills North

GRID REFERENCE: SP 783123

PARKING: Space in Eythrope Road, Hartwell

❶ From the A418 turn into Bishopstone Road and keep to the left of the church. Walk along to a footpath beside Manor Farm Close and cross pasture to a kissing gate leading out to the recreation ground. Pass the ornate gate pillars on the left, recalling village men who died in World Wars. Exit to the road by the railings. Cross over to footpath sign and gate for Woodspeen and follow the drive to the timber garage and shed. Bear right to the gate and follow the path to the road. Turn right, walk up to the A418. The Rose and Crown is on the right.
❷ Swing left at the corner. Follow the path beside the stone wall. Head for the road, bear right and walk to Hartwell House entrance.

Veer left at gate pillars. Follow the waymarked path through the hotel grounds. Go through the kissing gate, keeping the church right and the graveyard left. Turn right at the road and pass the pavilion. Avoid North Bucks Way to the left, pass Lower Hartwell Farm. Turn left at the footpath. Cross 2 fields via 3 stiles. Turn right just beyond the plank bridge.
❸ Skirt the field, making for a stile ahead. Keep the hedge on left and continue on North Bucks Way, heading towards Waddon Hill Farm. Cross stile, walk ahead alongside timber barns; turn left at waymark. Follow track across fields. When it eventually sweeps left, leave it and proceed along a path to a stile.

Cross meadow and head for River Thame. Swing left at river bank to gate and join the Thame Valley Walk.
❹ After about 60yds (55m) the path reaches 2nd gate, where the river begins a wide loop away to the right. Follow the stream to the next gate and rejoin the river bank. Follow the Thame, avoiding the bridleway branching away from the river, and continue on waymarked trail. Make for footbridge and weir, on opposite bank is ornate lodge. Join concrete track and follow it towards trees.
❺ Once in the trees, river is on left and Eythrope Park is on right. Bear right at next junction. To continue, keep left and follow tarmac drive. Begin the moderately lengthy ascent before reaching Stone.

The Five Arrows
Buckinghamshire

The Inn

Standing at the gates to the National Trust-owned Waddesdon Manor, this delightful Victorian confection was built by the Rothschild family in 1887 to house the architects and artisans working on the Manor. The name comes from the Rothschild family crest, with its arrows representing the five sons sent out by the dynasty's founder to set up banking houses in the financial capitals of Europe. Enter straight into the bar, from which open several civilised yet informal dining rooms, with a Pugin-style refurbishment that boasts antique tables, colourful chairs, crackling log fires, and pictures from Lord Rothschild's collection hanging on custard-coloured walls.

The good-sized bedrooms are individually decorated in classical style with antiques and original pieces of furniture from the Manor – all are named after Rothschild Houses. Both the Garden and Colonial suites in the converted courtyard stables feature big brass beds, separate sitting areas and all modern comforts – Freeview TV, internet access, telephones, fresh fruit and newly refurbished bathrooms.

The Five Arrows, High Street, Waddesdon, Aylesbury, Buckinghamshire HP18 0JE

The Food

Locally sourced ingredients, plus herbs from the garden, influence the imaginative seasonal menus that combine modern British and Mediterranean-style dishes. Terrine of foie gras with home-made toasted brioche, pickled grapes and sauternes jelly, honey and spiced braised pork belly on red cabbage, or cream of Jerusalem artichoke soup with truffle oil may kick off a memorable meal. Follow with braised lamb shoulder with shallot tarte tatin and quince jus, rib-eye steak with chunky chips and béarnaise sauce, roast sea bass with fennel and parmesan crisps, beef Wellington with red wine jus, or the vegetarian option, perhaps leek and tallegio risotto.

To finish, choose the cheese table or brioche bread and butter pudding, and home-made honeycomb ice cream. There are also daily blackboard specials and lighter lunchtime meals. Wash down with a pint of Fuller's London Pride or splash out and delve into the magnificent wine list, which majors on Rothschild wine interests that extend to Portugal and Chile.

The Essentials

Time at the Bar!
11am-11pm
Food: 12-2.15pm, 7-9.15pm

What's the Damage?
Main courses from £12.50

Bitter Experience:
Fuller's London Pride

Sticky Fingers:
Children welcome; smaller portions available

Muddy Paws:
No dogs

Zzzzz:
11 rooms, £85-£120; suite £150; single £65

Anything Else?
Garden, terrace, car park

What To Do

Shop

ANTIQUES IN BUCKINGHAM

Buckingham is a mecca for antiques – you'll find everything from clocks and paintings to shabby chic garden furniture and vintage clothes.

Buckingham Antiques Centre
54 West Street, Buckingham,
Buckinghamshire MK18 1HL
01280 824464

Flappers Antiques
High Street, Buckingham,
Buckinghamshire MK18 1NJ
01280 813115

Goodwins Home & Garden
2 High Street, Buckingham,
Buckinghamshire MK18 1HL
01280 813115

MODERN ART OXFORD

Working with international artists, Modern Art Oxford is the largest contemporary gallery outside London. With a reputation for pioneering exhibitions, there's plenty to see and do here. The gallery shop sells cards, art books, and jewellery by local designers. Treat yourself to lunch in the cafe.

30 Pembroke Street, Oxford,
Oxfordshire OX1 1BP
01865 722733
www.modernartoxford.org.uk

SUSTAINABLE LIFESTYLES RESEARCH CO-OP

This workers' co-operative offers free-range eggs, seasonal organic vegetables and fruit, especially Victoria plums, which are grown using the permaculture method. Occasionally, you can buy lamb and mutton from Jacob sheep at the on-site farm shop.

Pond Cottage East, Cuddington Road,
Dinton, Buckinghamshire HP18 0AD
01296 747737

Visit

ASCOTT

Originally a half-timbered Jacobean farmhouse, Ascott was bought in 1876 by the Rothschild family and enlarged and transformed. It now houses an exceptional collection of paintings, and oriental, English and French furniture. The extensive gardens mix formal and natural – don't miss the topiary sundial.

Wing, Leighton Buzzard,
Bedfordshire LU7 0PS
01296 688242
www.nationaltrust.org.uk

CLAYDON HOUSE

Claydon is a Georgian country house, built at a time when the craze for chinoiserie was at its height. The result is a remarkable series of rooms lavishly decorated with intricately carved white woodwork, covered with motifs based on oriental birds, pagodas and summerhouses. Florence Nightingale was a regular visitor here, and you can see some mementos of her life.

Middle Claydon, Buckinghamshire MK18 2EY
01296 730349
www.nationaltrust.org.uk

THE UNIVERSITY OF OXFORD BOTANIC GARDEN

Situated on the banks of the River Cherwell, this is a haven of tranquillity – a classic but contemporary garden full of stunning plants. It's the oldest botanic garden in the country, with over 7,000 species of plant in the Grade I listed walled garden, glasshouses and water gardens.

Rose Lane, Oxford, Oxfordshire OX1 4AZ
01865 286690
www.botanic-garden.ox.ac.uk

Activity

RIVER CRUISE

Oxford River Cruises ply the same stretch of water taken by Lewis Caroll and his muse Alice Liddell 150 years ago. You, too, can cruise the tranquil Thames – have a lazy lunchtime picnic or a sunset dinner on board an elegant Edwardian craft. Most boats depart from opposite Christchurch Meadows, off Folly Bridge.

Oxford River Cruises
34 West Street, Osney Island, Oxford,
Oxfordshire OX2 0BQ
08452 269396
www.oxfordrivercruises.com

STEAM TRAIN RIDE

Take the 7-mile (11km) round trip through delightful countryside at a relaxing pace on a lovingly restored locomotive. There are lots of interesting features to look out for, including Whiteleaf Cross, which is etched into the chalk hillside above Princes Risborough.

Chinnor & Princes Risborough Railway
Station Road, Chinnor,
Oxfordshire OX39 4ER
01844 354117
www.cprra.co.uk

THEATRE/FILM/EXHIBITIONS

There's something to interest all culture vultures at the Queens Park Art Centre: a good gallery with changing exhibitions, art and craft fairs, weekly music shows, comedy nights, dance, film and theatre. There is also a very good cafe for a spot of lunch.

Queens Park Art Centre
Queens Park, Aylesbury,
Buckinghamshire HP21 7RT
01296 424332
www.qpc.org

The Walk - *Making Tracks at Quainton*

A lengthy stroll that will recall the great days of steam.

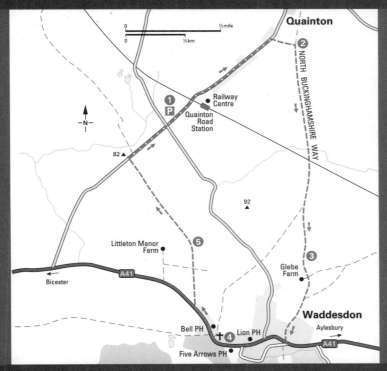

Walk Details

LENGTH: 5 miles (8km)

TIME: 2hrs

ASCENT: Negligible

PATHS: Mainly field paths, some stretches of road, parts of North Buckinghamshire Way and Midshires Way, 22 stiles

SUGGESTED MAP: aqua3 OS Explorer 181 Chiltern Hills North

GRID REFERENCE: SP 736189

PARKING: Brill Tramway Path car park, parking on the extreme left. Permission given by Buckinghamshire Railway Centre

1 Leave the car park, turn left and cross the road bridge over the railway. The entrance to the site is on the right. Exit the railway centre, bear right and follow Station Road towards Quainton. Pass the houses and, when the road curves to the left by a bus stop, turn right at a footpath sign and a stile to follow the track between fields. Quainton and a windmill are on the left. Go through the gateway. Turn right to join the North Buckinghamshire Way.

2 Follow the field edge to reach the gate. Continue to the stile in the far boundary. Cross 3 more stiles before reaching the railway line; Quainton Road Station lies to the right. Cross 2 stiles and follow the track to the righthand bend. The outline of Waddesdon Manor can be seen to the right of church. As the track bends right, cross the stile leading into the field. Turn immediately right.

3 Skirt Glebe Farm and cross the track via 2 stiles, continuing on the North Buckinghamshire Way. Aim diagonally right to 2 stiles and continue alongside the hedgerow in the next field. Cross 2 stiles and join the enclosed path running into Waddesdon. On reaching the A41, turn right, crossing Quainton Road and Frederick Street. Pass the Lion pub, church and post office before reaching the parish church of St Michael and All Angels on the right.

4 Follow the road out of the village, passing the Bell pub. Keep to the A41 and look out for the old stone milepost. In 50yds (46m), beyond the speed derestriction sign, turn right at the stile and the waymark. Cut through the trees to reach the 2nd stile and continue ahead in the field. Cross the concrete farm track, pass underneath the power lines and aim for the stile in the boundary hedge. Littleton Manor Farm buildings can be seen near by.

5 Aim slightly left in the next field to reach the stile. Go diagonally left across the next pasture to the far corner. Look for the narrow gap in the hedgerow, cross 2 stiles and walk ahead, passing beside the corrugated animal shelters. Make for 2 stiles, turn right and follow the road back to the start.

Three Horseshoes Inn

Buckinghamshire

The Inn

After a decade in the London hothouses of Le Gavroche and the Connaught Hotel, in 2005 chef Simon Crawshaw swapped the city for this 18th-century red-brick pub deep in the Chiltern Hills. He hasn't looked back. Lost down narrow leafy lanes, with valley views across rolling fields, the place draws walkers for ale and sandwiches, and foodies for accomplished modern cooking. Step through the latch door to find a cracking snug bar, replete with blackened beams, a flagstone floor and a blazing log fire in the original brick fireplace – the perfect spot for a post-walk pint of locally brewed Marlow Rebellion. Rooms ramble beyond, and from the split-level rear restaurant the view of the duck pond and its gradually sinking red telephone box will keep you amused between courses.

The quirky, individually decorated bedrooms are named after local shoots; all are done out in calming Farrow & Ball colours, with plump down duvets on big brass and wooden beds, an eclectic mix of furnishings, fluffy towels and Molton Brown toiletries in the tiled bathrooms.

The Essentials

Time at the Bar!
12-3pm, 6-11pm; closed Mon lunch
and Sun from 8pm
Food: 12-2.30pm, 6.30pm-9.30pm

What's the Damage?
Main courses from £12.50

Bitter Experience:
Rebellion ales

Sticky Fingers:
Children welcome

Muddy Paws:
Dogs welcome in the bar only

Zzzzz:
6 rooms, from £85

Anything Else?
Garden, car park, views

The Food

Everything is freshly prepared on the premises from local ingredients, and Simon's daily menus are varied and versatile to please both the booted walkers who call by at lunchtime for soup and sandwiches and the evening diners who travel miles to sample his innovative modern cooking. In the bar, tuck into tomato, lettuce and potato soup, served with olive and pesto bread, and a thick sandwich filled with roast Oxfordshire beef, wild rocket and horseradish, or you may like to try the home-made beef burger or, perhaps, wild mushroom and tarragon risotto. If you have time to linger, opt for the excellent-value set lunch menu, perhaps starting with chicken liver parfait with home-made piccalilli and following with steak and kidney pie.

The cooking style moves up a gear in the evening, with the short, imaginative menu offering the likes of seared scallops with chorizo and cauliflower fritter ahead of lamb rump with aubergine caviar and black olive jus or pan-fried cod with crushed peas and shrimp butter. Lemon cheesecake with confit of pineapple makes a tangy choice for afters. Don't miss the popular monthly live jazz and tapas evening.

What To Do

Shop

THE ANTIQUES TRAIL

Pick up a map and guide to buying antiques in the Thames Valley and you'll find a range of choice from the conventional to the positively quirky. The extent is best represented by the Swan at Tetsworth, near Thame. In this 40-room Grade II-listed Elizabethan coaching inn, you'll find antiques from more than 70 dealers. There's even an award-winning restaurant.

The Swan at Tetsworth
Thame, Oxfordshire OX9 7AB
01844 281777
www.theswan.co.uk

BURGERS

Head for Burgers, Marlow's long-established tea room on The Causeway, to enjoy the civilised ritual of afternoon tea after some serious shopping in the High Street, West Street and Spittal Street with their mixture of quality shops and independent retailers.

Tourist Information Centre, 31 High Street, Marlow, Buckinghamshire SL7 1AU
01628 483597
www.visitbuckinghamshire.org

THE GRANARY DELICATESSEN

Foodies will want to seek out this fantastic deli for its mind-boggling stock of 150 cheeses, ranging from top-grade parmesans and continental soft cheeses to a huge choice of English farmhouse cheeses. Watlington also has a very fine cookshop (The Galley) and a quality old-fashioned butchers (Calnan Brothers).

30 High Street, Watlington, Oxfordshire OX49 5PY
01491 613583
www.granarydeli.co.uk

Visit

HUGHENDEN MANOR

Looking at this striking Georgian house and its glorious rural setting, it's easy to see why Benjamin Disraeli chose Hughenden as his country seat in 1848. Now the property of the National Trust, the house holds letters from Queen Victoria, who regarded Disraeli as her favourite prime minister.

High Wycombe, Buckinghamshire HP14 4LA
01494 755565
www.nationaltrust.org.uk

WEST WYCOMBE HOUSE

If this National Trust treasure looks familiar, that's because it featured in the film version of Oscar Wilde's *The Importance of Being Earnest*, starring Judi Dench. The house dates back to the 18th century and was built for Sir Francis Dashwood, founder of the Dilettanti Society and the notorious Hellfire Club. Have a look at the nearby caves, open to Trust members.

West Wycombe Park, West Wycombe, Buckinghamshire HP14 3AJ
01494 513569
www.nationaltrust.org.uk

STONOR HOUSE & PARK

Home of Lord and Lady Camoys and occupied by the Stonor family for 800 years, the house dates back to 1190 but features a Tudor façade. View fine works of art, including paintings by old Italian masters, visit the medieval Catholic chapel, wander through the walled Italianate garden and explore the surrounding deer park.

Stonor, Henley-on-Thames, Oxfordshire RG9 6HF
01491 638587
www.stonor.com

Activity

GLIDING

Get away from it all in a lofty world of summer thermals and endless views by booking a trial lesson at the Booker Gliding Centre, one of Britain's top sites. The flight includes membership of the club for the day, so you can use all the facilities, and the lesson allows you plenty of time to get the feel of piloting a glider.

Wycombe Air Park, Marlow, Buckinghamshire SL7 3DP
01494 442501
www.bookergliding.co.uk

RED KITE-SPOTTING

This striking bird of prey was reintroduced to Britain in the 1990s and today the Chilterns are home to England's largest population, with around 200 pairs breeding in the area. Use the Red Kite Walks leaflet to guide you on a series of rambles exploring their haunts, or visit the cafe in Charwood Garden Centre, near Stokenchurch, to watch live CCTV images of a pair of kites nesting and rearing their chicks (April to mid-July).

High Wycombe Tourist Information Centre
Pauls Row, High Wycombe, Buckinghamshire HP11 2HQ
01494 421892
www.visitbuckinghamshire.org

Charwood Garden Centre
Wycombe Road, High Wycombe, Buckinghamshire HP14 3XB
01494 483761

The Walk - Disraeli's Des Res at West Wycombe

Visit Hughenden Manor, home of famous British statesman Benjamin Disraeli.

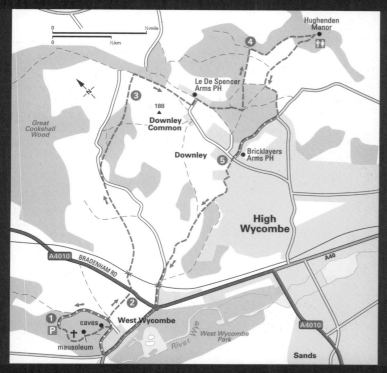

Walk Details

LENGTH: 7 miles (11.3km)

TIME: 2hrs 45min

ASCENT: 280ft (85m)

PATHS: Field, woodland and parkland paths, some roads, 5 stiles

SUGGESTED MAP: aqua3 OS Explorer 172 Chiltern Hills East

GRID REFERENCE: SU 826952

PARKING: Car park by church and mausoleum at West Wycombe

❶ From the car park pass to the immediate right of the church. Continue to the mausoleum and line up with the A40 below. Take the grassy path down hillside, avoiding path on right, and walk to fork. Keep right to steps; descend to the road. Bear left and pass Church Lane on right. Take next path on right; keeping to field righthand boundary. Look for stile and maintain same direction to the stile by the road.
❷ Cross over, making for the gate; pass under railway. At the field keep ahead, keeping right of fence. Follow the path to stile; cross track and continue up the slope. Make for 2 stiles by gate and barns. Join the lane, swing right at the waymark and follow ride through woodland.

Eventually reach a stile with the path crossing the field beyond.
❸ On reaching the track, turn right and cut through the wood. Veer left at fork and head for road. Bear left into Downley. Turn left for pub or right to continue. Pass houses; when track bends left, keep ahead briefly, veering left at the waymark. Cross the common, following the path through clearings and into trees. At the National Trust sign, turn sharp left and follow the path through woods. Avoid path on left following white arrows. Pass the gate and continue ahead, up a fairly steep slope to the junction.
❹ Keep right; follow path to track. Swing left to visit Hughenden Manor or right to continue. Follow path

through parkland, making for trees. Bear immediately left, up the slope. Look for the house; turn right at the road. Pass the Bricklayers Arms and go straight ahead at junction.
❺ Keep ahead through the trees to the housing estate. Go forward for several paces at road, bearing right at 1st footpath sign. Follow path as it bends left and leads to the junction. Swing left for several steps; veer right by the houses, heading through trees to the galvanised gate. Take the sunken path to right of the gate, follow it to fork and continue ahead. Head for lane and follow it towards West Wycombe. Cross Bradenham Road; proceed into the village. Turn right into West Wycombe Hill Road. Head uphill to the car park.

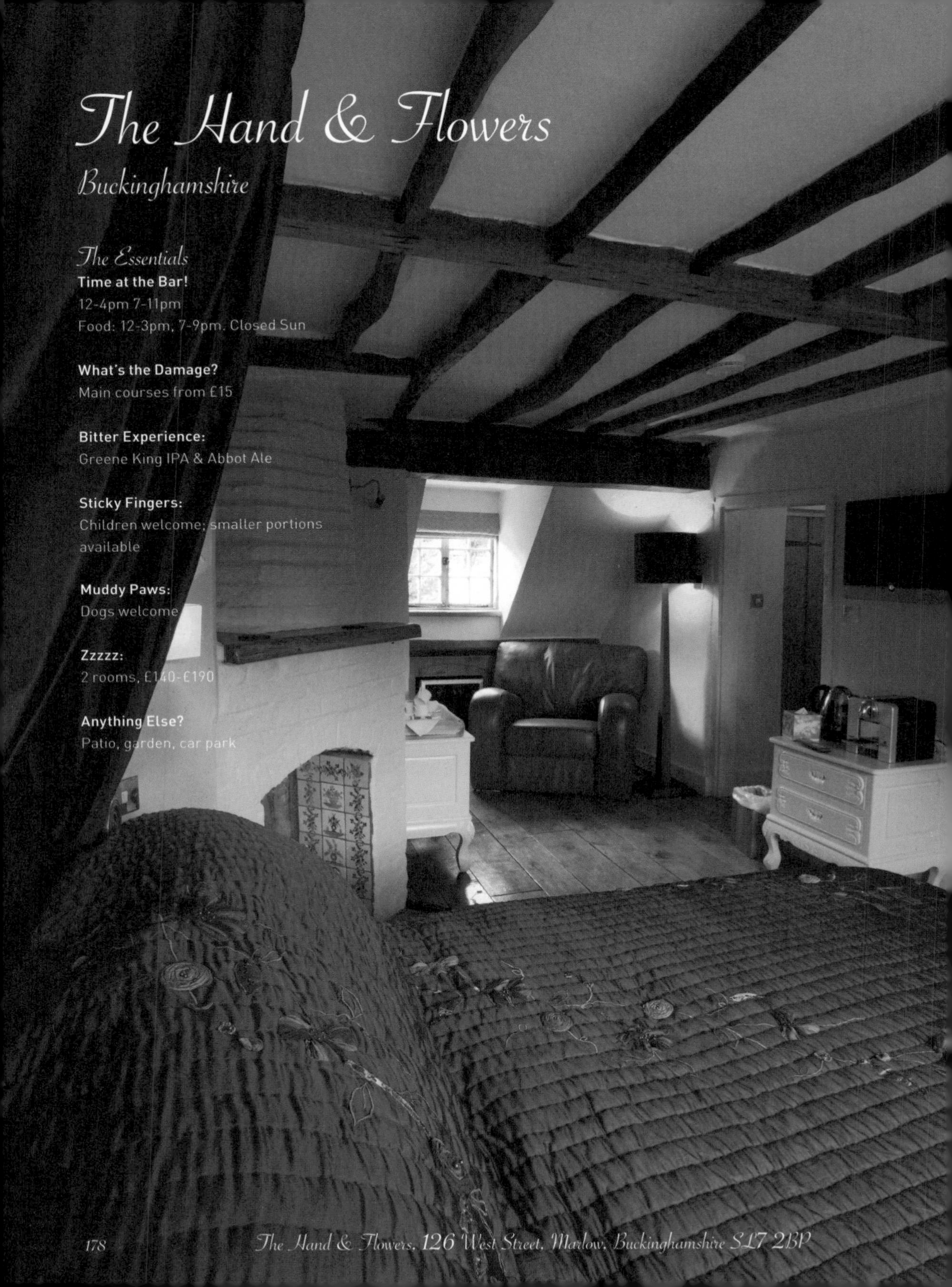

The Hand & Flowers

Buckinghamshire

The Essentials

Time at the Bar!
12-4pm 7-11pm
Food: 12-3pm, 7-9pm. Closed Sun

What's the Damage?
Main courses from £15

Bitter Experience:
Greene King IPA & Abbot Ale

Sticky Fingers:
Children welcome; smaller portions available

Muddy Paws:
Dogs welcome

Zzzzz:
2 rooms, £140-£190

Anything Else?
Patio, garden, car park

The Hand & Flowers, 126 West Street, Marlow, Buckinghamshire SL7 2BP

The Inn

Behind the Hand & Flowers' unpretentious pub exterior, chef-proprietor Tom Kerridge is a dynamo of energy and culinary dedication. The stylishly converted hostelry is nothing short of a masterclass in relaxed neighbourliness. With its, by turns, bare brick and stone interior, beams, timbers, open fire, diminutive pubby bar serving a short bar menu backed up by real ales and country casual restaurant, it certainly flies the flag for rural chic.

Small, cosy and decorated in modern neutrals, the cash has certainly been splashed on two small suites (four are planned), housed in a pair of converted cottages 100yds (180m) away. Named after different breeds of cattle, the rooms sport luxury beds and cowhide furnishings, cool bathrooms, and there are extras such as dressing gowns, bespoke mini bars, espresso machines, teas from teapigs, artisan chocolates, flat-screen TVs, DVD players, and a continental picnic breakfast (if you don't fancy sauntering to the pub for a full English). With all that on offer, you're going to find it hard to leave, especially if you are in a ground-floor suite with a terrace and hot tub.

The Food

The restaurant follows on from the bar, a charming, unpretentious dining room with a wood floor and plainly laid wood tables, while big mirrors create an illusion of space. From the tiny kitchen come dishes from a menu that's an intelligent and well-balanced selection of classic combinations with modern flourishes. That might translate as salt cod Scotch egg with red pepper sauce, or an intensely flavoured cooked tomato soup with pesto and black olive palmier to start. Braised belly of Middle White pork, teamed with broad beans, squash and sage, could follow, or roasted fillet of Dorset plaice with artichokes, mustard leaves, potato gnocchi and beurre noisette.

Desserts are a strong point – perhaps date and toffee pudding with caramel banana and ginger ice cream, or dark chocolate torte with coffee mousse and malted milk ice cream. Prices are not cheap, but if you're in for just a snack, the short bar menu delivers exemplary fish and chips and rare roast beef and horseradish sandwiches (with chips, too).

What To Do

Shop

CASTLEMAN'S FARM

The Rayner family run their own shoot here, using pheasants and partridges that they've raised themselves. Also available are wild venison, duck and rabbit and free-range poultry, along with unpasteurised cream and milk from their Guernsey herd.

Green Common Lane, Wooburn Common,
Buckinghamshire HP10 0LH
07900 886459

JUNGS BAKERY & PATISSERIE

Jungs specialises in continental breads, using recipes the owner brought back after many years training on the continent. Everything is hand-made, including rye, corn and olive bread.

6 The Broadway, Beaconsfield New Town,
Buckinghamshire HP9 2PD
01494 673070
www.hpjung.com

MARLOW ANTIQUES CENTRE

Home to over 35 dealers, the Marlow Antiques Centre sells a wide range of collectables – you're sure to find that special something in this huge space.

35 Station Road, Marlow,
Buckinghamshire SL7 1NW
01628 473223

ROOTS DELI

Les Root stocks the very best of British and international wines, cheeses, beer and charcuterie, most of it organic. Traditional British cheeses are a speciality, along with hams and pies.

33 Crendon Street, High Wycombe,
Buckinghamshire HP13 6LJ
01494 524243
www.rootsdeli.co.uk

Visit

FAWLEY COURT

Fawley Court is a unique surviving example of a Wren country house. Set on the banks of the Thames, in parkland that has remained unchanged for 150 years, the current house was designed by Sir Christopher Wren in 1663. The breathtaking ceiling in the drawing room, carved by Grinling Gibbons in 1690, is one of only three of its kind in the country.

Fawley, Henley on Thames,
Oxfordshire RG9 3AE
01491 574917
www.marians-uk.org/eng/fawleycourt

MILTON'S COTTAGE

This Grade I listed 16th-century cottage, where John Milton lived and finished *Paradise Lost* and started *Paradise Regained*, houses important first editions of poetry, prose and other examples of the work of this blind genius. The lovely garden features many of the plants mentioned in his poetry.

Deanway, Chalfont St Giles,
Buckinghamshire HP8 4JH
01494 872313
www.miltonscottage.org

PRINCES RISBOROUGH

As old as the Domesday Book, Princes Risborough is an attractive small town with a long curving high street with half-timbered Georgian houses and shops. Church Street, too, is full of interesting old houses, and leads to the mainly 14th-century parish church. Robert Louis Stevenson and Roald Dahl lived in the town, which has been a regular location for the popular TV detective shows *Midsomer Murders* and *Inspector Morse*.

Activity

COLNE VALLEY PARK

In this 40-square mile (105-sq km) mosaic of woodland, farmland and waterways, there's lots to do – spend a day fishing, birdwatching or take to the water. The Colne Valley Trail is a 7-mile (11-km) cycle route, running through lovely countryside and with spectacular views of the river, lakes and Grand Union Canal.

Colne Valley Park Visitor Centre, Denham
Court Drive, Uxbridge, Middlesex UB9 5PG
01895 833375
www.colnevalleypark.org.uk

Classic Bike Hire
114 Bushey Road, Ickenham, Uxbridge,
Middlesex UB10 8JX
01895 675402

GOLF

The course at Harewood Downs Golf Club has chalk downland and undulating parkland, and some of the finest holes in the country – tricky but fair tests for both experienced and new golfers. The views over tranquil Misbourne Valley and the rolling Chilterns are truly delightful.

Harewood Downs Golf Club
Cokes Lane, Chalfont St Giles,
Buckinghamshire HP8 4TA
01494 762184
www.hdgc.co.uk

LEARN TO FLY

Take a trial flying lesson in a 1950s De Havilland Chipmunk or a Piper Warrior – before you know it, you'll be looping the loop!

British Airways Flying Club
Wycombe Air Park, Booker, Marlow,
Buckinghamshire SL7 3DP
01494 529262
www.bafc.co.uk

The Walk - *Space in a Bustling World*

Enjoy the spacious clearings and sunny glades of a National Nature Reserve.

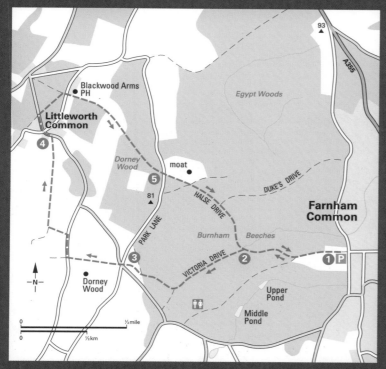

Walk Details

LENGTH: 4.5 miles (7.2km)

TIME: 1hr 45min

ASCENT: 150ft (46m)

PATHS: Woodland paths and drives, field paths, tracks and stretches of road, 9 stiles

SUGGESTED MAP: aqua3 OS Explorer 172 Chiltern Hills East

GRID REFERENCE: SU 957850

PARKING: Car park at Burnham Beeches

① Follow the drive away from Farnham Common, keeping the car parking area on your left. Pass the refreshment kiosk and veer right at the fork just beyond. Soon reach a gate where you enter the National Nature Reserve's car-free zone. Follow Halse Drive as it curves left and down between the trees. When you reach the bottom of the hill swing left into Victoria Drive.

② Follow the broad stony drive between the beeches, avoiding turnings either side of route; eventually reach a major junction with a wide path on left and right. On the right is a large beech tree with 'Andy 6.9.97' carved on the trunk. If you miss the path, you shortly reach the road. Bear right and go up the slope, keep left at the fork and cross some clearings to reach road junction; Green Lane and Park Lane.

③ Cross the road to the stile and waymark and go straight ahead, keeping the boundary on the left. Make for the stile and descend into the field dip, quickly climbing again to pass alongside the grounds of Dorney Wood. Walk ahead to the field corner, cross the stile and turn right at the road. Head for the waymarked footpath on the left and cross the field to the gap in the trees and hedgerow. Turn right and skirt the fields, making for the belt of trees and banks of undergrowth. The path cuts between 2 oak trees in the next field before reaching the gap in the hedgerow.

④ Cross the stile out to the road; turn left. Pass Common Lane and Horseshoe Hill; turn right at the next bridleway. Follow the track through the wood to the next road at Littleworth Common. Cross the stile to right of Blackwood Arms and follow Beeches Way. Beyond the next stile, continue ahead alongside the wood, crossing 2 stiles before following the fenced path. Go through the gate and take the path between the trees of Dorney Wood.

⑤ On reaching the stile, cross over to the road and continue ahead on Beeches Way. Make for the next major intersection and keep right along Halse Drive. Pass Victoria Drive and then retrace your steps back to the car park.

The White Hart

Hertfordshire

The Inn

Congenial and comfortable is a fair description of this civilised red-brick coaching inn in the centre of Welwyn. The recent total makeover reveals quite an eye for metropolitan sophistication – it is plush without being unduly lavish – with the bar going in for a solidly traditional look that runs to lots of dark wood and the odd leather sofa. The restaurant, meanwhile, is a cool mix of muted modern colours, timbered walls and a high-beamed ceiling offset by quirky touches such as flock wallpaper in elaborate gilded frames.

Bedrooms vary, the three boutique rooms in the inn itself are the best – moody and modern with Sky TV, CD players, dressing gowns, slippers and mini bars, along with hydrotherapy baths, double basins and power showers in the ultra-modern bathrooms. Those with more traditional tastes will love the two four-poster rooms for their classic good looks and claw-foot, roll-top baths, while those in the stables across the courtyard deliver good-sized, softly styled contemporary rooms with flat-screen TVs.

The Essentials

Time at the Bar!
11am-11pm (10.30pm Sun)
Food: 12-2.30pm, 6.30-9.30pm
No food Sun evening

What's the Damage?
Main courses from £7.50

Bitter Experience:
Fuller's London Pride, IPA

Sticky Fingers:
Children welcome; small portions

Muddy Paws:
No dogs

Zzzzz:
13 rooms, £118-£170

Anything Else?
Terrace, car park

The White Hart, 2 Prospect Place, Welwyn, Hertfordshire AL6 9EN

The Food

There may be no surprises on the menu but that is not to say that it's dull. Although the likes of beer-battered cod with mushy peas, hand-cut chips and tartare sauce, home-made pies, and pork and leek sausages with creamy mash, battered onion rings and onion gravy are based on popular pub fare, the dishes rely on first-rate raw materials, much of it local, as well as talent in the kitchen. Among livelier modern offerings, substantial first courses may run to crayfish, bacon and watercress salad or hot beef salad with asparagus, soft egg, cherry tomatoes and parmesan served with a sweet chilli dressing, while a main-course roasted belly of pork is teamed with champ potato, stem broccoli, capers and red onion.

Hot chocolate and orange fondant with white chocolate ice cream is a popular dessert. The cooking doesn't aim to dazzle, but steers a steady course through the prime ingredients that constitute the foundation of the menu. Service is pleasant, and the wine list can be relied on to furnish a sound bottle at a reasonable price.

What To Do

Shop

HARRIET KELSALL JEWELLERY DESIGN

Harriet Kelsall designs beautiful jewellery in a converted Tudor barn with workshops and a light, airy gallery space. Watch the goldsmiths at work, commission a one-off or buy a limited edition piece.

North Barn, Fairclough Hall Farm, Halls Green, Weston, Hertfordshire SG4 7DP

01462 790565

www.hkjewellery.co.uk

HATFIELD FARMERS' MARKET

At this Rick Stein-recommended Farmers' Market, you can find all the best locally grown, reared and sourced food – eggs, cheeses, meat, organic flour, seasonal veg, beer, pies and pickles.

White Lion Square, Hatfield, Hertfordshire

REAL MEAT COMPANY

This traditional butchers' shop is tucked down a back street by the river. Home-made sausages include pork, venison, caramelised onion and pistachio, and you can also take home high-quality, ready-made meals and delicious pies.

Mill Walk, Wheathampstead, Hertfordshire AL4 8DT

01582 834656

www.realmeat.co.uk

TISSIMAN & SONS

This gentlemen's outfitters was established in 1601 as a tailor, draper and undertaker, though parts of the timbered building date back to 1360. The clothes, though, are entirely modern.

3–12 High Street, Bishops Stortford, Hertfordshire CM23 2LT

01279 654009

www.tissimans.co.uk

Visit

CAPEL MANOR GARDENS

Take the opportunity to see behind the scenes at London's specialist college of horticulture, a colourful, scented oasis surrounding a Georgian manor house and Victorian stables. There's plenty to see in the 30-acre grounds, including historical, modern and Japanese gardens, and a striking Italianate maze.

Bullsmoor Lane, Enfield, Middlesex EN1 4RQ

08456 122122

www.capelmanorgardens.co.uk

HATFIELD HOUSE

Built in 1607 and home to the Cecil family for 400 years, this fine Jacobean house and garden is in a spectacular setting. The house was sumptuously decorated for entertaining the Royal Court, and the state rooms are rich with paintings, fine furniture and tapestries. Enjoy the scented and knot gardens, fountains, topiary and elegant parterre.

Hatfield, Hertfordshire AL9 5NQ

01707 287010

www.hatfield-house.co.uk

KNEBWORTH HOUSE & GARDENS

Now famous worldwide for hosting large-scale pop concerts in the grounds, Knebworth was once the home of the Victorian novelist Edward 'the pen is mightier than the sword' Lytton. The impressive house has turrets, domes and gargoyles – and 500 years of history. The drawing room is Edwardian, the study Victorian, and in the Jacobean banqueting hall there are paintings by Sir Winston Churchill. The herb, walled and rose gardens are remarkable. See, too, the maze and sunken lawn.

Knebworth, Hertfordshire SG3 6PY

01438 812661

www.knebworthhouse.com

SHAW'S CORNER

Home to George Bernard Shaw for 40 years, this stunning Arts and Crafts house contains many literary and personal effects, and remains as it was when he died in 1950. Rooms open for viewing include his bedroom, study, the kitchens and extraordinary revolving writing hut at the bottom of the garden.

Ayot St Lawrence, Welwyn, Hertfordshire AL6 9BX

01438 820307

www.nationaltrust.org.uk

Activity

CANAL TRIP

Take a trip on a narrow boat, through locks and the ancient and fascinating village of Marsworth – the surrounding countryside is lovely, and you'll see plenty of birdlife. Go on the Cream Tea Tour, or hire a boat and take a picnic.

Grebe Canal Cruises, Pitstone Wharf, Cheddington Road, Pitstone, Buckinghamshire LU7 9AD

01296 661920

www.grebecanalcruises.co.uk

DOG RACING

Expect a friendly atmosphere and a great night out at Harlow Dogs. There's a good bar and restaurant with a view of the track.

Harlow Greyhound Stadium, The Pinnacles, Roydon Road, Harlow, Essex CM19 5DY

01279 426804

www.harlowgreyhounds.co.uk

The Walk – Ebenezer's Vision at Welwyn Garden City

A walk around the first garden city.

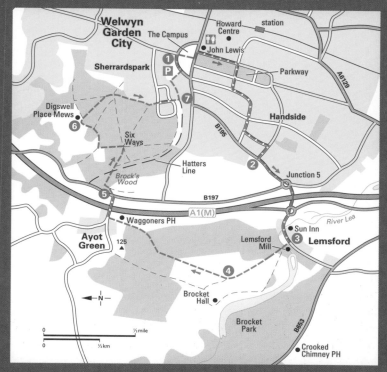

Walk Details

LENGTH: 4 miles (6.4km)

TIME: 2hrs

ASCENT: 120ft (37m)

PATHS: Town roads, parkland paths and woodland tracks, 3 stiles

SUGGESTED MAP: aqua3 OS Explorer 182 St Albans & Hatfield

GRID REFERENCE: TL 235133

PARKING: Campus West Long Term car park (free on Sunday) off B195 in Welwyn Garden City

❶ Cross The Campus; pass to the right of the John Lewis department store, along Parkway. At the traffic lights cross right, into Church Road. At the end turn left into Guessens Road. Cross Handside Lane into Youngs Rise and then turn left into Elm Gardens. At the end turn right into Applecroft Road.

❷ Turn left into Valley Road. Leaving Welwyn, go under the A1(M) bridge and straight on into Lemsford village, with the River Lea to the left.

❸ At Lemsford Mill turn right to cross the river on the modern bridge. Follow the footpath and bear right at the junction, now on the Lea Valley Walk. Soon enter Brocket Park, this part a golf course. Carry straight on where the righthand fence ends. Cross the tarmac path to the footpath post – thatched tennis pavilion behind fence here.

❹ Turn right, follow the drive for 20 paces, then carry on across the golf course, following the waymarkers. The footpath climbs right, out of the dry valley. Pass the cottage, climb the stile out of Brocket Park. Over another stile, turn left into Brickwall Close, with the Waggoners pub on the right. At Ayot Green turn right and cross over the A1(M).

❺ At the T-junction turn left and almost immediately right, down to the stile leading into the woods. Go diagonally left, not sharp right. At the bridleway junction bear right, the path descends to cross the course of the old railway line. At Six Ways (carved totem poles) turn sharp left on to the bridleway. Pass through the car park to the lane. Turn right, with the parkland of Digswell Place on the left.

❻ At Digswell Place Mews turn right by a waymarker post, to return to the woods. At the bridleway post bear right uphill through the woods. Ignore turns left and right until you near gardens of houses. Turn right to walk beside fences, eventually bearing left to merge with track and leave woods. Go straight over Reddings into Roundwood Drive and on to tarmac path between gardens.

❼ Turn left on to the old railway (Hatters Line). Turn right up the fenced ramp, out of the cutting and into the car park.

The Bell Inn

Essex

The Inn

Family-run for some 70 years, this 500-year-old coaching inn is a legend in these parts, with a reputation for good food and accommodation maintained over many years. An unprepossessing façade gives way to a historic beamed interior, full of exposed timbers and panelling, cushioned oak settles, flagstones, rug-strewn wooden floors and lots of foundry memorabilia to go with the pub name. That it works well on all levels is a tribute to Christine and John Vereker, especially as they manage to keep in sight the Bell's origins as a pub, offering real ales in an informal, chatty drinkers' bar, warmed by a real fire.

Stylish bedrooms are divided between the inn and Hill House, a few steps down the road. All are thoughtfully equipped and beautifully furnished, none more so than the four atmospheric suites at the inn, where exposed beams and timbers complement antique beds, comfortable sofas and smart bathrooms. At Hill House, which has its own breakfast room, there's an additional suite, and the more expensive rooms make the most of the character of the building.

The Essentials

Time at the Bar!
12-1.45pm; 6.30-9.45pm

What's the Damage?
Main courses from £10.50

Bitter Experience:
Greene King IPA, Brewers Gold

Sticky Fingers:
Children welcome only in restaurant; half portions available

Muddy Paws:
Dogs welcome in the bar only

Zzzzz:
16 rooms, £50-£85

Anything Else?
Courtyard garden, car park

The Food

If you fail to get a reservation in the restaurant, don't panic. The same menu is served at unbookable tables in the bar – you just need to get there early to secure one or else they take your name and you wait, propping up the bar, until a table is free. It's no hardship and worth the wait – the daily changing blackboard lists some dazzling modern pub food, often with an Asian twist.

Starters such as peppermint tea-smoked duck with Chinese cabbage and pimento salad, a robust foie gras with Puy lentils, crispy pancetta, salsa verde and red wine syrup, or even mustard and dill monkfish with Colchester oyster and mustard mayonnaise would sit well on any restaurant menu. For mains, there's turbot imaginatively teamed with Jerusalem artichoke cream, samphire and baby turnip sauté, or lamb chump with saffron pasta and spaghetti vegetables. Desserts such as glazed lemon tart are exemplary, but the cheeseboard is worth pursuing if you want to continue exploring the very good wine list.

What To Do

Shop

BATTLESBRIDGE ANTIQUES CENTRE

Set up 40 years ago, and with over 80 dealers in five fine old buildings, this is the largest antiques centre in Essex, and a great place for that special something. There's a motorcycle museum here, too.

Battlesbridge, Basildon, Essex SS11 7RE

01268 734005

www.battlesbridge.com

NEW HALL VINEYARD

Established in 1969, this 164-acre vineyard is one of the oldest and largest in the country. The grapevines have been carefully selected over the years from Europe, from which New Hall produce a range of different wines each year. Taste award-winning Ruby Royale, a full-bodied red, and Ortega, a dessert wine, and, of course, take some home with you.

Chelmsford Road, Purleigh, Chelmsford, Essex CM3 6PN

www.newhallwines.co.uk

Visit

HYDE HALL

This 24-acre dynamic RHS garden contains The National Collection of Viburnum. The Dry Garden is designed to show how a garden can be created with the minimum of irrigation – in fact, water-wise techniques are employed throughout the gardens. The Plantsman's garden has a woodland area, spring bulbs and ornamental ponds. The Barn Restaurant sells home-made cakes and good coffee.

Rettendon, Chelmsford, Essex CM3 8ET

01245 400256

www.rhs.org.uk

HYLANDS HOUSE

Hylands is a stunning white stucco Grade II listed mansion built in 1730, sitting resplendently in 600 acres of ancient parkland landscaped by Repton. Inside, there's an exquisitely gilded and painted drawing room, a sumptuously ornate baroque banqueting suite and grand staircase. The house was used during World War II as the HQ for the SAS, when much of the interior was neglected, but Chelmsford Council, along with English Heritage, have completed an extensive and sensitive renovation. The beautiful woodland, lakes and gardens are a delight to wander round, and there's a good cafe and a shop.

Hylands Park, London Road, Chelmsford, Essex CM2 8WQ

01245 605500

KELVEDON HATCH SECRET NUCLEAR BUNKER

A simple bungalow, built by the Air Ministry in 1952, guards the entrance to the biggest and deepest Cold War bunker open to view in south east England – 80ft (24m) below the Essex countryside. It's designed for up to 600 military and civilian personnel, possibly even the Prime Minister, who would be in charge of organising the survival of the population in the aftermath of a nuclear war. You can view the communication rooms, a fully operational BBC broadcasting studio, government rooms, a canteen and dormitories.

Crown Buildings, Kelvedon Hall Lane, Brentwood, Essex CM14 5TL

01277 364883

www.secretnuclearbunker.com

Activity

BIRDWATCHING

Rainham Marshes is the largest remaining expanse of wetland bordering the upper reaches of the Thames estuary, and the RSPB reserve is noted for its diverse birdlife, namely breeding wading birds and wintering wildfowl. Visit the Educational Centre for fine views across the marshes.

New Tank Hill Road, Purfleet, Essex

01708 899840

www.rspb.org.uk/rainham

KITE SURFING

Essex is very proud of its Blue Flag beaches. Here you can enjoy the simple pleasures of building sand castles or bird watching, but if you want to go up a gear or two, take a course at the BSKA-approved Essex Kitesurf School.

Essex Kitesurf School

East Beach, Shoeburyness, Southend on Sea, Essex

07751 705558

www.essexkitesurfschool.co.uk

TRAIN RIDE

What better way to explore and enjoy the beautiful Essex countryside than on a slow train, travelling over viaducts, through leafy woodland, open farmland and alongside river valleys? The journey through Epping Forest is delightful, and the train passes through several pretty villages, where you can see the restored station buildings and signal boxes.

Eppping Ongar Railway

Ongar Station, High Street, Ongar, Essex CM5 9BN

01277 366616

www.eorailway.co.uk

The Walk - Weald Country Park

A fairly strenuous walk taking in a great Tudor mansion and a royal deer park.

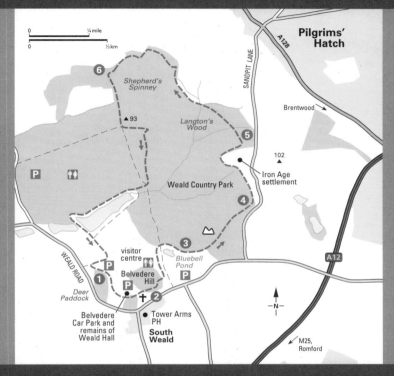

Walk Details

LENGTH: 5 miles (8km)

TIME: 2hrs 45min

ASCENT: 117ft (35m)

PATHS: Open parkland, forest tracks and some cross-field footpaths

SUGGESTED MAP: aqua3 OS Explorer 175 Southend-on-Sea & Basildon

GRID REFERENCE: TQ 568940

PARKING: Free car parks at visitor centre, Belvedere and Cricket Green on Weald Road and Lincolns Lane

① With your back to Weald Road, turn right out of the car park past the golden willow tree. Keep the red-brick wall on your right and continue to Belvedere car park – site of the foundations of Weald Hall. An information board (left) tells the story of Weald Hall. Walk into the car park and take earth path uphill. Turn left, keeping the church on your right. At the end of the church wall, turn left through the trees and go on to the grassy knoll overlooking the original gardens.

② Keeping the gardens to your left, walk up the steps to the site of Belvedere Hill where, in Tudor times, spectators would watch hunting and enjoy banquets. Walk down the steps, turn right and take

the path downhill, between conifers, to open parkland. Maintain direction and turn left through the gap in the fence, keeping Bluebell Pond and the cricket field on your right.

③ Turn right through the kissing gate and follow the grassy path uphill, passing bridleway waymarks on your right. At the top of the hill, pass through a thickly wooded area of ancient hornbeam and silver birch, and continue along the bridleway, which runs parallel with Sandpit Lane.

④ As the path veers away from the road, note the steep embankment to your right – the remains of an Iron-Age settlement. You are now walking around what was a moat. Keep to the path through meadow

and parkland and, at a tree-clad embankment to your right, continue clockwise to join hard track.

⑤ Turn left through the gap in the fence on the left and continue downhill through Langton's Wood. Follow this hard bridleway, which hugs the edge of the woods, to pass an avenue of sweet chestnut trees by Shepherd's Spinney.

⑥ At fingerpost turn left on to public footpath. After 400yds (366m), at the cross path, turn left and then right between a wide avenue of chestnut trees. After 500yds (457m), turn right before the kissing gate to walk with the lake on your left. At the end of the lake, turn left over the footbridge and return to the car park, passing the deer paddock.

The Sun Inn

Essex

The Sun Inn, High Street, Dedham, Essex CO7 6DF

The Essentials

Time at the Bar!
11am-11pm
Food: 12-2.30pm (Sat-Sun 3pm),
6.30-9.30pm (Fri-Sat 10pm)

What's the Damage?
Main courses from £10.50

Bitter Experience:
Adnams Broadside, Crouch Vale

Sticky Fingers:
Children welcome

Muddy Paws:
Dogs welcome in the bar

Zzzzz:
5 rooms, £85-£130

Anything Else?
Terrace, garden, car park

The Inn

As country pubs go in this historic part of the world, the 16th-century Sun Inn presents a pretty typical look, with beamed ceilings, exposed timbers, several open fires and plenty of panelling. But it sets itself apart as a laid-back pub serving local ales; as a great place for lingering meals in a rambling, atmospheric restaurant; and, with its classy rural-chic bedrooms, as the perfect weekend getaway. In summer the terrace is an additional lure.

Half-timbered walls, beams, wonky wood floors and some imaginative auction-room finds make up the five character bedrooms on the first floor. They come with super-sized beds, crisp white linen, plump pillows and extras like CD players, alongside the ubiquitous TV, mineral water and morning newspaper. Bathrooms are compact, but put together with the same modern eye for detail and have great showers (only one can fit a bath in).

The Food

Behind all the ancient beams and timbering is a kitchen with a young, modern attitude, working away and producing a breezy line-up of appealing modern Mediterranean dishes with a strong Italian accent. Short and to the point, the seasonal repertoire is built around top-notch produce (the greengrocers next door, selling locally grown fruit and veg, is owned by the inn). Purple sprouting broccoli and duck egg frittata with mixed salad leaves and pecorino, and grilled squid with borlotti beans, grilled red chilli, rocket and lemon could appear alongside unfussy mains such as Colne Valley lamb with roast green pumpkin and fennel, grilled polenta and salsa rossa, or local sea bass accompanied by potatoes, ceps, rosemary and spinach.

Desserts offer rich pickings: a glorious coffee, walnut and hazelnut cake with melted chocolate and cream, perhaps, or a deliciously creamy pannacotta with baked rhubarb. English cheeses served with fruit and chutney make a savoury alternative, especially if the 30 wines offered by the glass and the interesting wine list tempt you.

What To Do

Shop

LONG MELFORD

If you love browsing antique shops, book shops and small, independent boutiques, then head for pretty Long Melford, which is a renowned antiques centre. Highlights of your visit may include the Lime Tree Gallery, which specialises in contemporary art and glass; Instep for quality Italian shoes and handbags; Swags and Bows for opulent fabrics, beautiful soft furnishings and design-led goods for the home; and Sue and Roger Kistruck's Posting House Pottery for individual handmade stoneware. Don't miss Long Melford Antiques Centre and its extensive range of antique furniture, silver, pictures and *objets d'art,* or to rest and refuel try The Lounge, a stylish cafe serving great coffee and lunches.

Lime Tree Gallery
Hall Street 01787 319036
www.limetreegallery.com

Instep
Hall Street 01787 313403

Swags & Bows
Hall Street 01787 379860

Posting House Pottery
Hall Street 01787 311165

Long Melford Antiques Centre
Chapel Maltings, Little St Marys
01787 379287

The Lounge
Little St Marys 01787 379279

DEDHAM ART & CRAFT CENTRE

A large selection of furnishings, jewellery, books and clothing, plus paintings and work by local artists. The centre was originally a congregational chapel built in 1738.

High Street, Dedham, Essex CO7 6AD
01206 322666
www.dedhamartandcraftcentre.co.uk

Visit

SIR ALFRED MUNNINGS ART MUSEUM

The well-proportioned Tudor and Georgian Castle House is where the artist Sir Alfred Munnings lived and painted for 40 years. He called it 'the house of my dreams'. Noted for painting racehorses and equestrian scenes, Munnings is probably best known for capturing on canvas the spirit and essence of the East Anglian countryside as it was in the early 20th century. Many examples of his work are on view, as is his original studio.

Dedham, Colchester, Essex CO7 6AZ
01206 322127
www.siralfredmunnings.co.uk

LAYER MARNEY TOWER

England's tallest Tudor gatehouse has magnificent views, gardens, wildlife walks and 120 acres of parkland. The tea room serves both light lunches and tea and cakes, and the shop stocks a good range of souvenirs, cards, gifts and local produce. The site is a venue for rallies and theatre productions.

Colchester, Essex CO5 9US
01206 330784
www.layermarneytower.co.uk

BRIDGE COTTAGE

Situated just upstream from Flatford Mill, the 16th-century thatched Bridge Cottage houses an exhibition on John Constable – several of his paintings depict the cottage. There is a tea garden, shop, information centre and boat hire, and walks across National Trust land through the Dedham Vale.

Flatford, East Bergholt, Suffolk CO7 6UL
01206 298260
www.nationaltrust.org.uk

Activity

PAINTERS' TRAIL

The Painters' Trail is a 70-mile (113km) circular route exploring an area of Suffolk renowned for its links with famous artists – among them Constable, of course. Discover this corner of East Anglia on foot or by cycle – the trail takes you to the heart of the English countryside, and the Dedham Vale area.

Tourist Information Centre, 1 Queen Street, Colchester, Essex CO2 2PG
01206 282920
www.colchesterwhatson.co.uk

VINEYARD NATURE TRAIL

Explore 40 acres of vines, wild flower meadows, lakes and woodlands at Carter's Vineyard at Boxted. Follow the nature trail, take a tour of the vineyard and winery, and taste several English wines.

Carter's Vineyards
Green Lane, Boxted, Colchester, Essex CO4 5TS
01206 271136
www.cartersvineyards.co.uk

WALKING TOUR OF COLCHESTER

Discover the people, places and drama of Britain's oldest recorded town on a walking tour with one of Colchester's qualified guides. Go on patrol with a Roman soldier as he describes his duties on the streets; then return to 1648 with Master Barton and Mistress Turner as they re-enact the time when Colchester was under siege.

Tourist Information Centre, 1 Queen Street, Colchester, Essex CO2 2PG
01206 282920
www.colchesterwhatson.co.uk

The Walk - *East Bergholt, Constable Country*

A gentle walk through the landscape that inspired one of England's greatest artists.

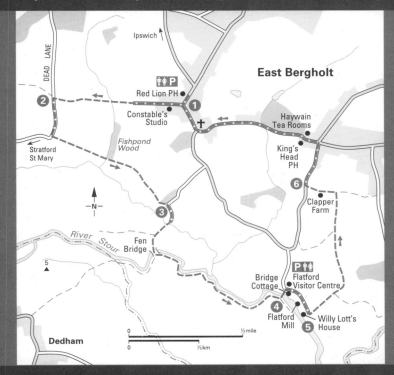

Walk Details

LENGTH: 3.75 miles (6km)

TIME: 1hr 30min

ASCENT: 246ft (75m)

PATHS: Roads, field paths and riverside meadows, 9 stiles

SUGGESTED MAP: aqua3 OS Explorer 196 Sudbury, Hadleigh & Dedham Vale

GRID REFERENCE: TM 069346

PARKING: Free car park next to Red Lion, East Bergholt

INFORMATION: This walk is over the county border in Suffolk

1 Turn right out of the car park, past the Red Lion pub and post office. Turn right along the lane, note Constable's studio on the left. Continue walking past the chapel and cemetery, through the gate and down lefthand side of the meadow to cross the footbridge. Climb the path on the far side for views of Stour Valley, church towers at Dedham and Stratford St Mary. **2** Turn left at the junction of paths to walk down Dead Lane, sunken footpath ('Dedham Road'). At the foot of the hill, turn left on to field-edge path. The path goes right then left to cross the stile on the edge of Fishpond Wood. Walk beside the wood for a few paces, then climb the stile into the field and walk beside a

hedge to your right. Follow the path, which switches to the other side of the hedge and then back again before bending left around the edge of the woodland to reach Fen Lane. **3** Turn right along the lane, crossing the cart bridge and ignoring footpaths to the left and to the right as you continue towards wooden-arched Fen Bridge. Cross this bridge and turn left beside the River Stour towards Flatford on the wide open pasture of flood plain. **4** Cross bridge to return to north bank of river beside Bridge Cottage. Turn right here, passing restored dry dock on the way to Flatford Mill. **5** Pass Willy Lott's House and turn left past the car park. An optional loop, on a National Trust permissive

path, leads right around the outside of Gibbonsgate Field beside a hedge. Otherwise, keep left on the wide track and go through the gate to join another National Trust path through Miller's Field. Stay on this path as it swings left and climbs to the top of the field, then go ahead through the kissing gate, crossing 2 stiles to the T-junction of footpaths. Turn left along the edge of the meadow and continue down the drive of Clapper Farm to Flatford Road. **6** Turn right along the road. At the crossroads, turn left passing by the King's Head pub and Haywain Tea Rooms on the way back to East Bergholt. Stay on the pavement on right side of road to walk through churchyard and return to the start.

The Mistley Thorn

Essex

The Inn

People come here from all over, and you can see at once why the Mistley Thorn is popular. It's a solid early 18th-century building overlooking the magnificent Robert Adam-designed Swan Basin, and the estuary views guarantee an instant holiday feel. The low-key contemporary interior (soft colours, modern art) blends comfortably with period features, and there's a relaxed yet orderly feel to the place. For informal eating and drinking in what can be thought of as a gentrified pub, it's nothing short of a find.

Upstairs in the five large bedrooms the style owes a lot to New England, with simple decor and the use of lots of crisp white on walls and beds – which are ultra-comfortable king- and super-king-size topped with plump pillows. There are quirky touches also, with high ceilings sporting the odd chandelier. The two best rooms have estuary views; all have TVs, DVD and CD players and positively gleaming modern bathrooms, while home-made biscuits and ironing boards are just two of many thoughtful touches.

The Food

Chef/proprietor Sherri Singleton's feeling for comfort food is finely tuned, and she sends out smoked haddock chowder, home-made burgers and chicken fricassee for lunch. The cooking is not formulaic, however, and the starting point is tip-top ingredients – from Mersea Island oysters to locally caught pollack to lamb and beef reared nearby. Dinner expands the choice, adding twice-baked Oxford Blue soufflé, or crispy duck salad with Asian leaves, almonds and sweet ginger dressing, and free-range chicken breast with Aspall's cyder-mustard sauce, to calamari with lime, coriander and chilli, and Harwich lobster with lemon butter.

It is completely impossible to resist the home-made bread (and the accompanying olive oil for dipping), so it's fortunate that lightness of touch pervades the cooking. The presentation is appealing, too, especially when it comes to desserts: chocolate and amaretto torte is delicious – be sure to order it when it's on the menu. Service is friendly and professional, and the wine list reflects the care taken elsewhere.

The Essentials

Time at the Bar!
11am-3pm, 6.30-11pm
Food: 12-3pm, 6.30-9.30pm;
Sat 12-10pm; Sun 12-9pm

What's the Damage?
Main courses from £8.95

Bitter Experience:
Adnams Bitter, Mersea Island Ales

Sticky Fingers:
Children welcome, children's menu

Muddy Paws:
Dogs welcome in bar and bedrooms

Zzzzz:
5 rooms, £90–£105

Anything Else?
Small terrace, car park

What To Do

Shop

ARNA FARRINGTON GALLERY & CERAMIC STUDIO

View and buy some of the best arts, crafts and design by established artists and emerging new talent at this contemporary gallery.

High Street, Thorpe le Soken, Colchester, Essex CO16 0EA
01255 862355
www.arnaandfarrington.co.uk

HALL FARM SHOP & CAFE

Opened in 2001, the shop has rapidly expanded from selling just prize-winning beef and lamb to offering an extensive range of local foods from small producers across East Anglia. Cakes, preserves and pickles, fine cheeses and wines, local milk and free-range eggs, and delicious olives and oils. Much of the produce on sale in the farm shop is used in the smart new cafe situated in a converted 16th-century cattle byre, which looks out across Dedham Vale to Dedham church.

Stratford St Mary, Colchester, Essex CO7 6LS
01206 322572
www.hallfarmshop.co.uk

H GUNTON

A long-established family grocer, Guntons is now a high-class deli selling fine East Anglian products, such as locally reared meat, salt from Maldon and even olive oil from olives grown and pressed down the road – plus they have a huge selection of local and continental cheeses. Coffee is roasted on the premises: try a cup in the cafe.

81-83 Crouch Street, Colchester, Essex CO3 3EZ
01206 572200
www.guntons.co.uk

Visit

THE BETH CHATTO GARDENS

Beth Chatto has transformed this six-acre site over the last 40 years into a stunning informal garden. Alliums, verbascums and flowering grasses now inhabit what was once a dried-up river bed, while shade-loving plants illuminate the woodland. You can buy most of the plants at the well-stocked shop.

White Barn House, Elmstead Market, Colchester, Essex CO1 2JQ
01206 822007
www.bethchatto.co.uk

PAYCOCKE'S

A fine half-timbered 15th-century merchant's house run by the National Trust, Paycocke's has intricate woodwork and panelling – testimony to the wealth of the East Anglian wool and lace trade. There's a lovely cottage garden, too.

West Street, Coggeshall, Colchester, Essex CO6 1NS
01376 561305
www.nationaltrust.org.uk

OLD HARWICH

Once a bustling port, Old Harwich has a rich nautical history. Start your journey at The Redoubt, the 180ft (55m) circular fort built in 1808 to defend Harwich against a Napoleonic invasion – part of it is now a military museum, and battle enactments are held in summer months. The Harwich Society, which restored and maintains the fort, runs guided tours starting from the Ha'penny Pier Visitor Centre on the quay. It's a town of great character, with cobbled criss-cross streets and narrow alleyways.

Harwich Redoubt Fort, Behind 29 Main Road, Harwich, Essex CO12 3LT

Activity

BOAT TRIP ALONG THE RIVER STOUR

Enjoy a trip through picturesque water meadows on *Rosette*, an elegant Edwardian launch. It starts at Sudbury – begin your journey with coffee and home-made cakes at The Granary on the quayside. The boat stops in a couple of pretty villages, and in Henny, where the Henny Swan pub is great for food and is right by the river.

The Granary, Quay Lane, Sudbury, Essex CO10 2AN
(Leaves at 11.30am, Sun only)

CYCLE THE PAINTER'S TRAIL

Hire a bike and explore scenes and skies painted by John Constable in this Area of Outstanding Natural Beauty. The length of the routes varies, but all are on well-established paths and quiet roads. Start at Manningtree station – but don't forget to pick up your Route Pack from Colchester Tourist Information Centre.

Colchester TIC: 01206 282920
www.realessex.co.uk/countryside
Bike hire at Colchester in Action Bikes: 01206 541744

THE ELECTRIC PALACE CINEMA

For all you fans of Cinema Paradiso! Built in 1911, this independent cinema is one of the oldest and least altered in the country, so it's a complete nostalgia-fest! It still has its silent screen, original projection room and rococo frontage. It's now run as a community cinema, showing films every weekend.

Kings Quay Street, Harwich, Essex CO12 3ER
01255 55333
www.electricpalace.com

The Walk - Manningtree, England's Smallest Town

Where Matthew Hopkins, the notorious Witchfinder General, was born and buried.

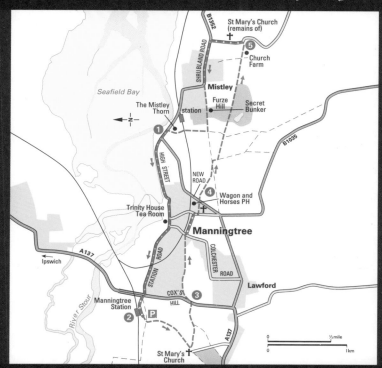

Walk Details

LENGTH: 7 miles (11.3km)

TIME: 3hrs 30min

ASCENT: 98ft (30m)

PATHS: Field paths, footpaths, tracks and sections of road, may be boggy, 5 stiles

SUGGESTED MAP: aqua3 OS Explorer 184 Colchester, Harwich & Clacton-on-Sea

GRID REFERENCE: TM 093322

PARKING: The Mistley Thorn car park, or pay-and-display at Manningtree Station; free at weekends

① From The Mistley Thorn, turn left into the High Street; follow The Walls by the River Stour to Manningtree, England's smallest town. Walk for about 1 mile (1.6km) along Station Road.

② Turn left after the station, following the fingerpost ('Lawford') along the steep, grassy path to St Mary's Church. Go through the black gate, keep the church on your right, cross the stile over the church wall. Turn left and, at the wooden post, follow the yellow waymark half right across the meadow. Cross the earth bridge over Wignell Brook, go left uphill keeping line of trees on your right. Just before the house at the top of the hill, cross the stile and bear left to Cox's Hill, on to the A137.

③ Cross Cox's Hill, turn left and after 40yds (37m), at the fingerpost ('Essex Way'), turn right. Walk downhill with the trees on your left and the pond on your right. Pass the housing estate on the left and cross the plank bridge over the stream. Follow the gravel path through the Owl Conservation Area. Ignoring the concrete path on the left, turn half-right on to cross-field path towards the playing fields. Cross Colchester Road, and at the T-junction turn right into Trinity Road, ignoring the signs for Essex Way. At the Evangelical church turn left between houses to New Road, Wagon and Horses pub is on the left.

④ Cross New Road and follow the yellow waymarked footpath between backs of houses. At a T-junction turn left on to the wide bridleway. After 70yds (64m) follow the waymark half-right and rejoin Essex Way. Continue, crossing the earth bridge over the brook and 2 stiles. Just after the 2nd stile, follow the track between 2 concrete posts into the wooded slopes of Furze Hill. Emerge from the woods, go ahead keeping to the field-edge path to Church Farm. Turn left on to Heath Road.

⑤ Cross the road to the low wall to the remains of St Mary's Church. Continue north and turn left on to the B1352 and into Shrubland Road, which becomes a green lane. Cross the 1st stile on the right and walk under railway. Turn left into Mistley Green, which joins the High Street.

Index